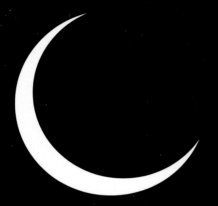

COLLECTION EDITOR: JENNIFER GRÜNWALD
ASSISTANT EDITOR: SARAH BRUNSTAD
ASSOCIATE MANAGING EDITOR: ALEX STARBUCK
EDITOR, SPECIAL PROJECTS: MARK D. BEAZLEY
SENIOR EDITOR, SPECIAL PROJECTS: JEFF YOUNGQUIST
SVP PRINT, SALES & MARKETING: DAVID GABRIEL
BOOK DESIGN: JEFF POWELL

EDITOR IN CHIEF: AXEL ALONSO
CHIEF CREATIVE OFFICER: JOE QUESADA
PUBLISHER: DAN BUCKLEY
EXECUTIVE PRODUCER: ALAN FINE

MOON KNIGHT VOL. 2: DEAD WILL RISE. Contains material originally published in magazine form as MOON KNIGHT #7-12. First printing 2015. ISBN# 978-0-7851-5409-9. Published by MARVEL WORLDWIDE, IN
a subsidiary of MARVEL ENTERTAINMENT, LLC. OFFICE OF PUBLICATION: 135 West 50th Street, New York, NY 10020. **Printed in Canada.** ALAN FINE, EVP - Office of the President, Mar
Worldwide, Inc. and EVP & CMO Marvel Characters B.V.; DAN BUCKLEY, Publisher & President - Print, Animation & Digital Divisions; JOE QUESADA, Chief Creative Officer; TOM BREVOORT, SVP of Publishing; DA
BOGART, SVP of Operations & Procurement, Publishing; C.B. CEBULSKI, SVP of Creator & Content Development; DAVID GABRIEL, SVP Print, Sales & Marketing; JIM O'KEEFE, VP of Operations & Logistics; DAN CA
Executive Director of Publishing Technology; SUSAN CRESPI, Editorial Operations Manager; ALEX MORALES, Publishing Operations Manager; STAN LEE, Chairman Emeritus. For information regarding advertising
Marvel Comics or on Marvel.com, please contact Niza Disla, Director of Marvel Partnerships, at ndisla@marvel.com. For Marvel subscription inquiries, please call 800-217-9158. **Manufactured between 2/20/20
and 3/30/2015 by SOLISCO PRINTERS, SCOTT, QC, CANADA.**

10 9 8 7 6 5 4 3 2 1

MOON KNIGHT

DEAD WILL RISE

WRITER
BRIAN WOOD

ARTIST
GREG SMALLWOOD
WITH GIUSEPPE CAMUNCOLI (#10)

COLOR ARTIST
JORDIE BELLAIRE

LETTERER
VC'S CHRIS ELIOPOULOS

COVER ART
DECLAN SHALVEY & JORDIE BELLAIRE

ASSISTANT EDITOR **CHARLES BEACHAM**   EDITOR **NICK LOWE**

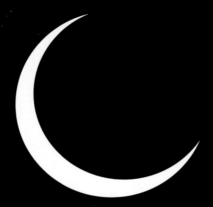

Mercenary Marc Spector died in Egypt, under a statue of the ancient deity Khonshu. He returned to life in the shadow of the moon god, and wore his aspect to fight crime for his own redemption. He went completely insane, and disappeared.

This is what happened next.

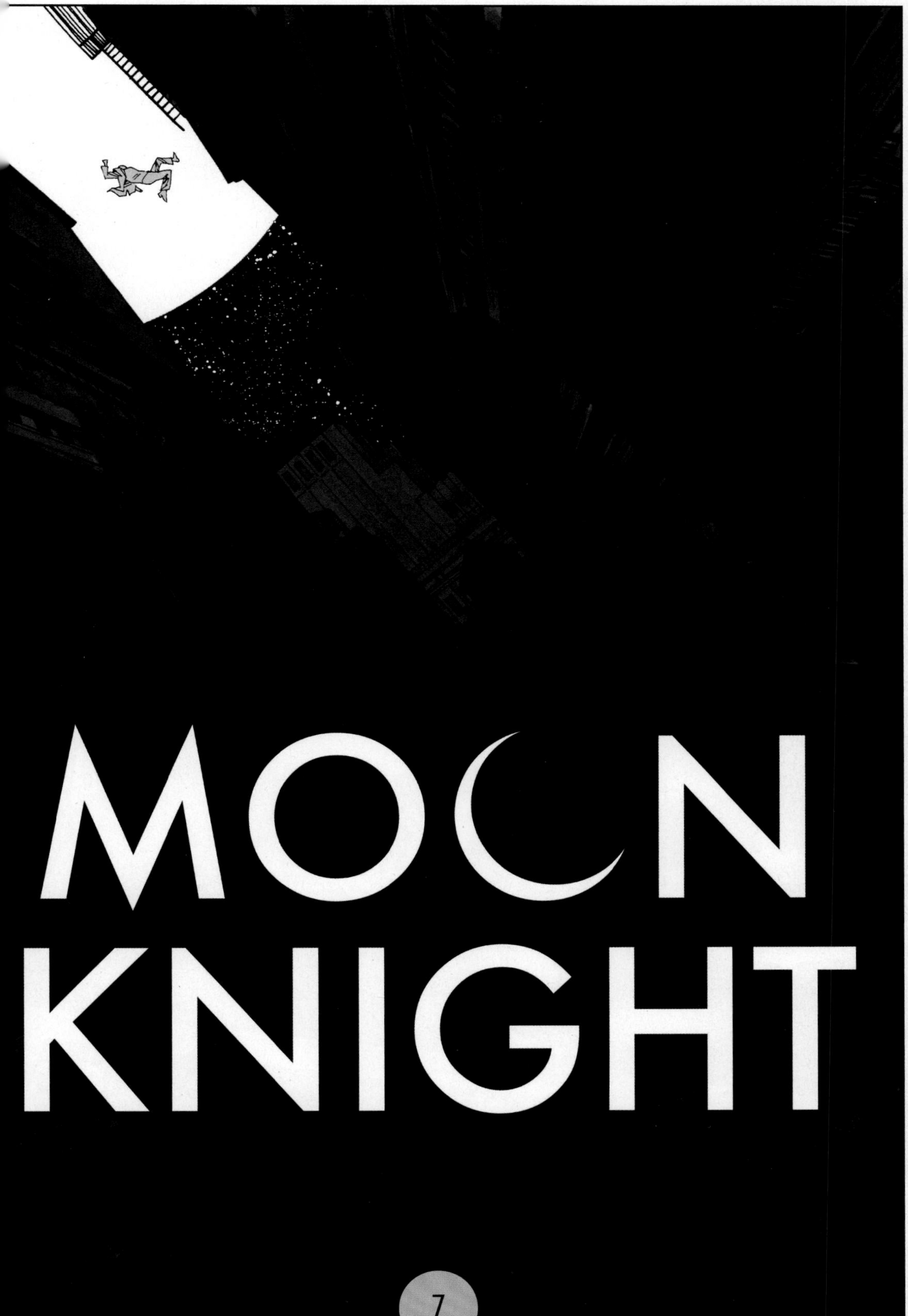
MOON
KNIGHT

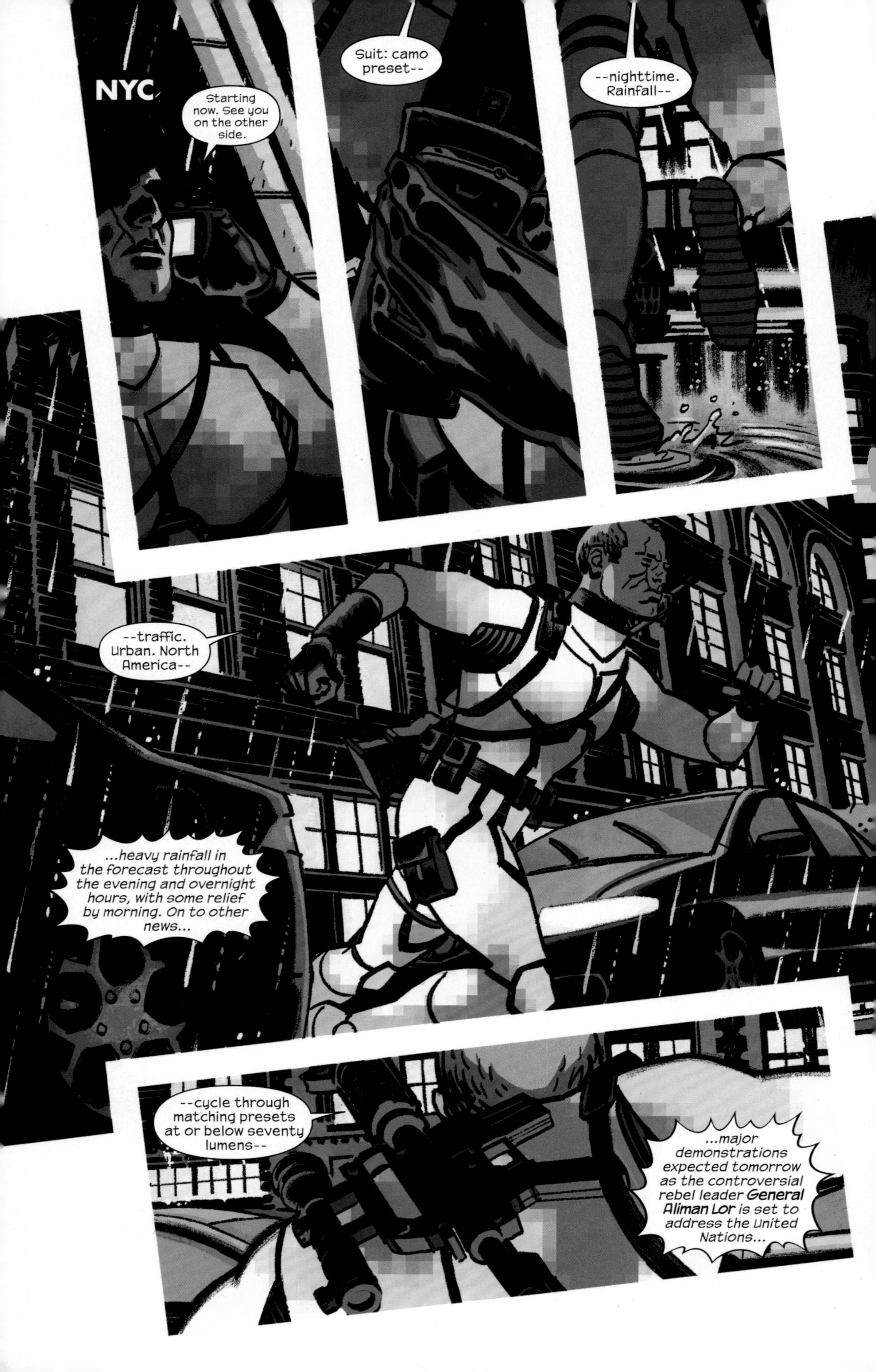
NYC
Starting now. See you on the other side.
Suit: camo preset--
--nighttime. Rainfall--
--traffic. Urban. North America--
...heavy rainfall in the forecast throughout the evening and overnight hours, with some relief by morning. On to other news...
--cycle through matching presets at or below seventy lumens--
...major demonstrations expected tomorrow as the controversial rebel leader **General Aliman Lor** is set to address the United Nations...

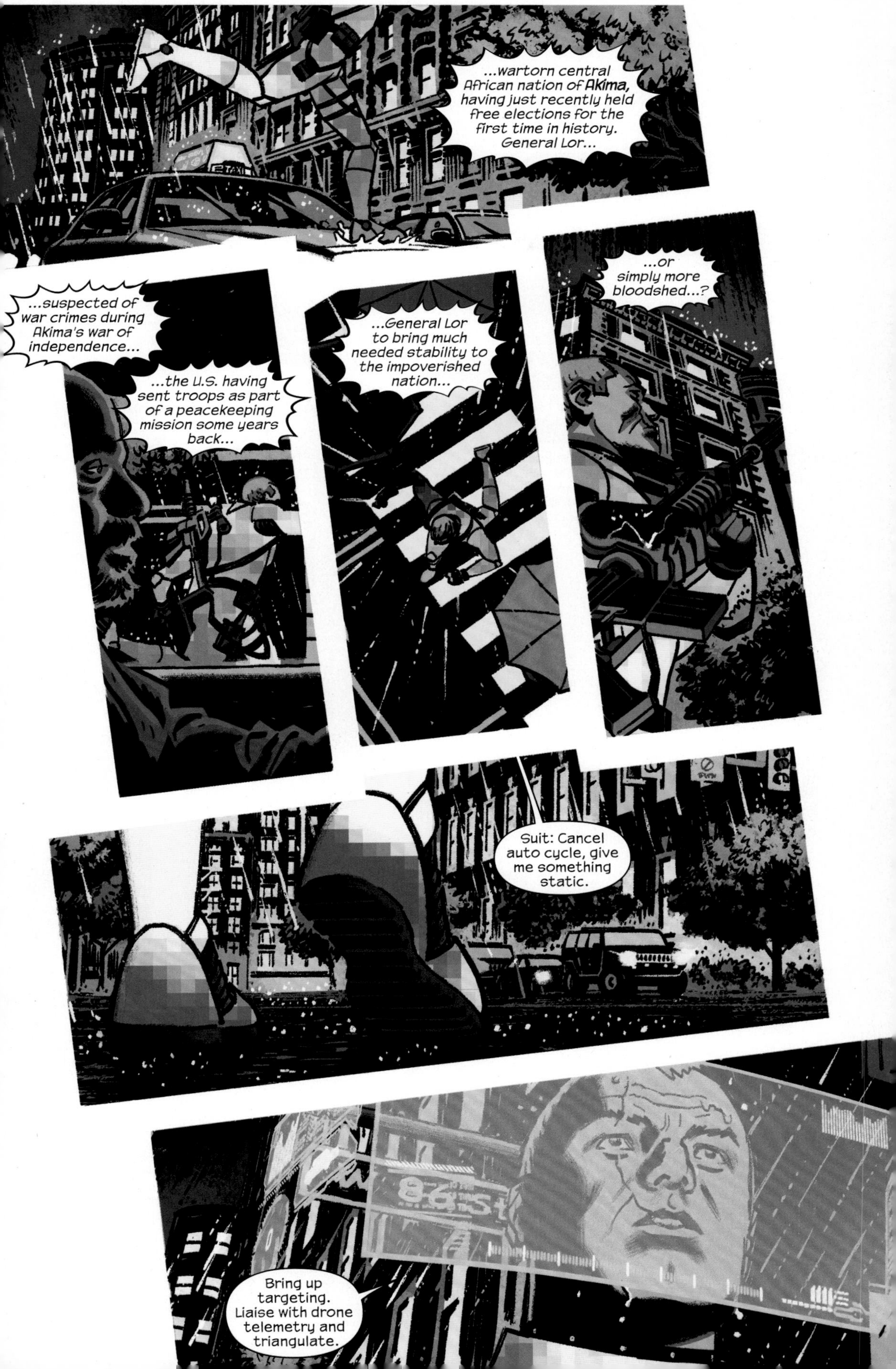
...wartorn central African nation of Akima, having just recently held free elections for the first time in history. General Lor...
...suspected of war crimes during Akima's war of independence...
...the U.S. having sent troops as part of a peacekeeping mission some years back...
...General Lor to bring much needed stability to the impoverished nation...
...or simply more bloodshed...?
Suit: Cancel auto cycle, give me something static.
86 St
Bring up targeting. Liaise with drone telemetry and triangulate.

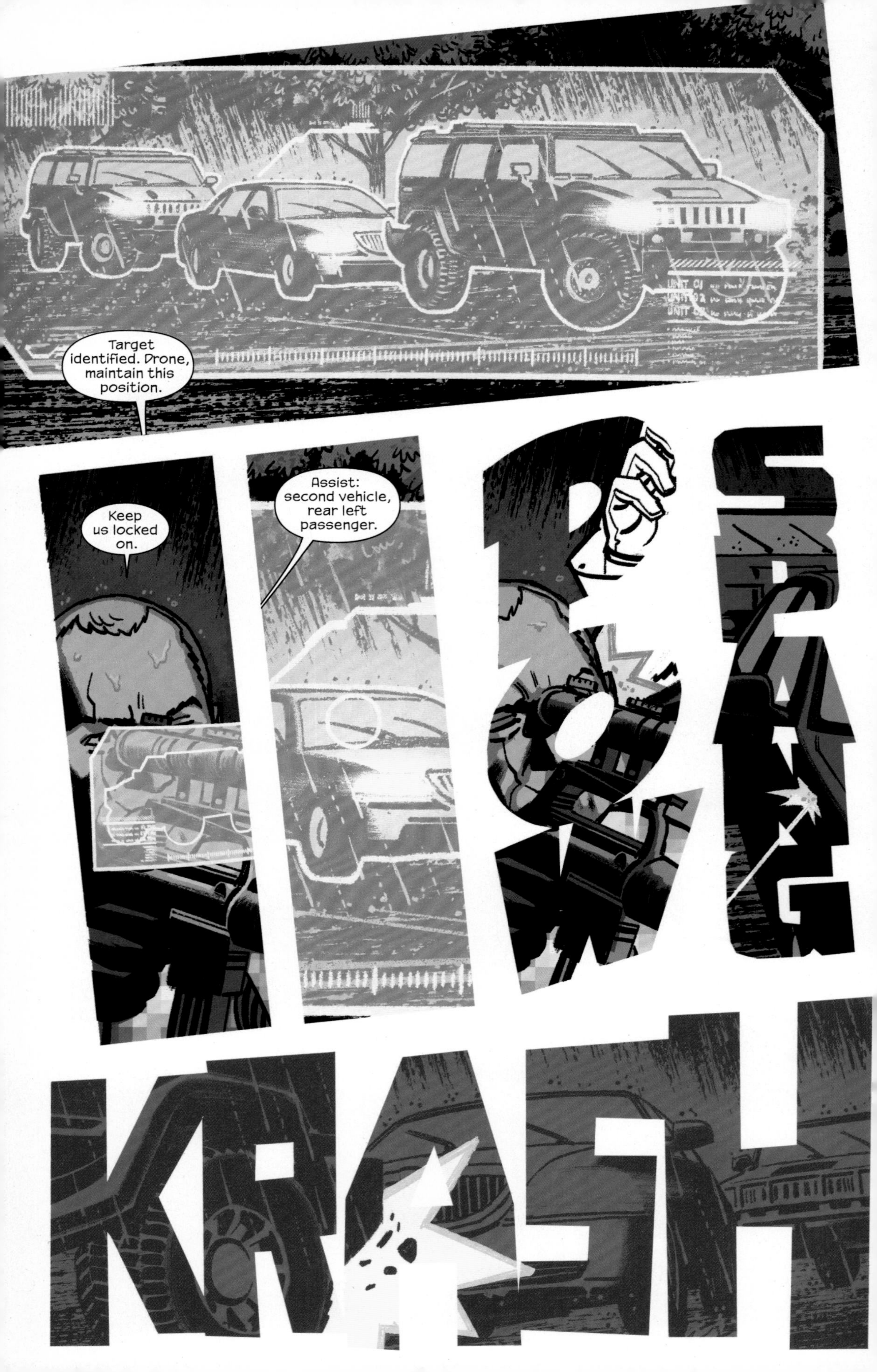
Target identified. Drone, maintain this position.
Keep us locked on.
Assist: second vehicle, rear left passenger.
KRASH

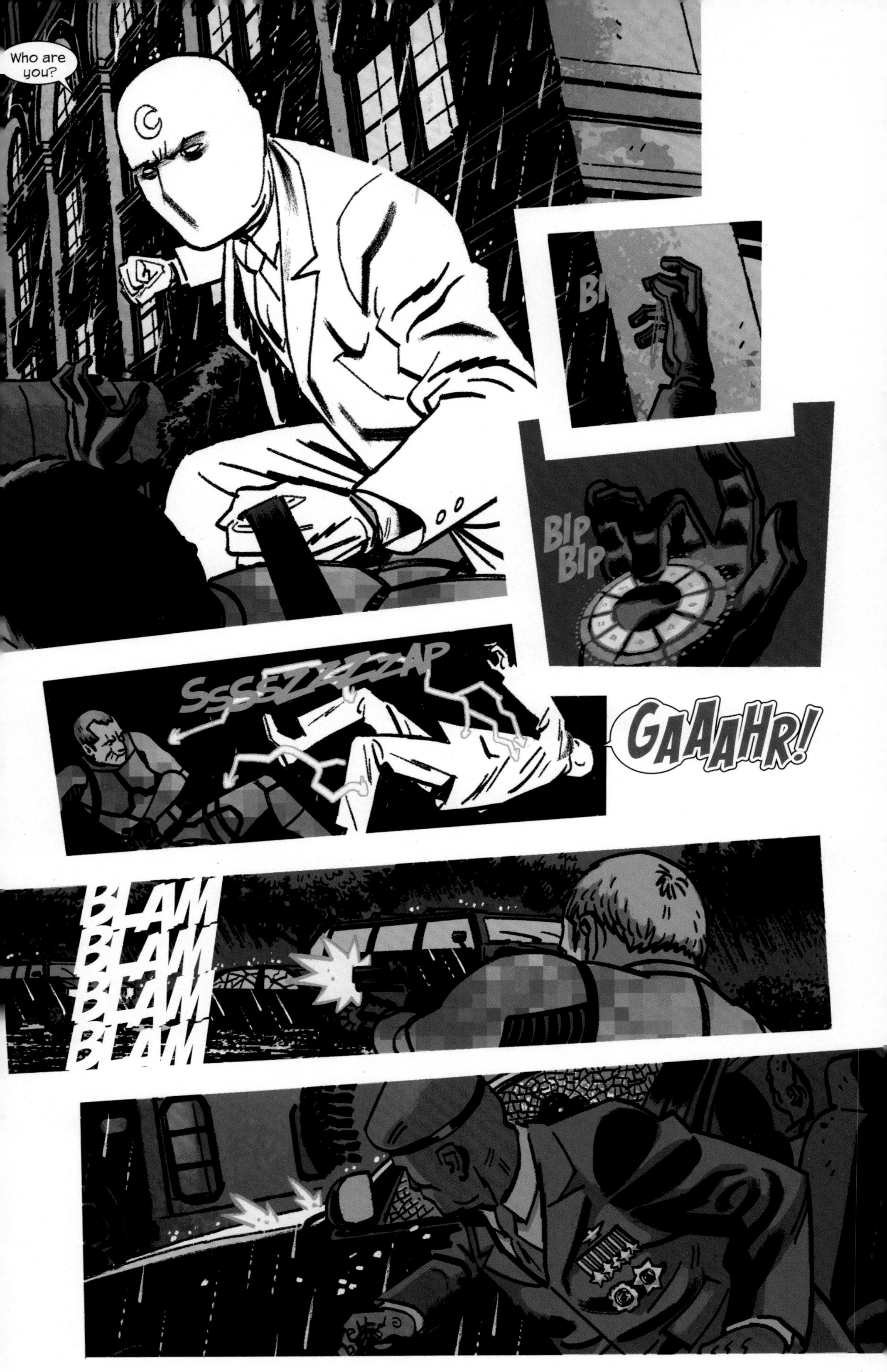
Who are you?
BIP BIP
SSSSZZZZZAP
GAAAHR!
BLAM BLAM BLAM BLAM

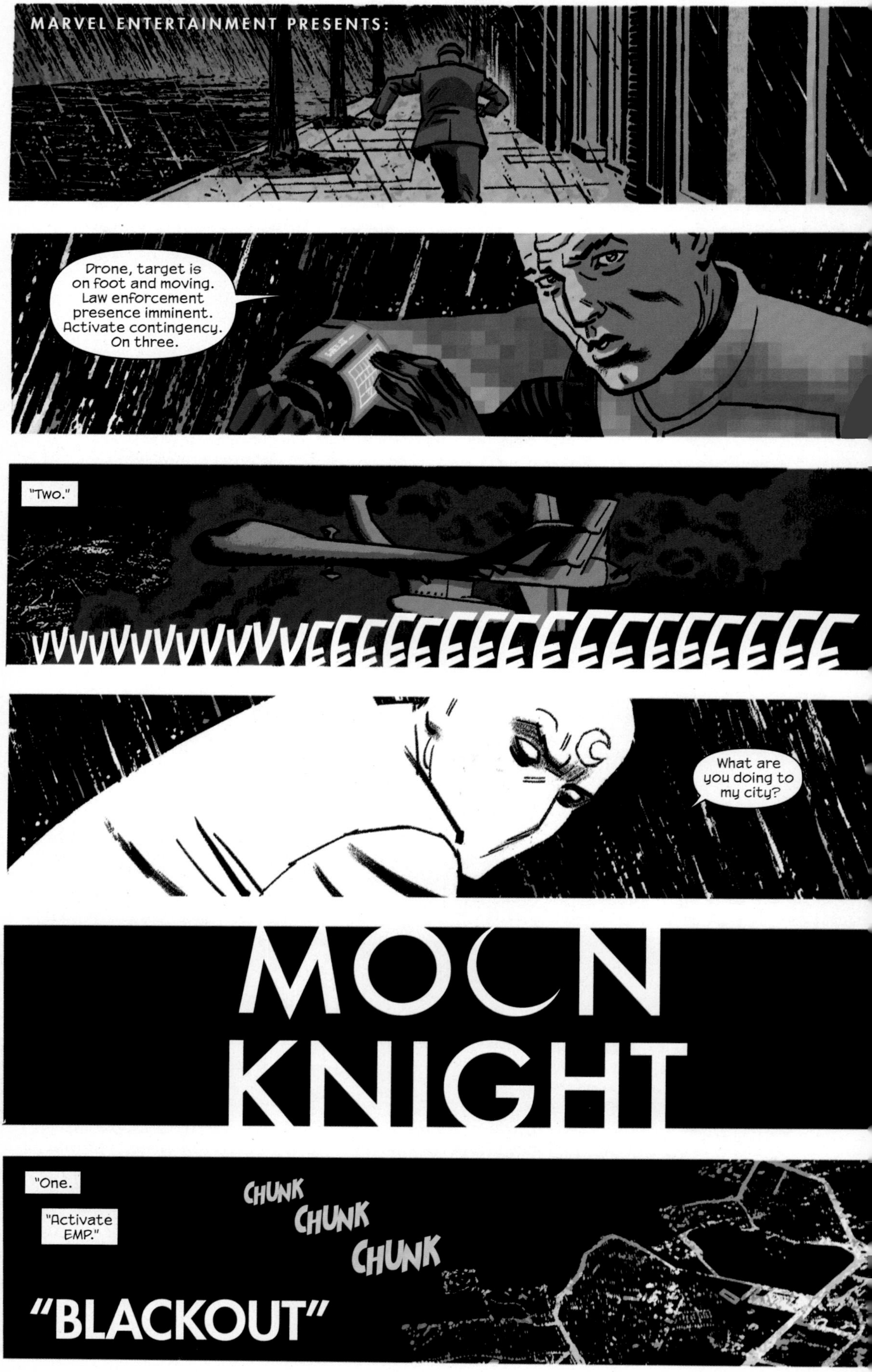
MARVEL ENTERTAINMENT PRESENTS:
Drone, target is on foot and moving. Law enforcement presence imminent. Activate contingency. On three.
"Two."
VVVVVVVVVVVVVVVEEEEEEEEEEEEEEEEEEEEE
What are you doing to my city?
MOON KNIGHT
"One.
"Activate EMP."
CHUNK
CHUNK
CHUNK
"BLACKOUT"

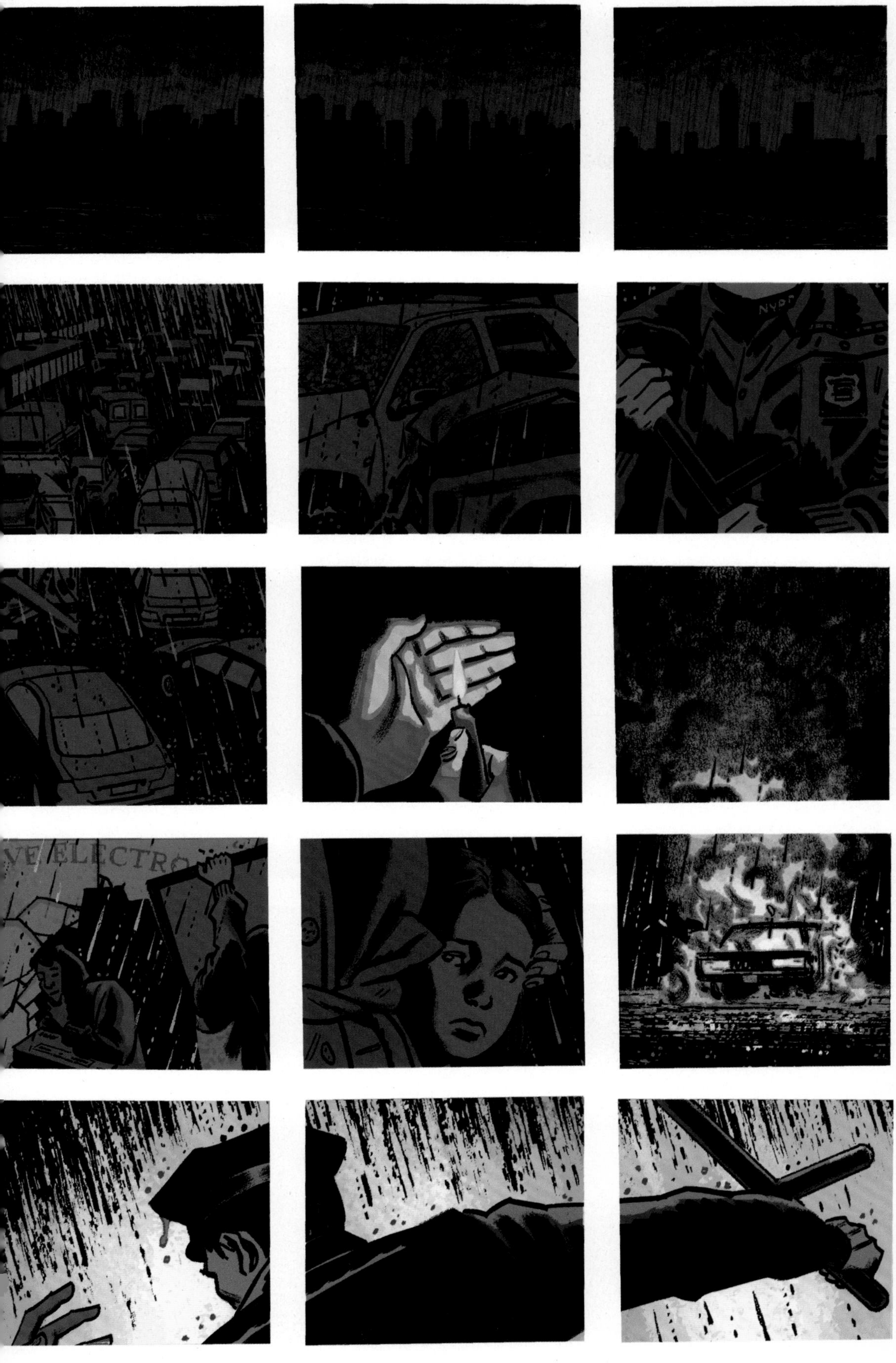
NYPD
VE ELECTRO

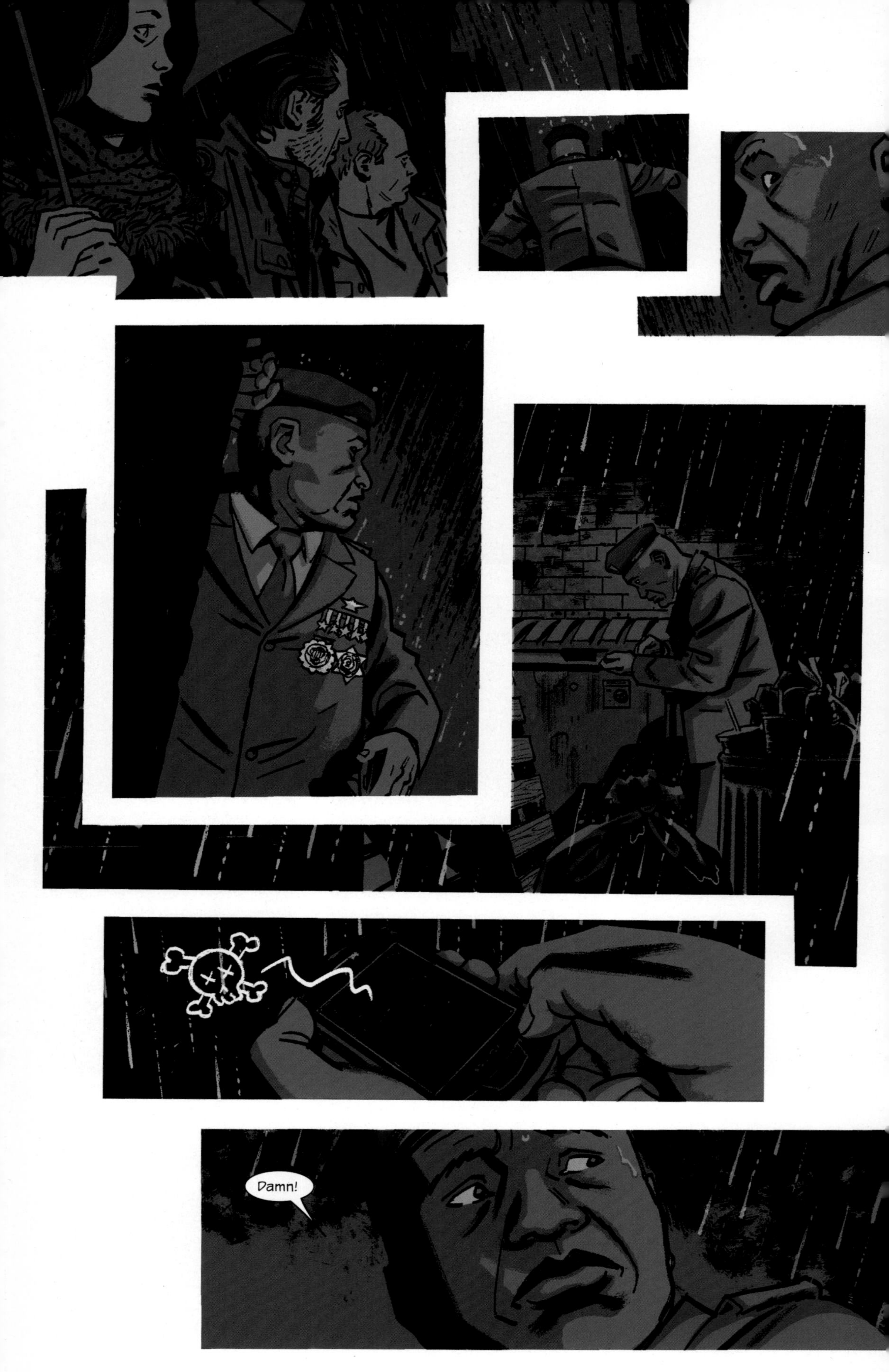
Damn!

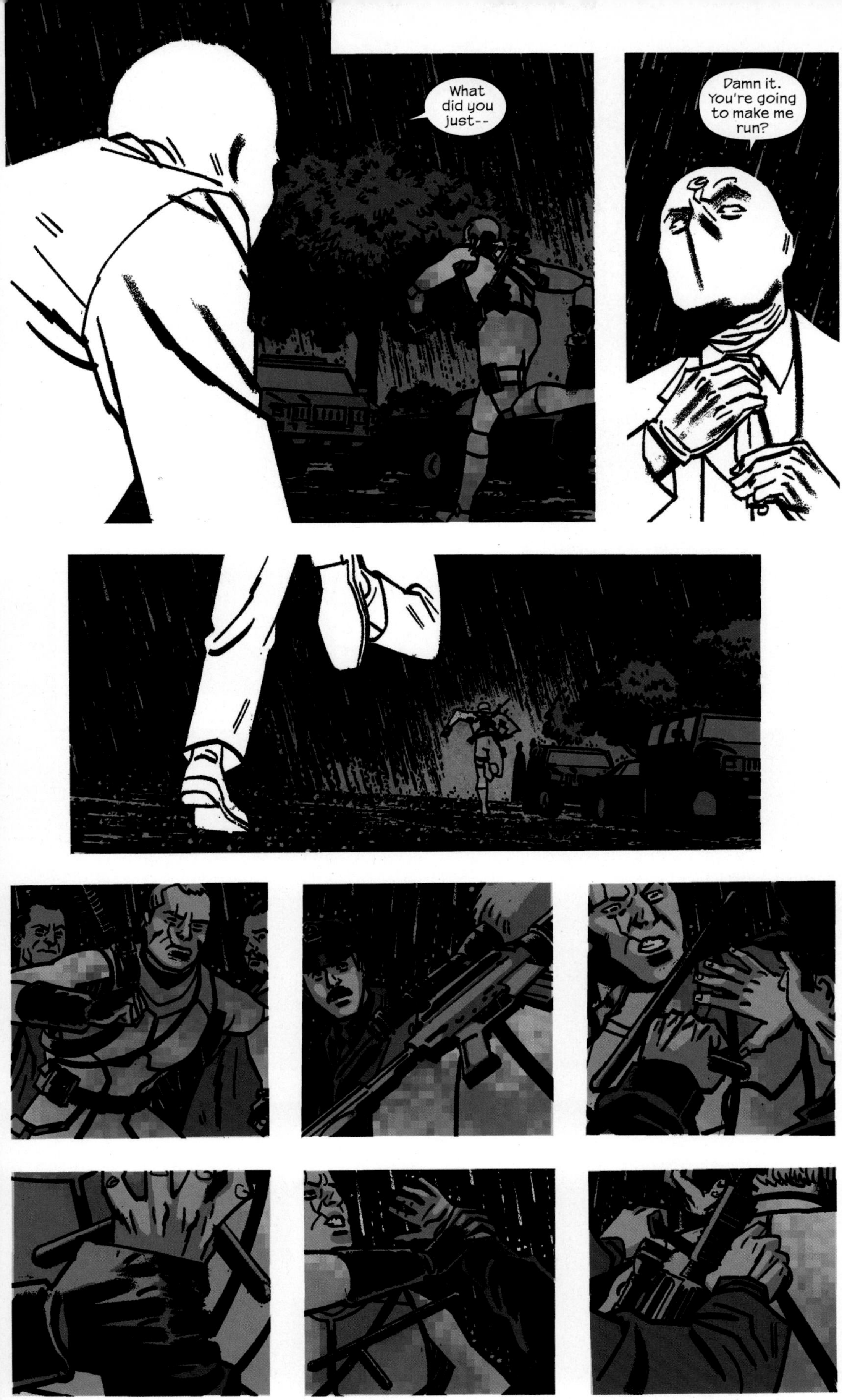
What did you just--
Damn it. You're going to make me run?

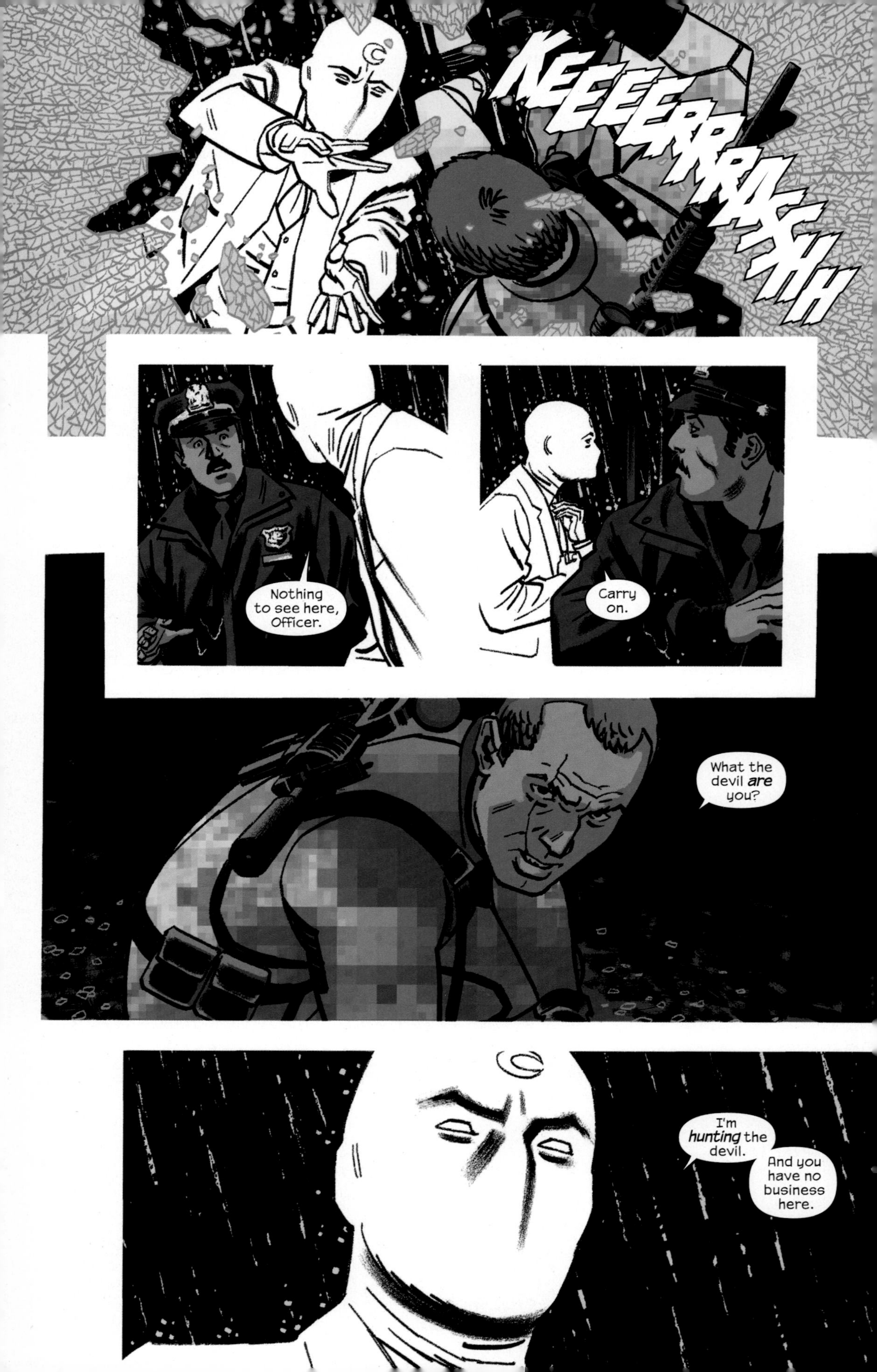
KEEEERRRAAASHH
Nothing to see here, Officer.
Carry on.
What the devil *are* you?
I'm *hunting* the devil.
And you have no business here.

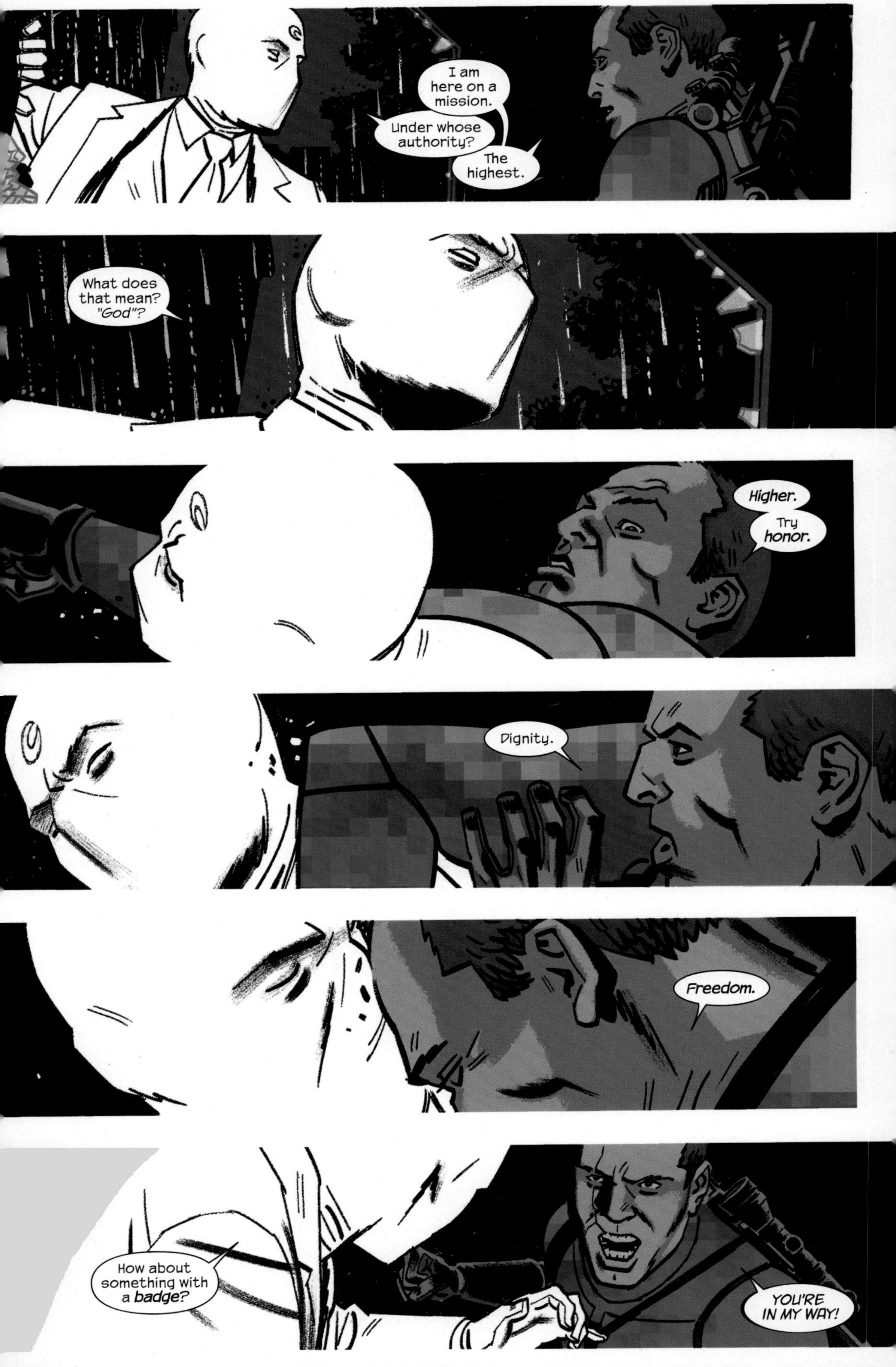
I am here on a mission.
Under whose authority?
The highest.
What does that mean? "God"?
Higher.
Try honor.
Dignity.
Freedom.
How about something with a badge?
YOU'RE IN MY WAY!

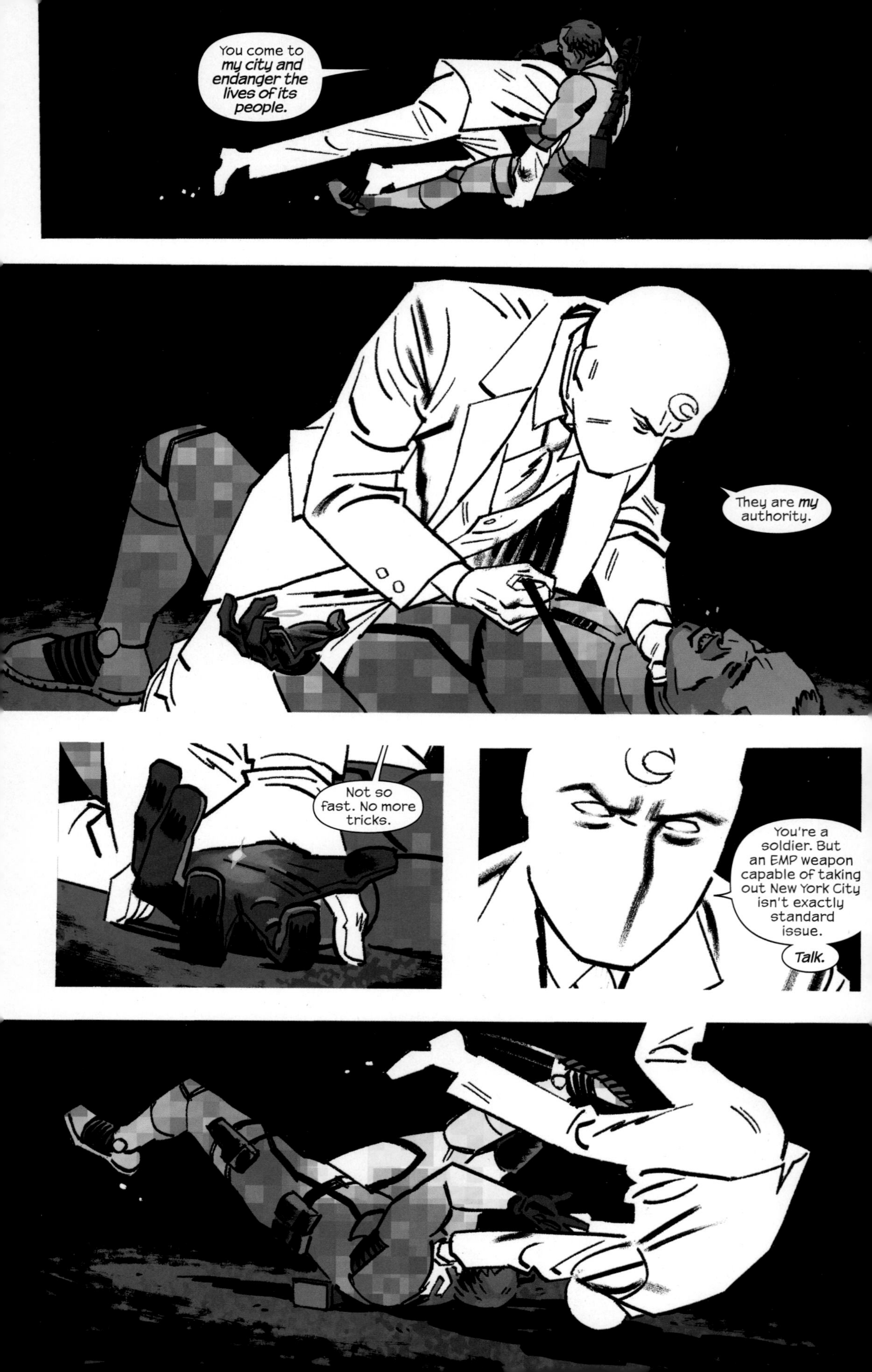
You come to *my city* and *endanger the lives of its people.*
They are *my* authority.
Not so fast. No more tricks.
You're a soldier. But an EMP weapon capable of taking out New York City isn't exactly standard issue.
Talk.

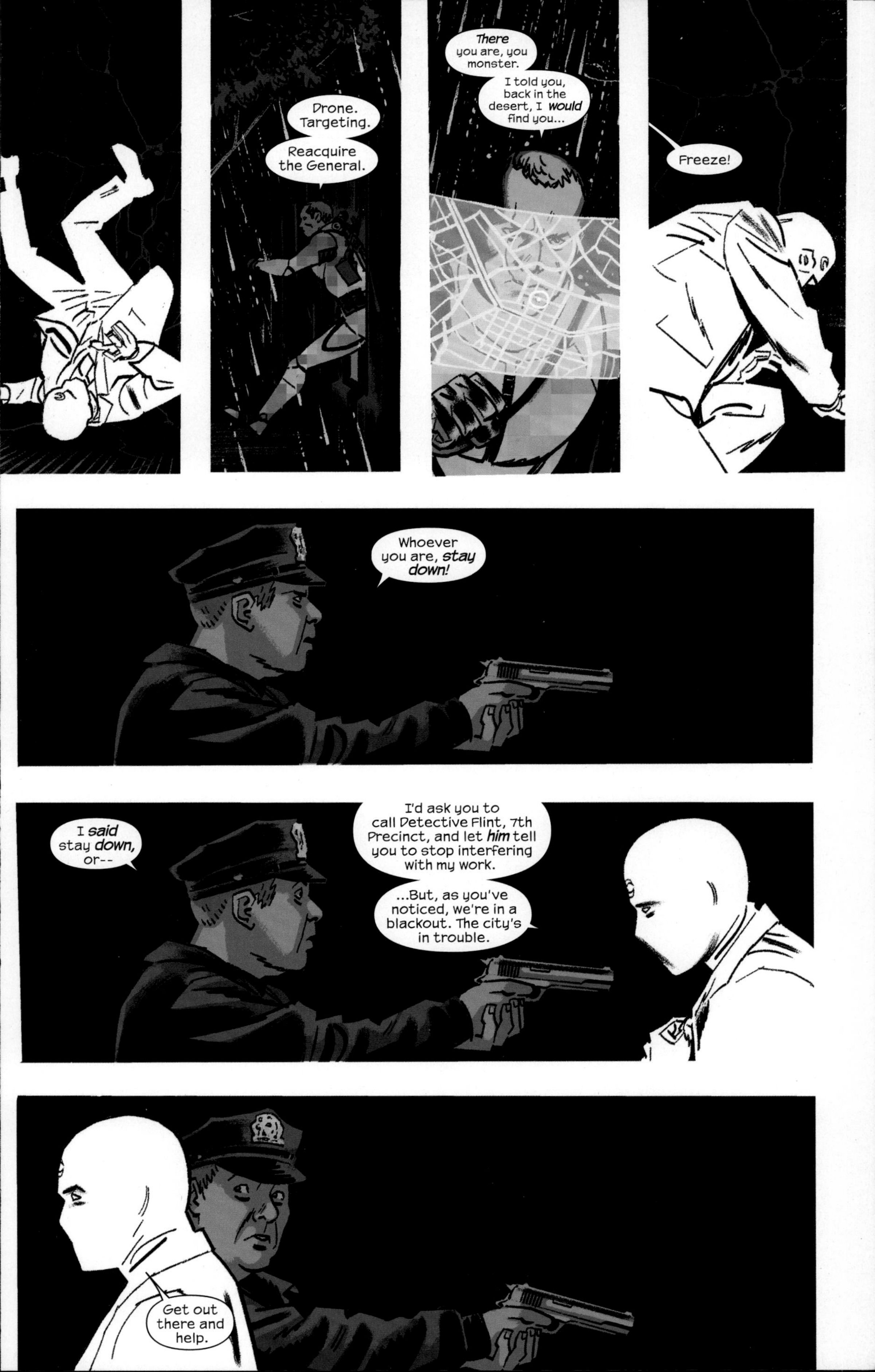
Drone. Targeting.
Reacquire the General.
There you are, you monster.
I told you, back in the desert, I would find you...
Freeze!
Whoever you are, stay down!
I said stay down, or--
I'd ask you to call Detective Flint, 7th Precinct, and let him tell you to stop interfering with my work.
...But, as you've noticed, we're in a blackout. The city's in trouble.
Get out there and help.

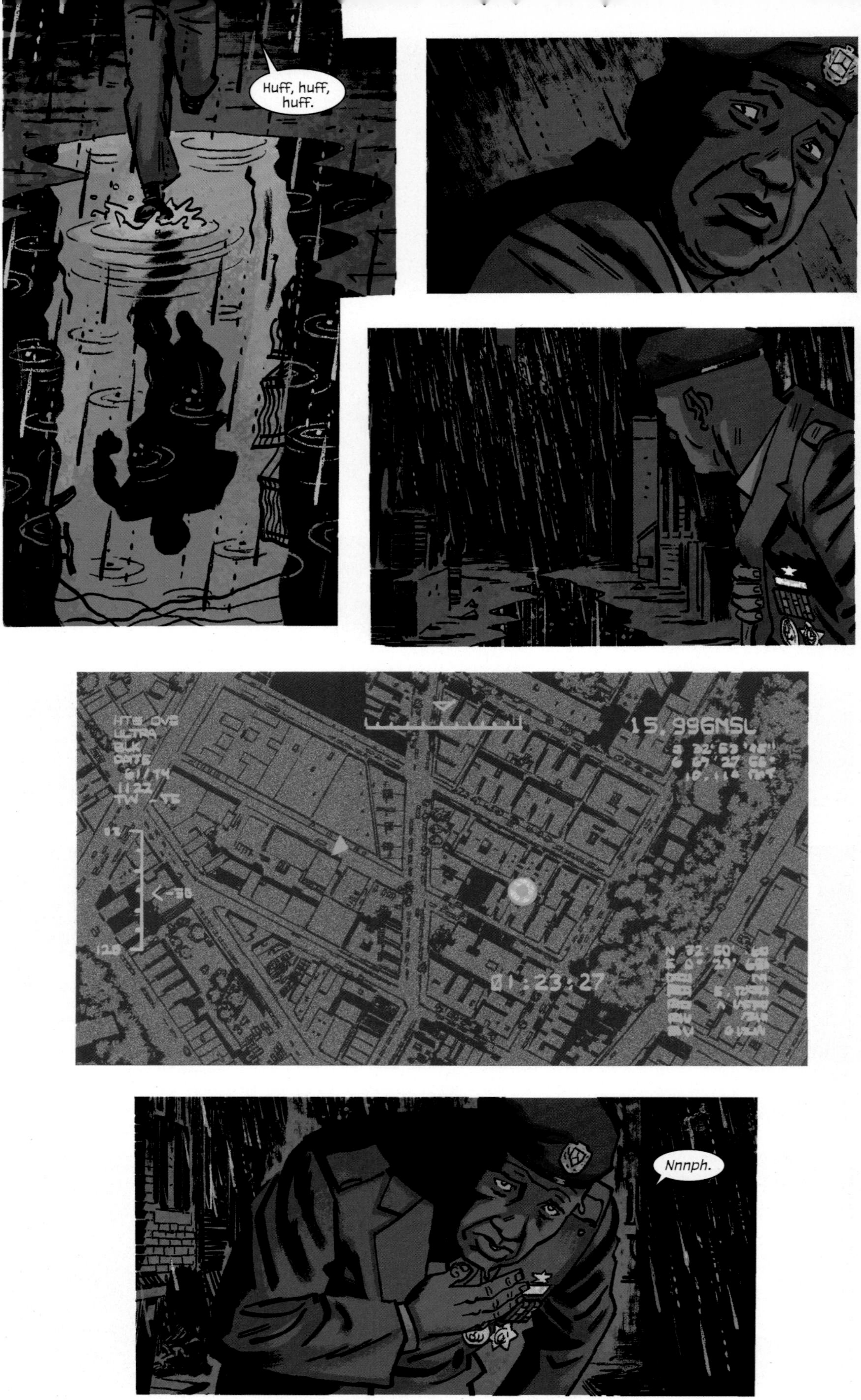
Huff, huff, huff.
15.996NSL
01:23:27
Nnnph.

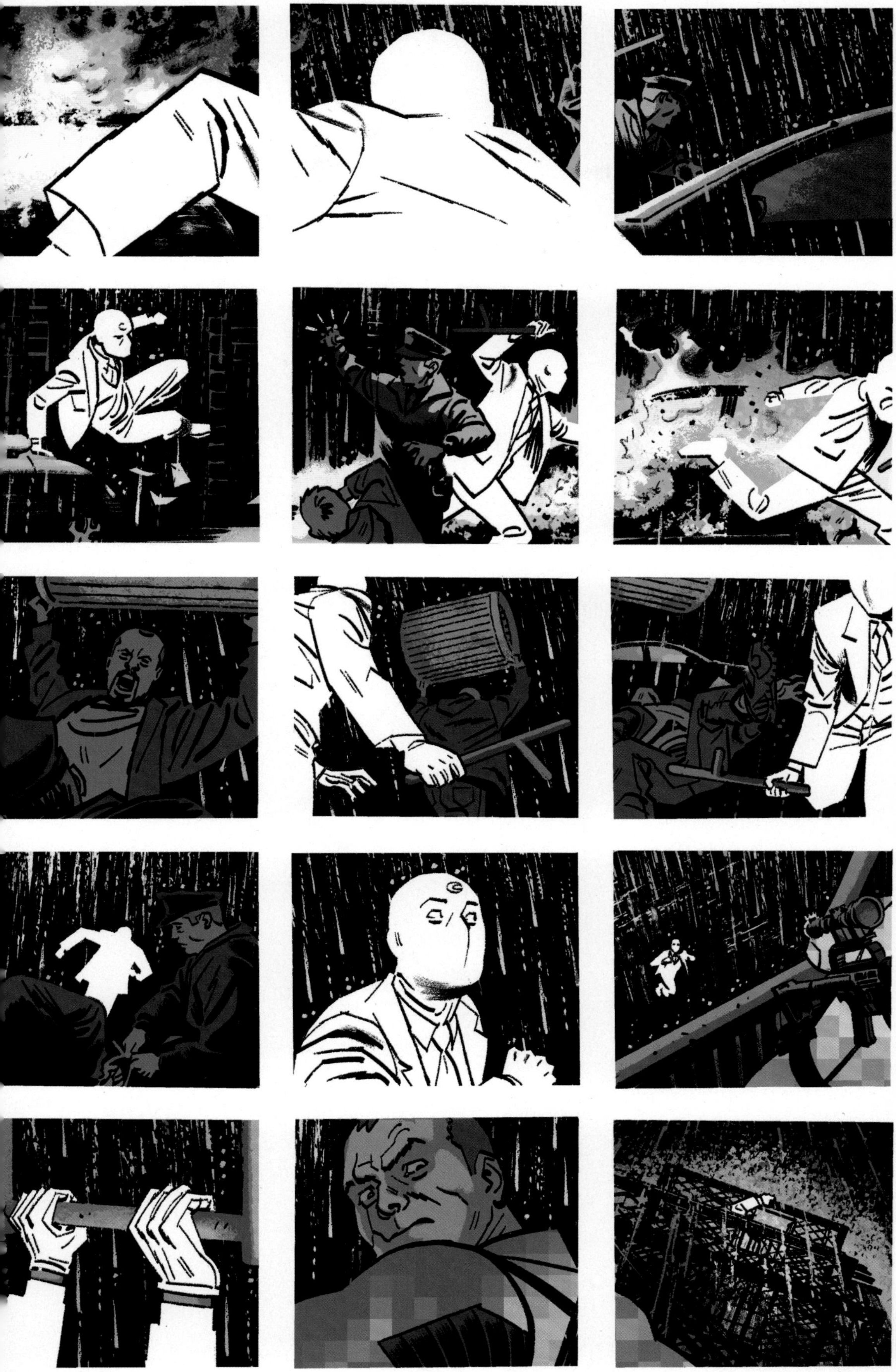

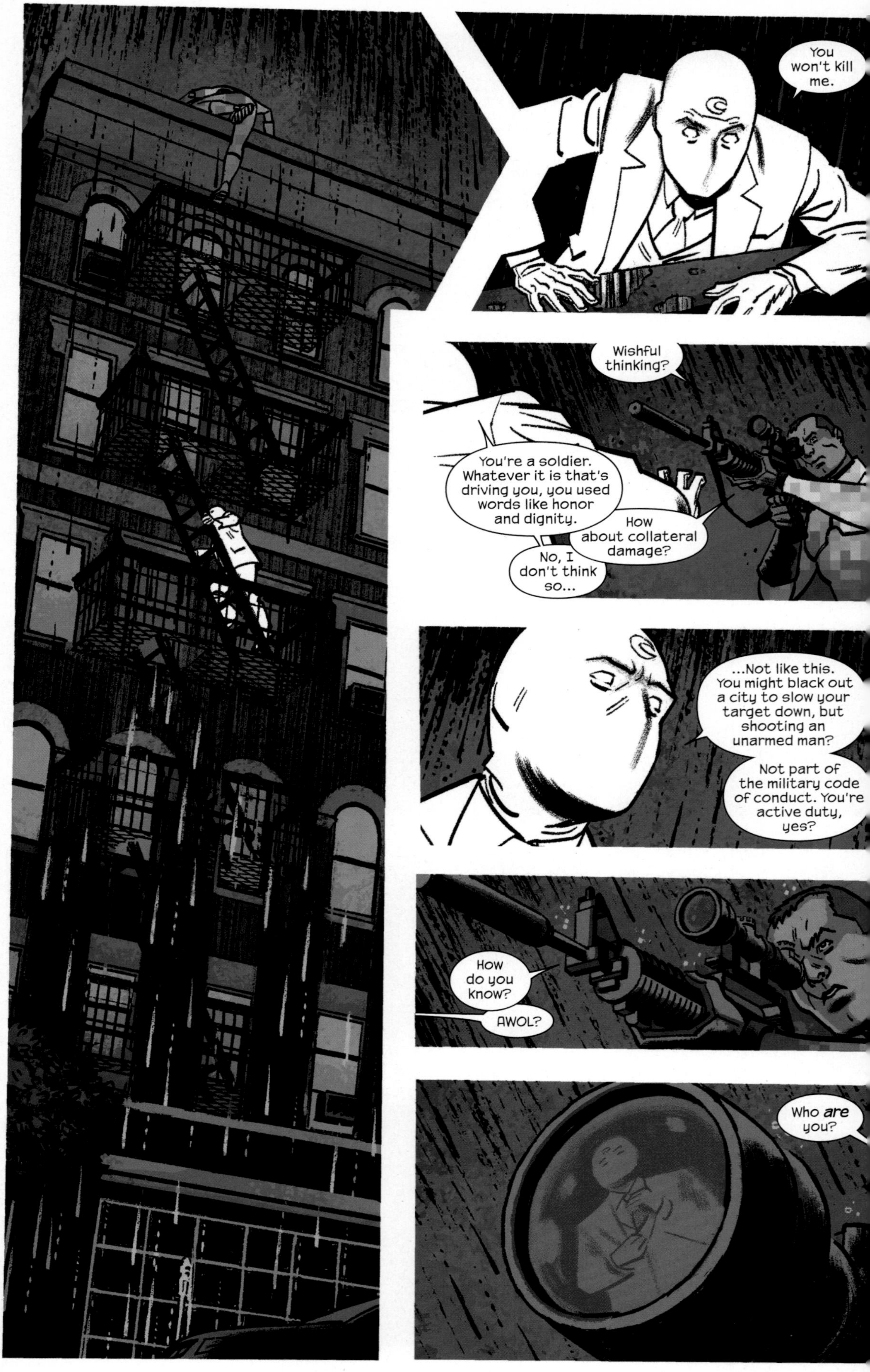
You won't kill me.
Wishful thinking?
You're a soldier. Whatever it is that's driving you, you used words like honor and dignity.
How about collateral damage?
No, I don't think so...
...Not like this. You might black out a city to slow your target down, but shooting an unarmed man?
Not part of the military code of conduct. You're active duty, yes?
How do you know?
AWOL?
Who *are* you?

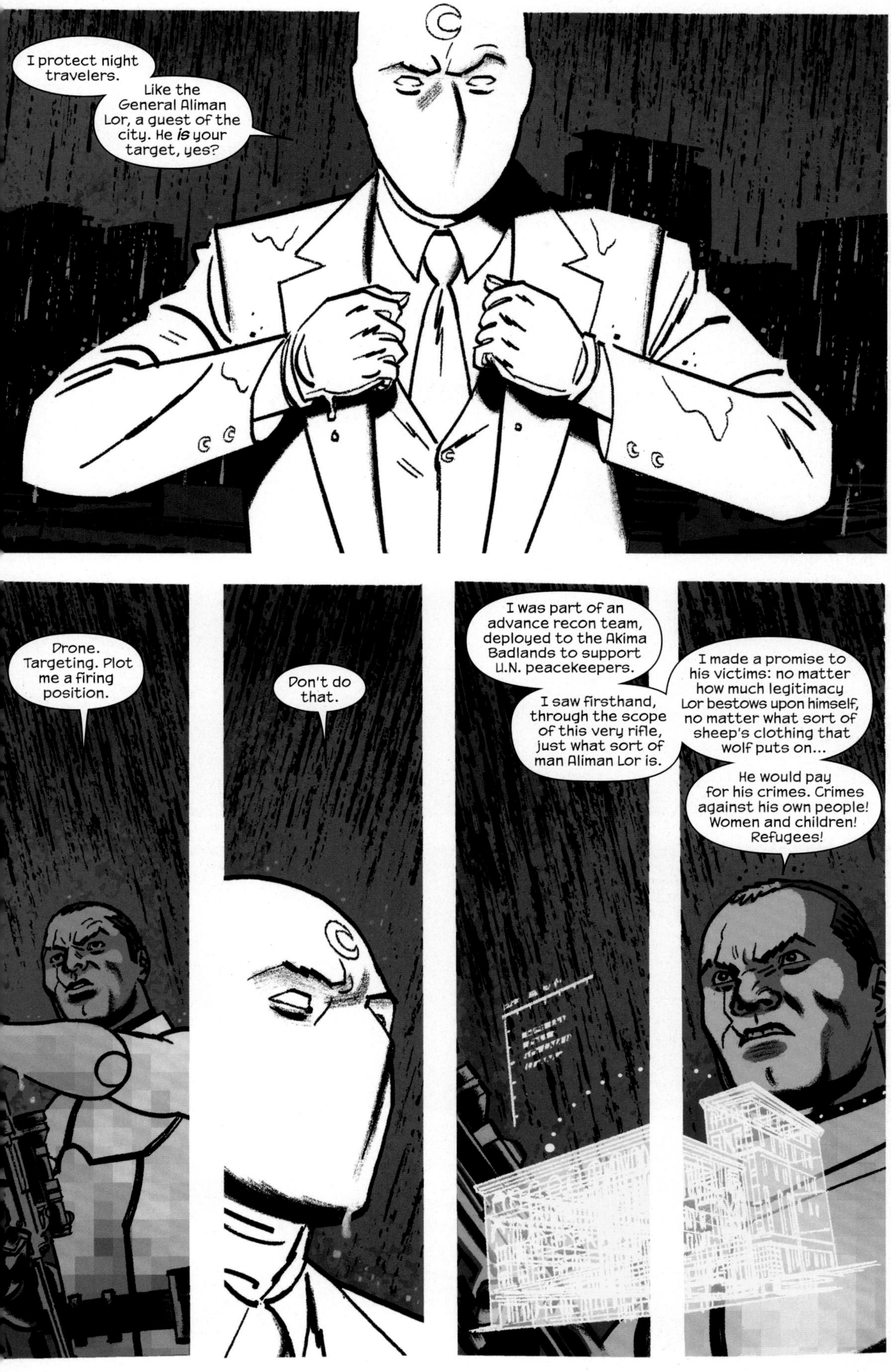
I protect night travelers.
Like the General Aliman Lor, a guest of the city. He *is* your target, yes?
Drone. Targeting. Plot me a firing position.
Don't do that.
I was part of an advance recon team, deployed to the Akima Badlands to support U.N. peacekeepers.
I saw firsthand, through the scope of this very rifle, just what sort of man Aliman Lor is.
I made a promise to his victims: no matter how much legitimacy Lor bestows upon himself, no matter what sort of sheep's clothing that wolf puts on...
He would pay for his crimes. Crimes against his own people! Women and children! Refugees!

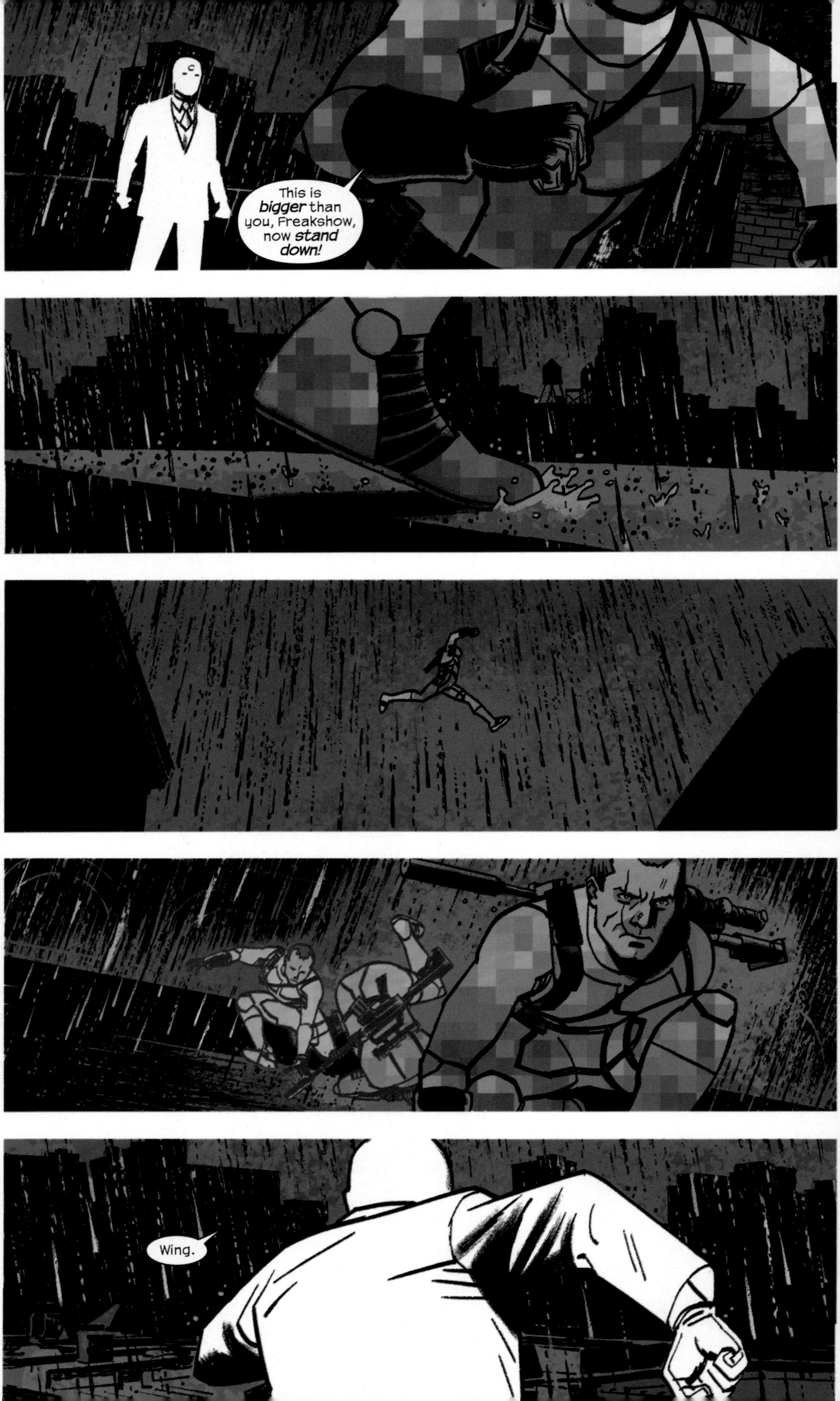
This is bigger than you, Freakshow, now stand down!
Wing.

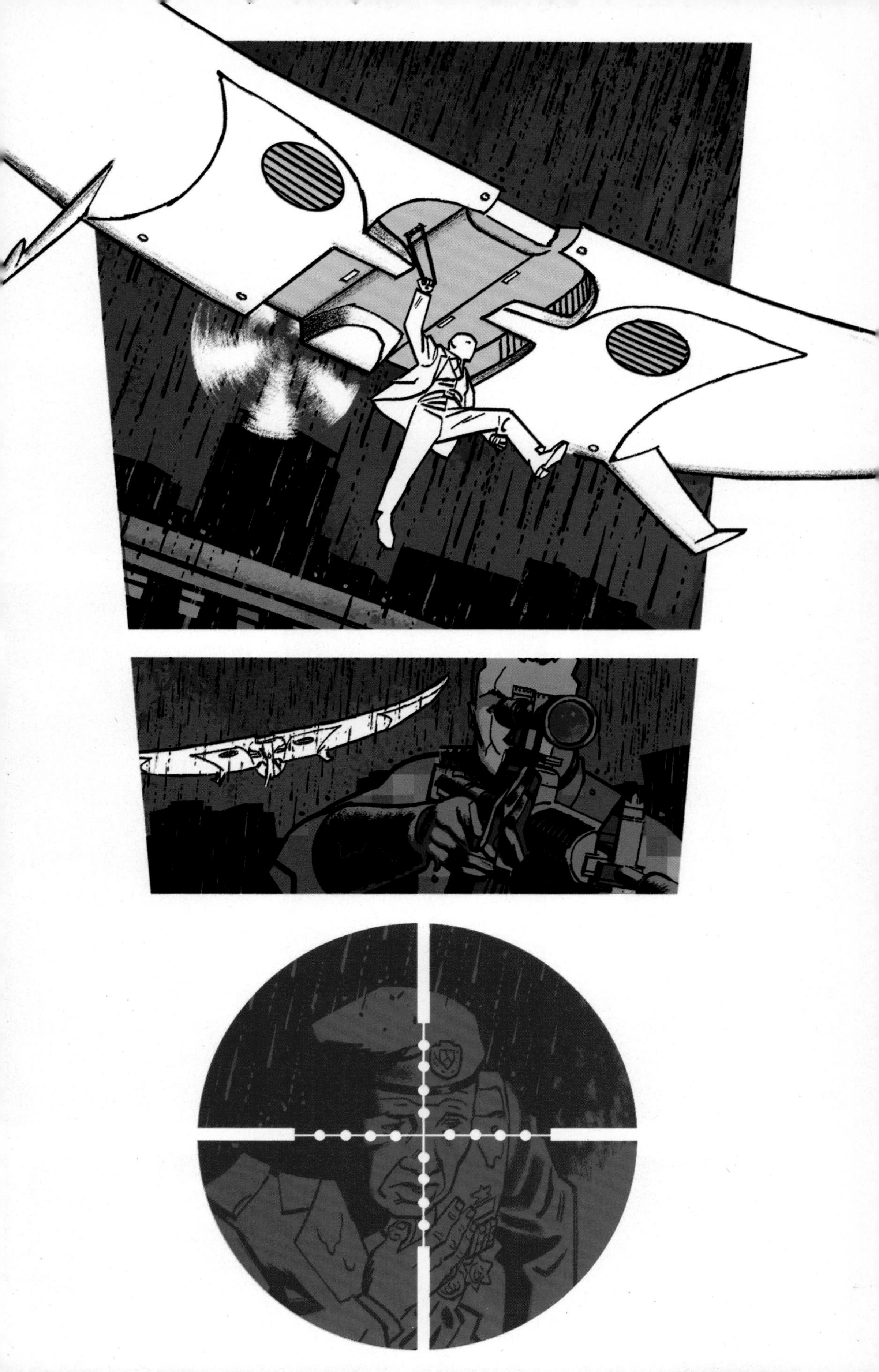

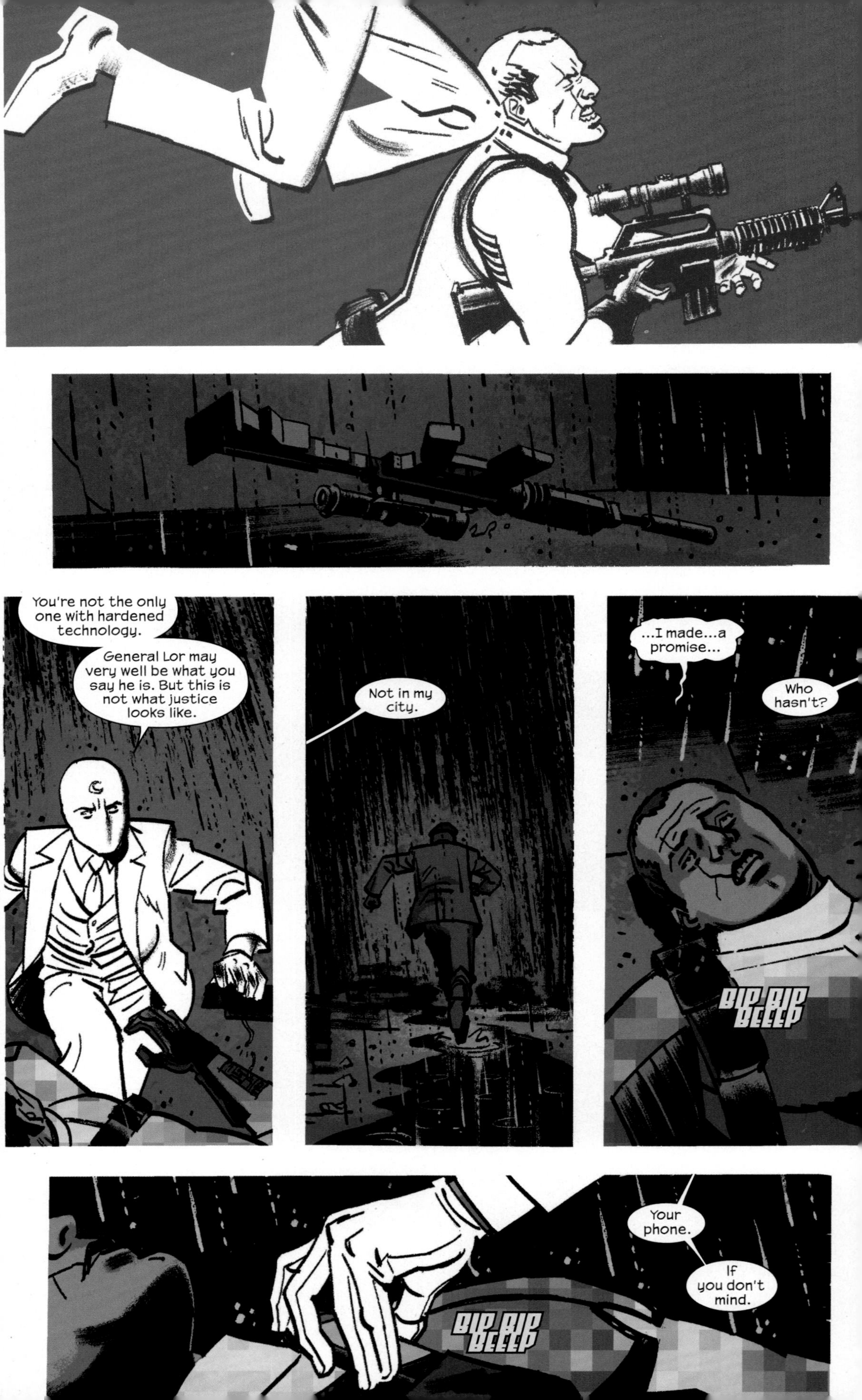
You're not the only one with hardened technology.
General Lor may very well be what you say he is. But this is not what justice looks like.
Not in my city.
...I made...a promise...
Who hasn't?
BIP BIP BEEEP
Your phone.
If you don't mind.
BIP BIP BEEEP

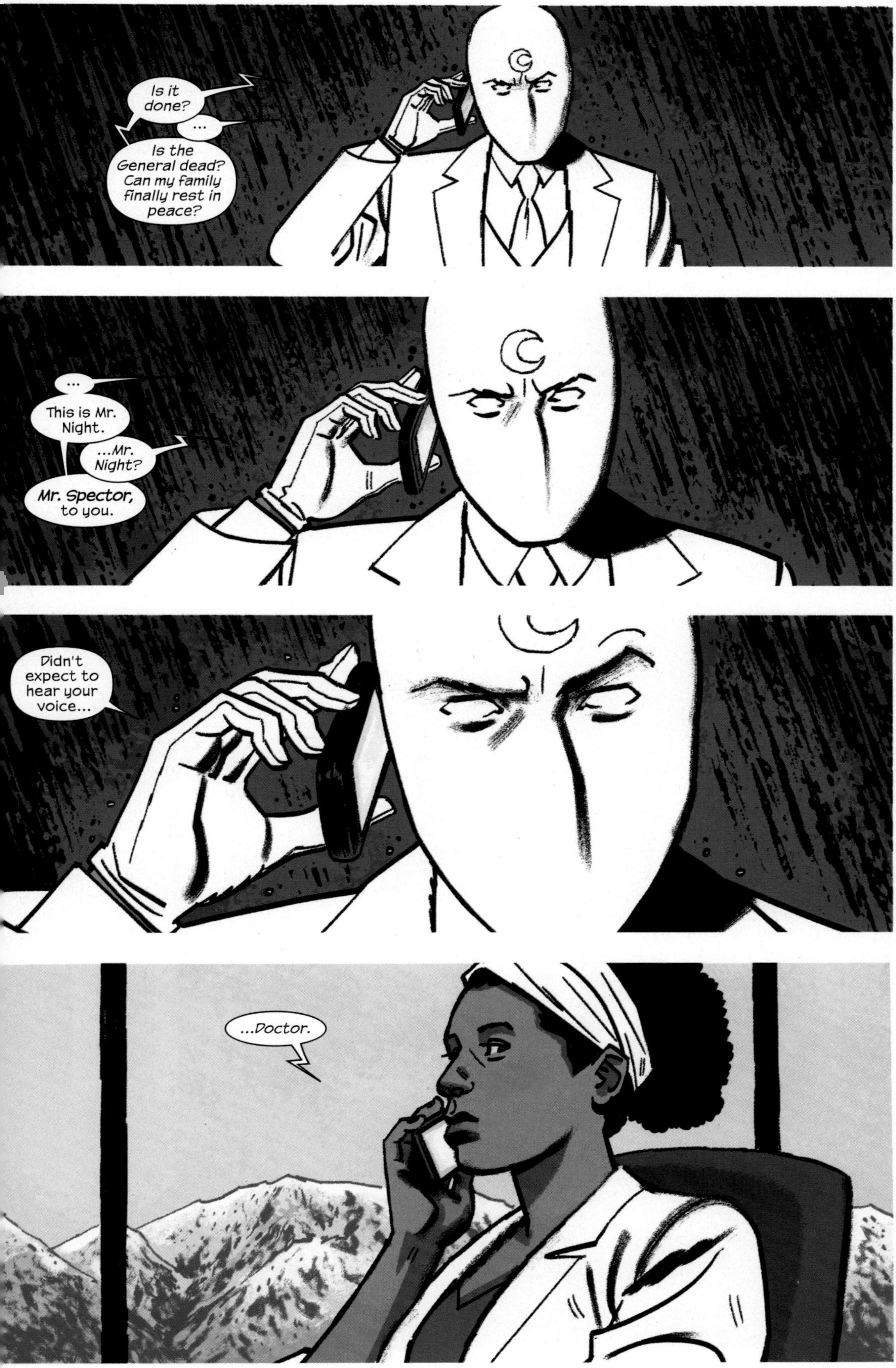
Is it done?
...
Is the General dead? Can my family finally rest in peace?
...
This is Mr. Night.
...Mr. Night?
Mr. Spector, to you.
Didn't expect to hear your voice...
...Doctor.

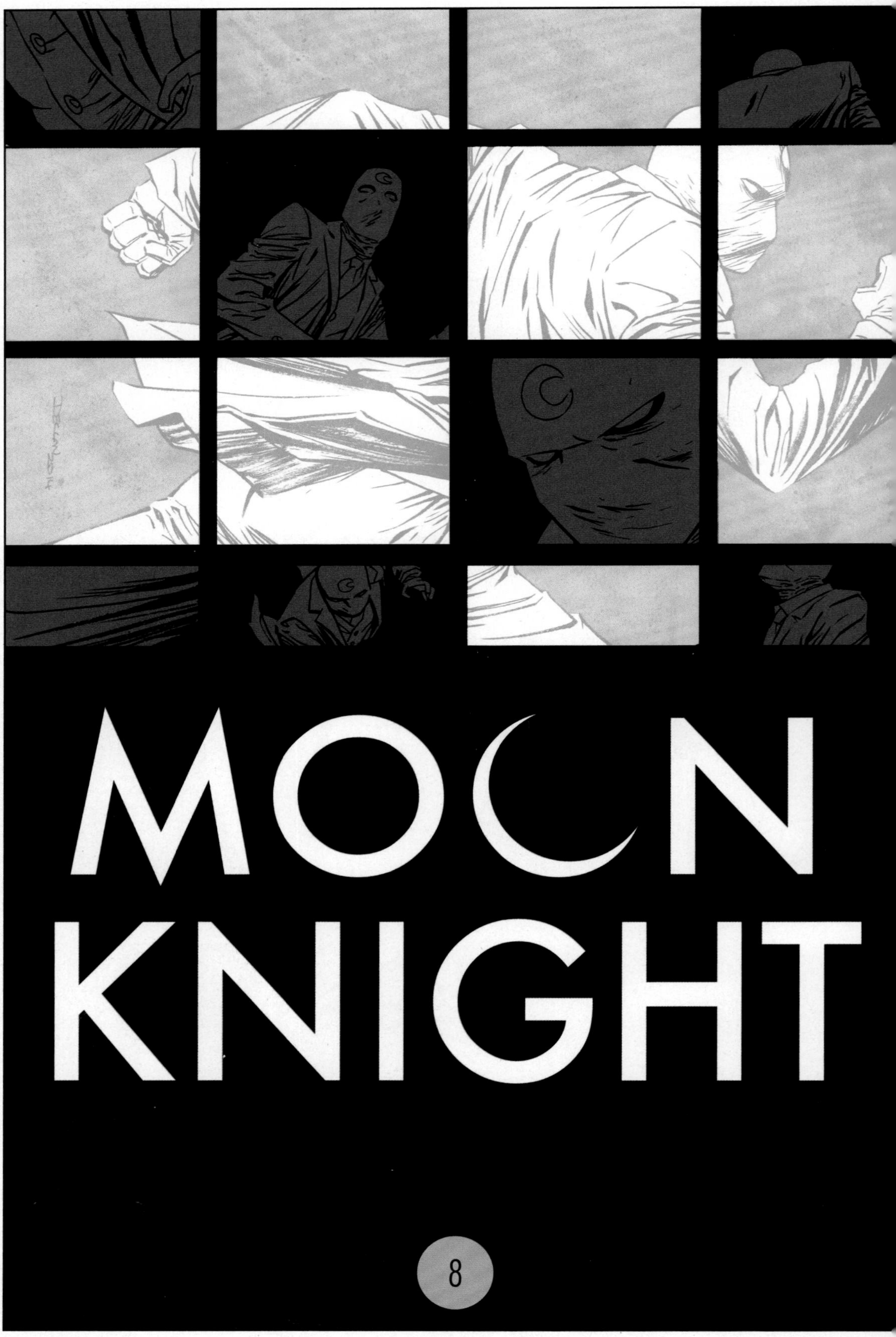
MOON
KNIGHT
8

NEW YORK CITY

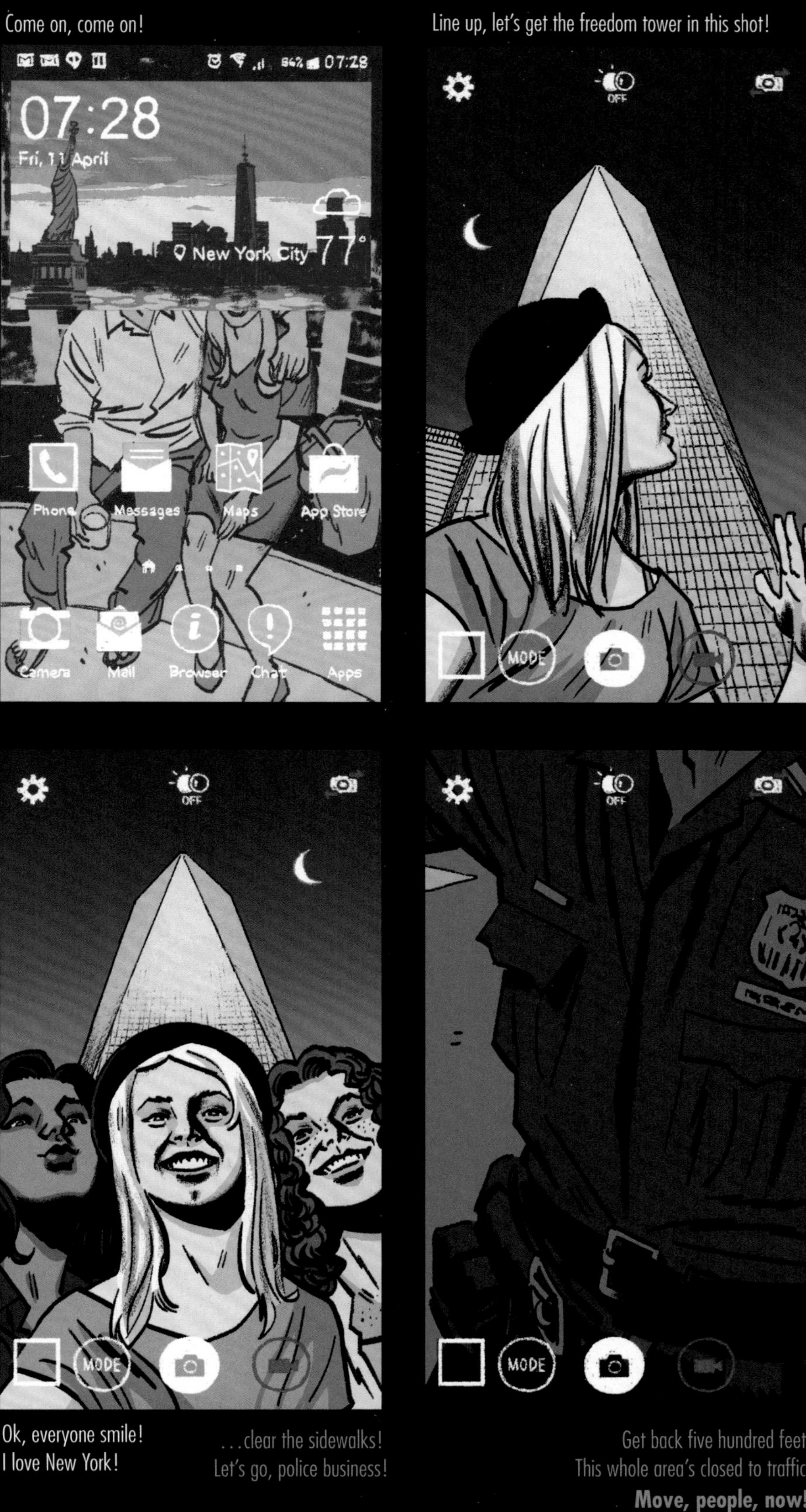

Come on, come on!
07:28
07:28
Fri, 11 April
New York City 77°
Phone
Messages
Maps
App Store
Camera
Mail
Browser
Chat
Apps
Line up, let's get the freedom tower in this shot!
OFF
MODE
OFF
MODE
OFF
MODE
Ok, everyone smile!
I love New York!
...clear the sidewalks!
Let's go, police business!
Get back five hundred feet
This whole area's closed to traffic
Move, people, now!

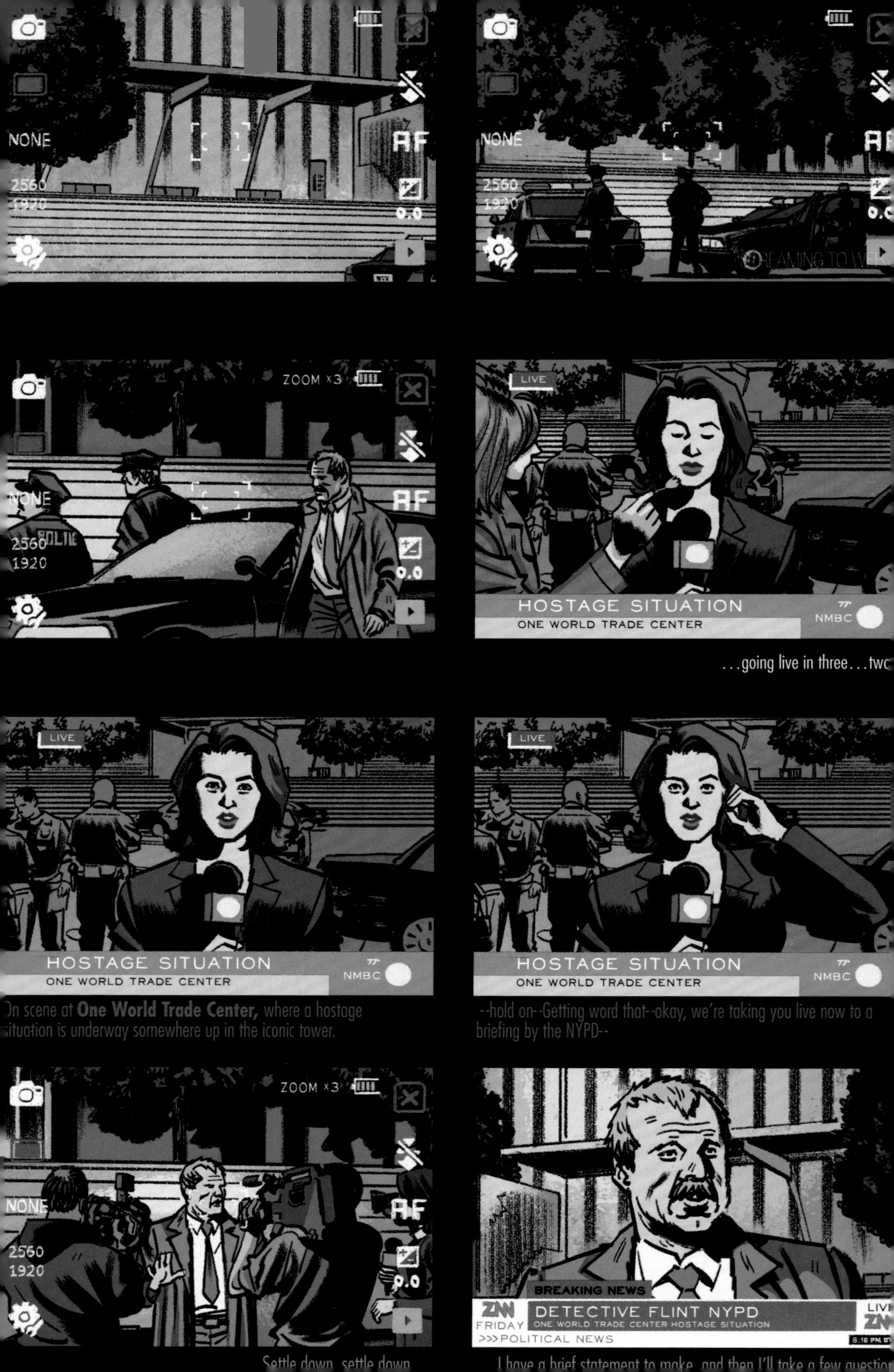

NONE
2560
1920
AF
0.0
STREAMING TO WEB
ZOOM x3
POLICE
LIVE
HOSTAGE SITUATION
ONE WORLD TRADE CENTER
NMBC
. . .going live in three. . .two
On scene at **One World Trade Center,** where a hostage situation is underway somewhere up in the iconic tower.
--hold on--Getting word that--okay, we're taking you live now to a briefing by the NYPD--
Settle down, settle down.
BREAKING NEWS
DETECTIVE FLINT NYPD
ONE WORLD TRADE CENTER HOSTAGE SITUATION
FRIDAY
>>>POLITICAL NEWS
I have a brief statement to make, and then I'll take a few questions.

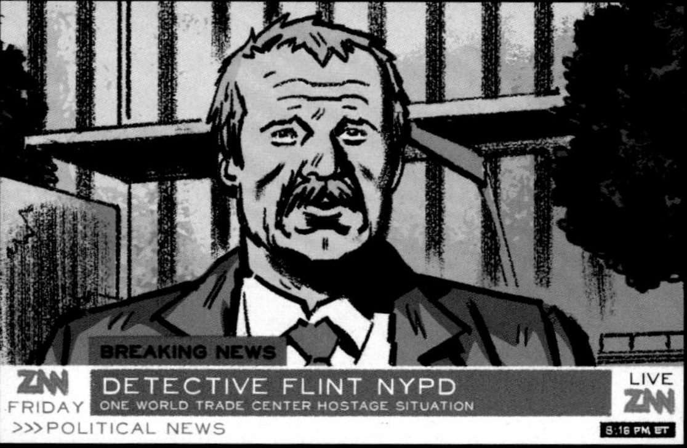
BREAKING NEWS
ZNN
FRIDAY
DETECTIVE FLINT NYPD
ONE WORLD TRADE CENTER HOSTAGE SITUATION
>>>POLITICAL NEWS
LIVE
ZNN
8:16 PM ET

At about 5:00 PM today, we received a call from an office on the 88th floor of One World Trade Center, reporting a physical assault between two coworkers. A couple uniforms were dispatched, but once arriving, were denied access to the office.

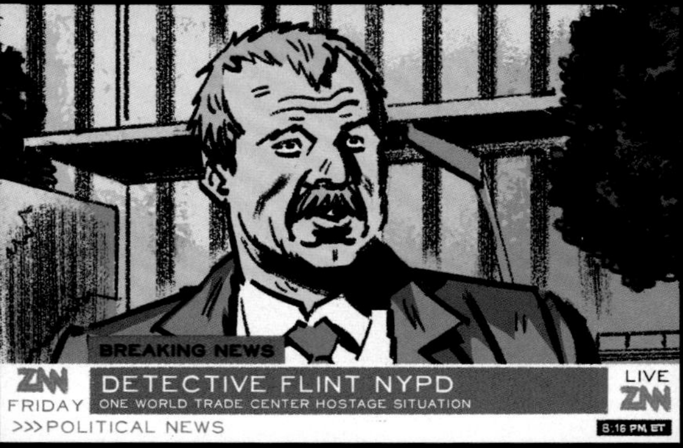
BREAKING NEWS
ZNN
FRIDAY
DETECTIVE FLINT NYPD
ONE WORLD TRADE CENTER HOSTAGE SITUATION
>>>POLITICAL NEWS
LIVE
ZNN
8:16 PM ET

Security feeds are still running, however, and we've been able to confirm, provisionally, that we have a hostage situation occuring in that office at this time.

We are attempting to establish contact with someone within--

Detective! Is this a terrorist act?

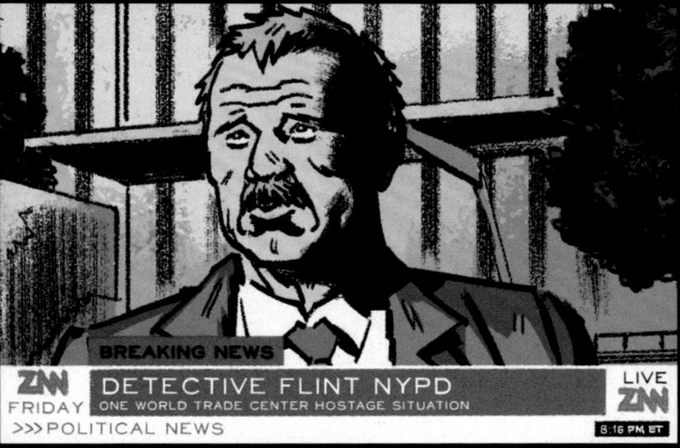
BREAKING NEWS
ZNN
FRIDAY
DETECTIVE FLINT NYPD
ONE WORLD TRADE CENTER HOSTAGE SITUATION
>>>POLITICAL NEWS
LIVE
ZNN
8:16 PM ET

We don't have information to support or discount terror, but as is usual these days, precautionary measures are in place. The commerical air corridor over Manhattan has been closed...

...and first responders have been mobilized and are on-site. In addition, the appropriate state and federal agencies have been notified.

Has anyone been sent inside?

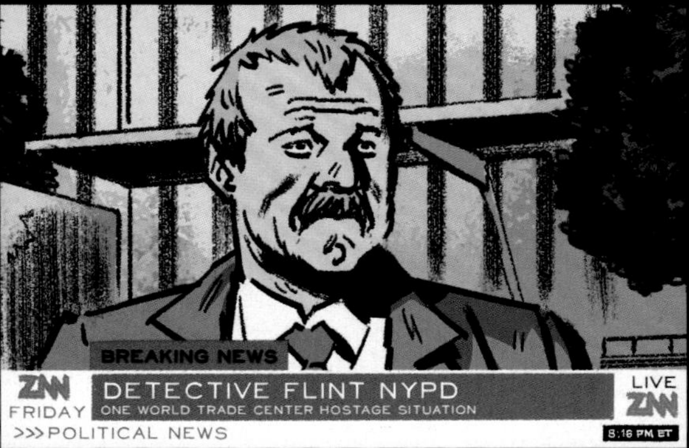
BREAKING NEWS
ZNN
FRIDAY
DETECTIVE FLINT NYPD
ONE WORLD TRADE CENTER HOSTAGE SITUATION
>>>POLITICAL NEWS
LIVE
ZNN
8:16 PM ET

We have deployed a team to monitor the situation.

Detective--

I can't comment further on operational matters, I'm sorry--

Has this turned into a **military** operation?

We have our **best men** in place.

I'm afraid that's all I can say at the moment.

Best man." Come on.

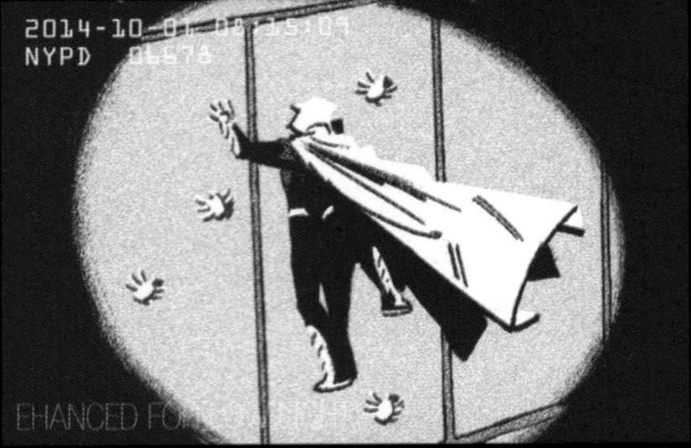
NYPD

don't even know who--
what--the hell he is.

Detective Flint's man.

Great.

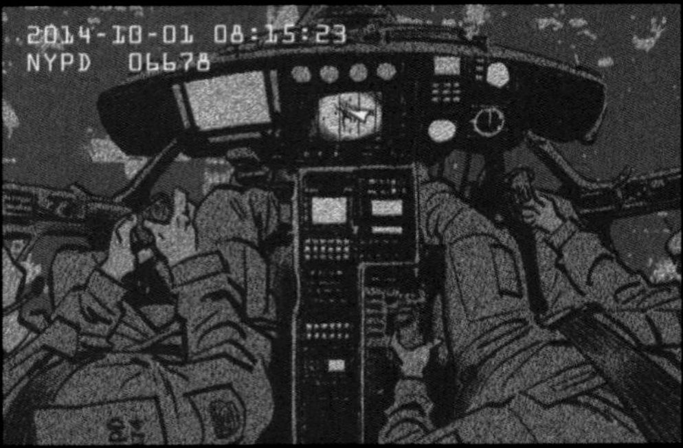
2014-10-01 08:15:23
NYPD 06678

Cut that spo

Now.

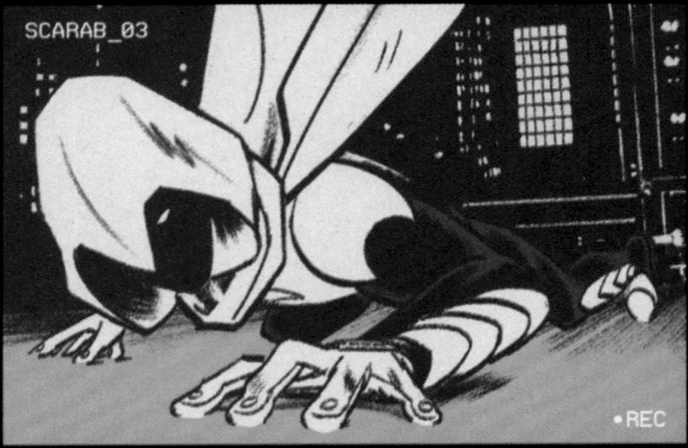
SCARAB_03
•REC

You're on you

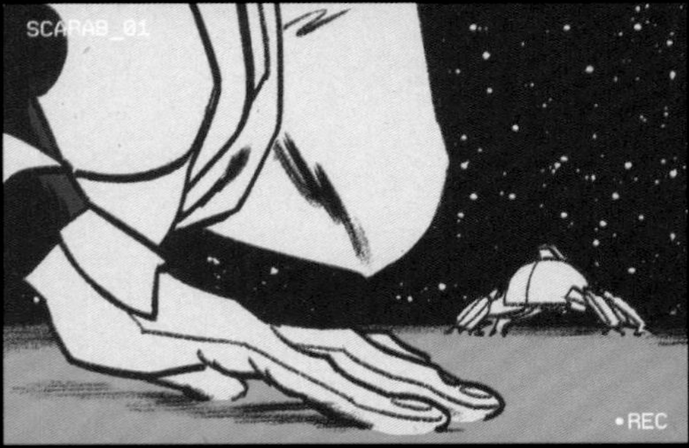
•REC

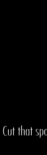

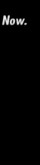

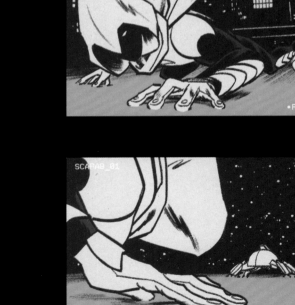

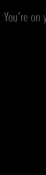

Thank you.

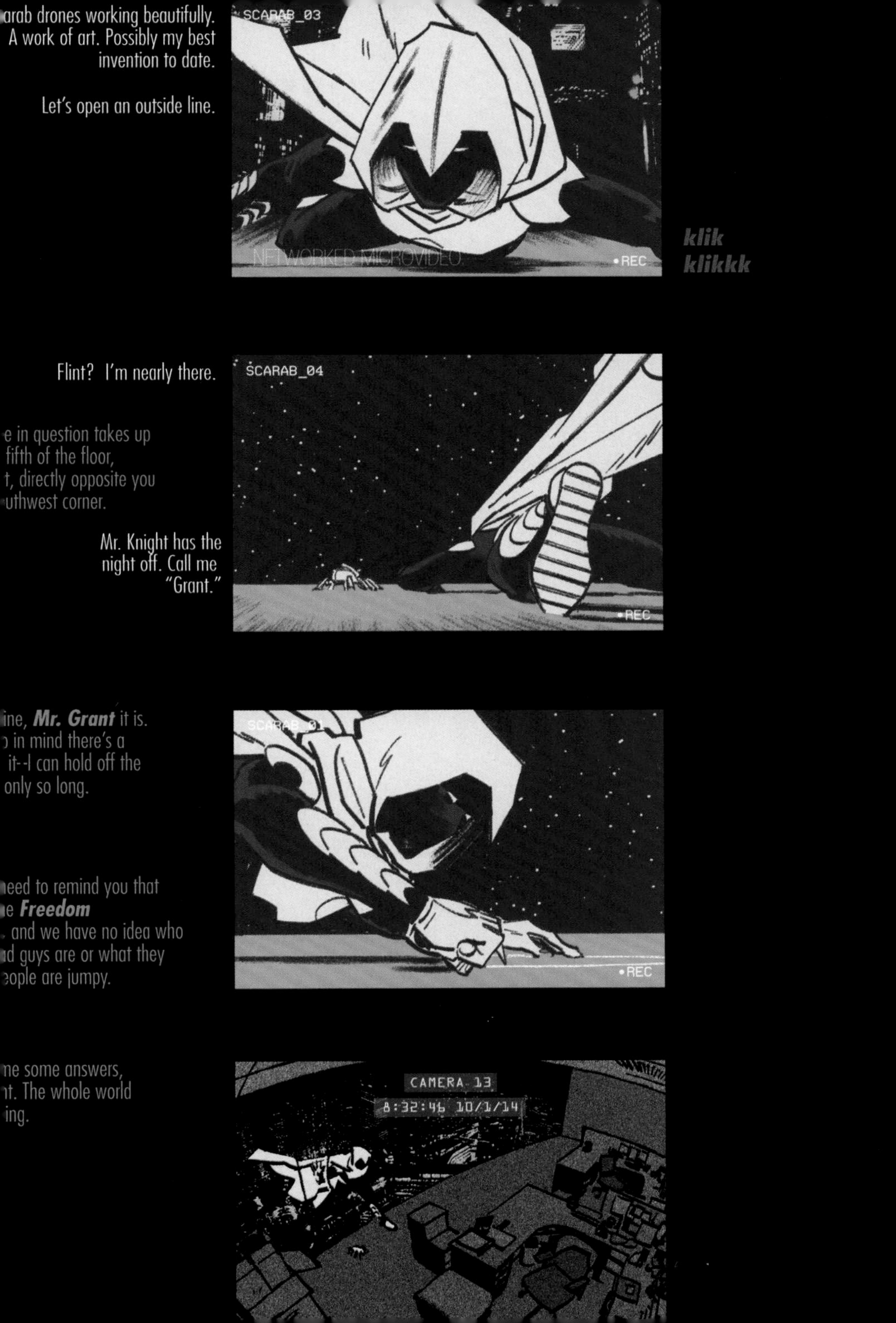
arab drones working beautifully. A work of art. Possibly my best invention to date.
Let's open an outside line.
SCARAB_03
NETWORKED MICROVIDEO
•REC
klik
klikkk
Flint? I'm nearly there.
e in question takes up
fifth of the floor,
t, directly opposite you
uthwest corner.
Mr. Knight has the night off. Call me "Grant."
SCARAB_04
•REC
ine, ***Mr. Grant*** it is.
in mind there's a
it--I can hold off the
only so long.
eed to remind you that
e ***Freedom***
and we have no idea who
d guys are or what they
eople are jumpy.
•REC
ne some answers,
t. The whole world
ing.
CAMERA 13
8:32:46 10/1/14

SCARAB_01
•REC
SCARAB_02
•REC
SCARAB_03
•REC
SCARAB_04
•REC
Still there. Don't move. Shut up until I tell you.
Please, sir, I have a fam--
REC
ust say what I told you and naybe you'll see them ıgain, understood? Three, wo, one.
n, this is a message for the, um, paymasters and puppet-string lders of our immoral and corrupt global industrial complex. Um, please listen carefully to the following.
REC
X-ray--Beta Kilo--

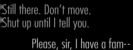

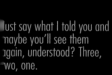

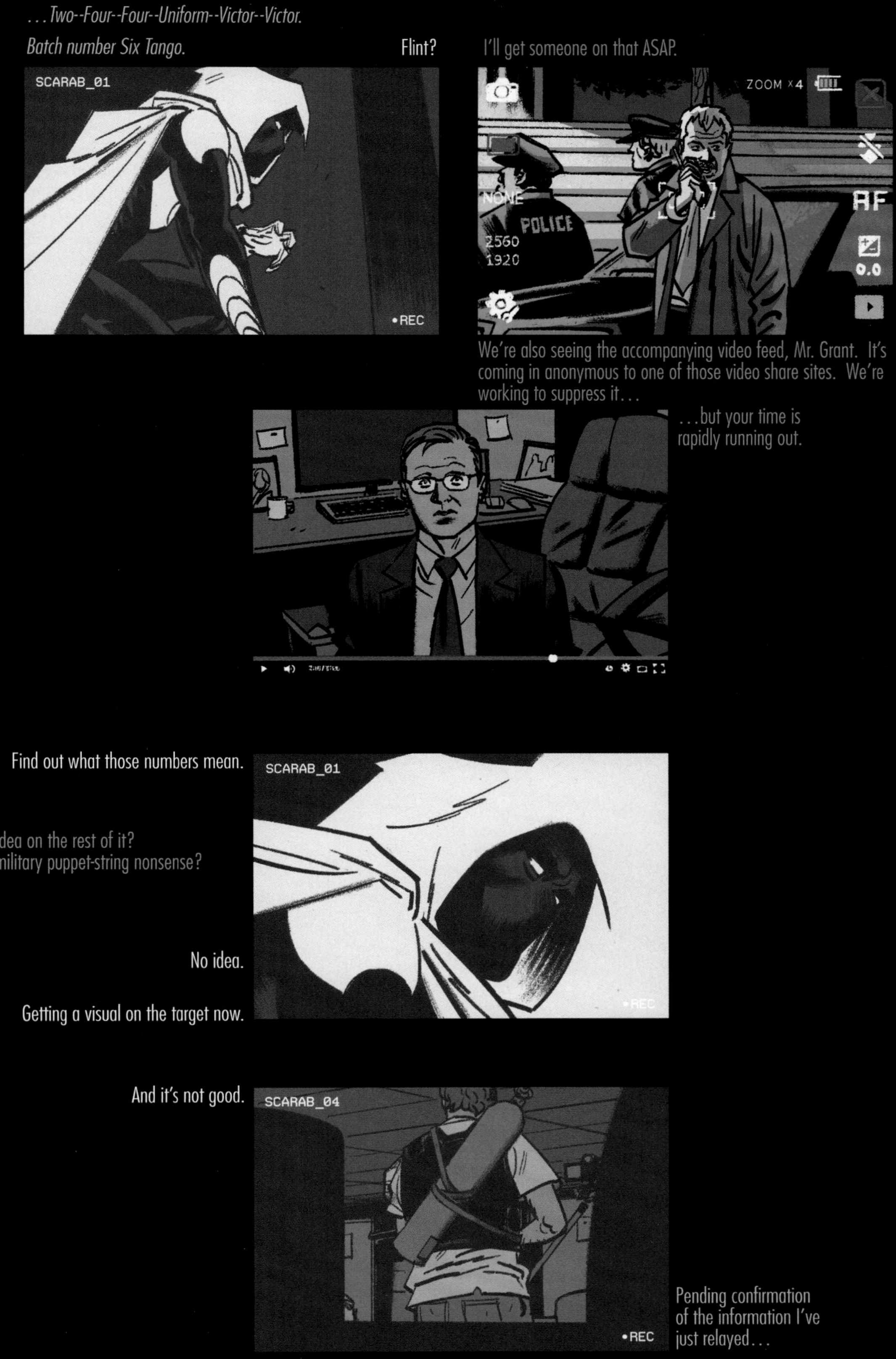

...Two--Four--Four--Uniform--Victor--Victor.
Batch number Six Tango.
Flint?
I'll get someone on that ASAP.
SCARAB_01
•REC
ZOOM x4
NONE
POLICE
2560
1920
AF
0.0
We're also seeing the accompanying video feed, Mr. Grant. It's coming in anonymous to one of those video share sites. We're working to suppress it...
...but your time is rapidly running out.
Find out what those numbers mean.
SCARAB_01
y idea on the rest of it?
e military puppet-string nonsense?
No idea.
Getting a visual on the target now.
•REC
And it's not good.
SCARAB_04
•REC
Pending confirmation of the information I've just relayed...

...you will receive further
instructions. In the meantime,
any moves to, um, bring a premature
end to this situation will result in
um um **complete destruction**
of both this bulding...

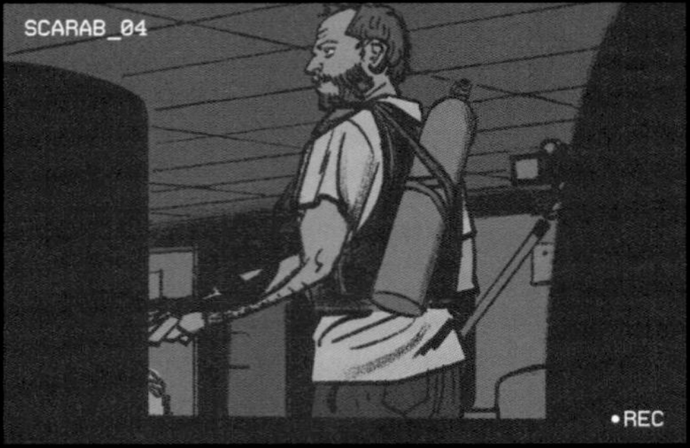
SCARAB_04
•REC

...and much of Lower
Manhattan...

Describe what I'm wearing.

...wait, what?

What do you
see me wearing?
Tell them.

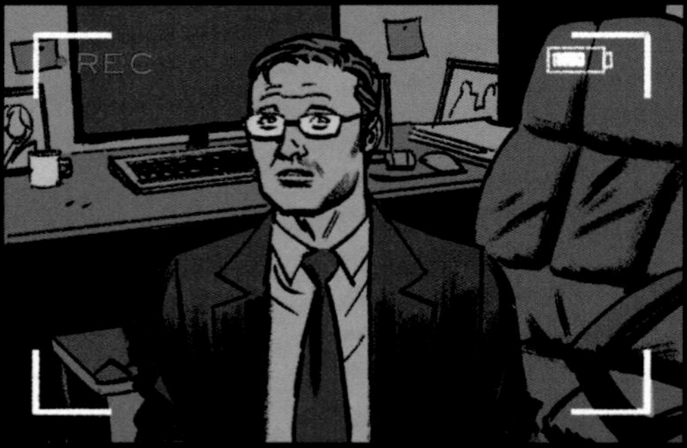
REC

Um, it's a bomb vest, like a suicide bom
Lots of wires, blocks of explosive materi
Um, maybe ten blocks? And a **tank,** li
a scuba tank.

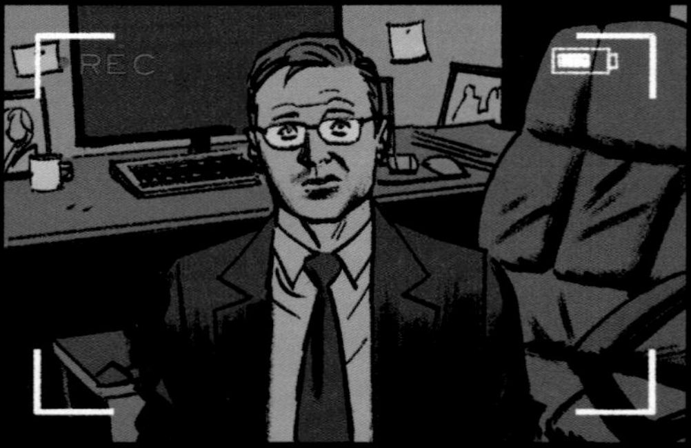
REC

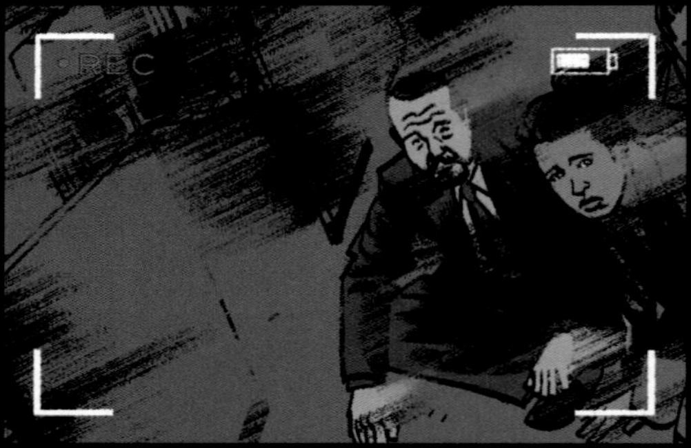
REC

It's not a--look, here--

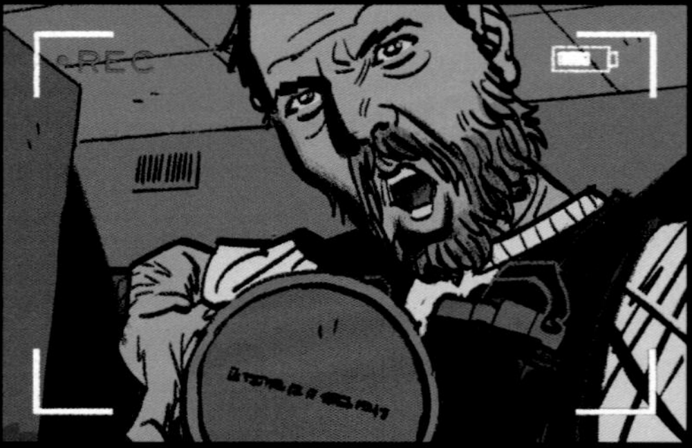
REC

This is **not** a **scuba tank. Look at it.** Confirm the numbers,
and then you'll realize. In the meantime...

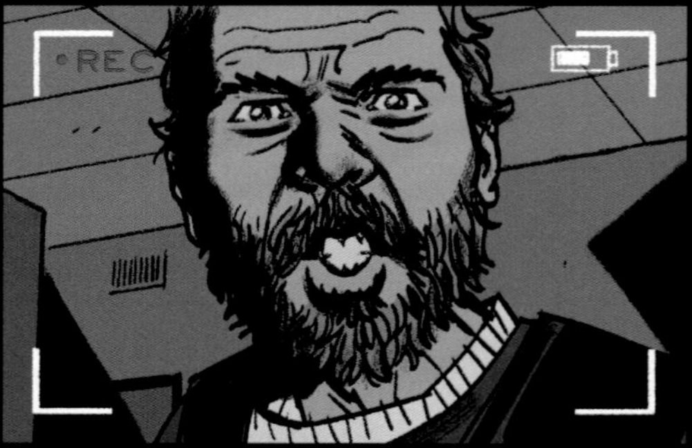
REC

...you come for me, I'll salt this earth.

Mr. Grant?

is is getting out of
ntrol. We have
ndreds or thousands
eyewitnesses here,
d once that video
eam hits social
edia, this'll go global.

is won't be an
PD jurisdiction
r much longer.
e FBI is en
ute. I'd say we
ve **minutes**
maining.

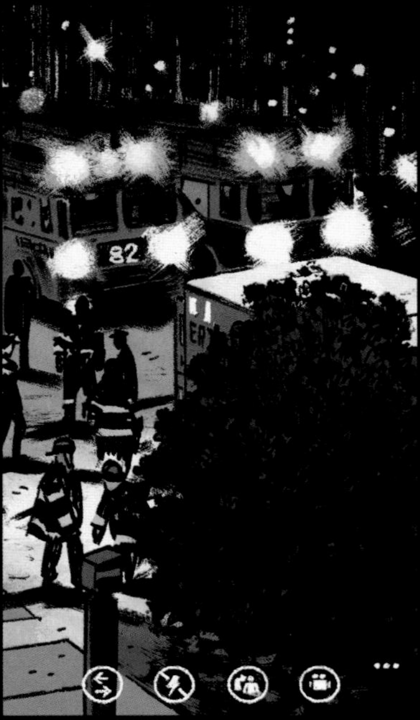
82

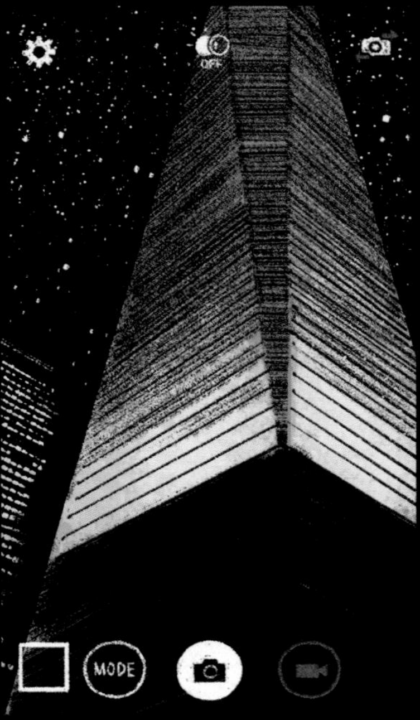
MODE

What about those serial
numbers?

Still waiting. But
understand that
information may
not be shared
with me.

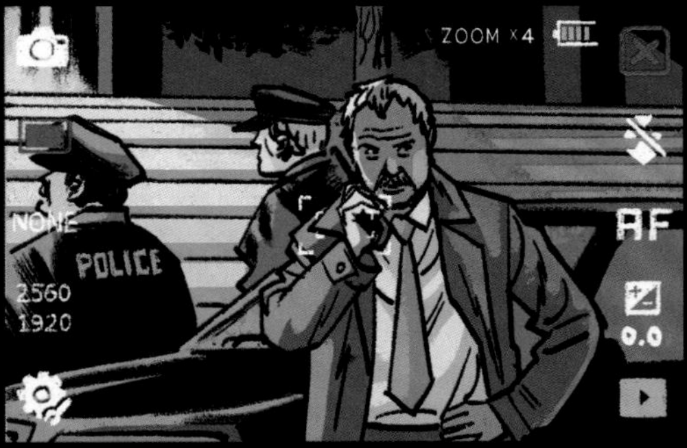
ZOOM ×4
POLICE
NONE
2560
1920
AF
0.0

We've confirmed there are two
dozen hostages, and while the
tower is still being evacuated,
if he sets off that bomb?
Any sort of bomb?

Do I need to talk
about that?

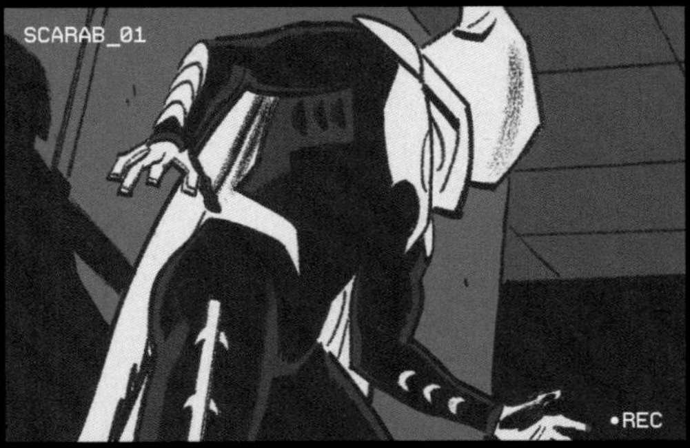
SCARAB_01
•REC

No.

Which is why I need **you** to
make a call for me, before all
of this escalates out of all
restraint and reason.

I need you to call
my doctor.

SCARAB_01

Flint?

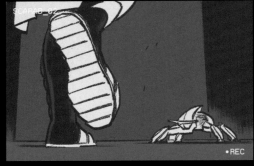

SCARAB_02

If you can't respond for whatever reason, just keep listening.
My scarab network is archiving this audio.

SCARAB_03

I can hear voices.

Correction: one voice.
The target's voice.

ZOOM ×4

NONE

2560
1920

AF

0.0

Detective Flint?

ZOOM ×4

NONE

POLI

2560
1920

AF

0.0

Be with you guys in a second.

SCARAB_01

I have the hostages in sight.

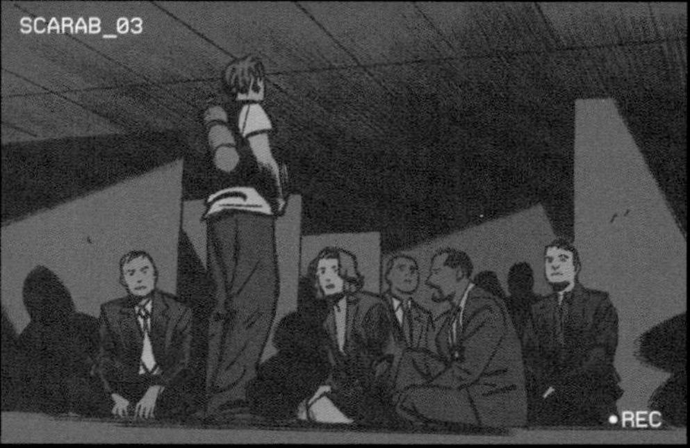
SCARAB_03
•REC

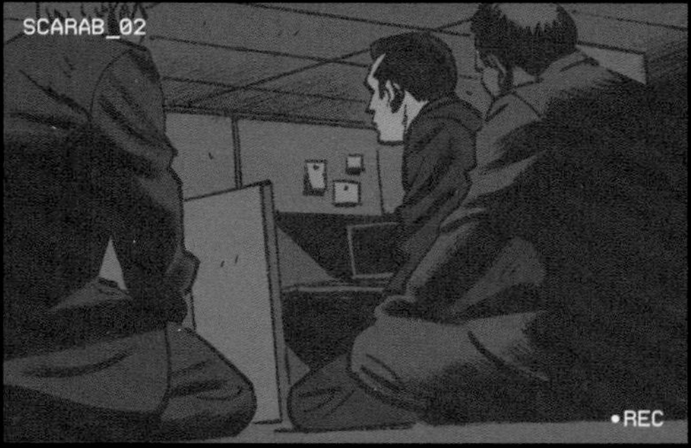
SCARAB_02
•REC

Sixteen hostages. One target.

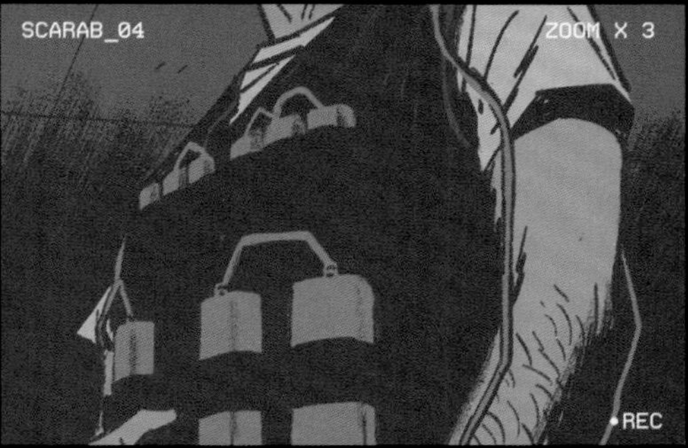
SCARAB_04
ZOOM X 3
•REC

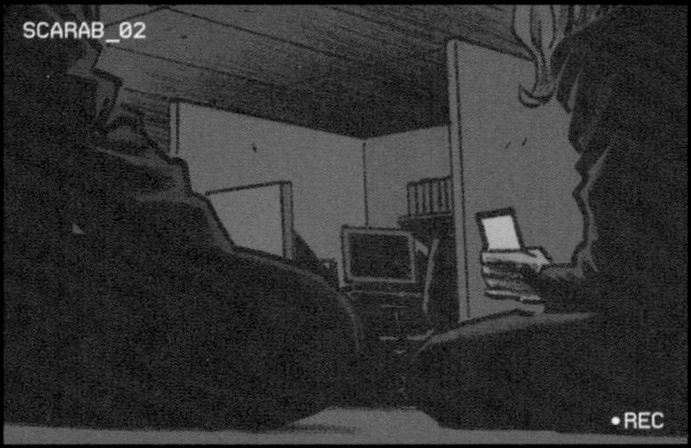
SCARAB_02
•REC

Sending you shots of the bomb.

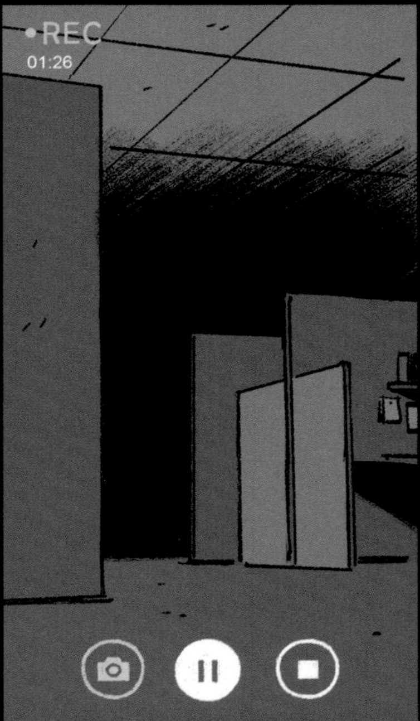
•REC
01:26

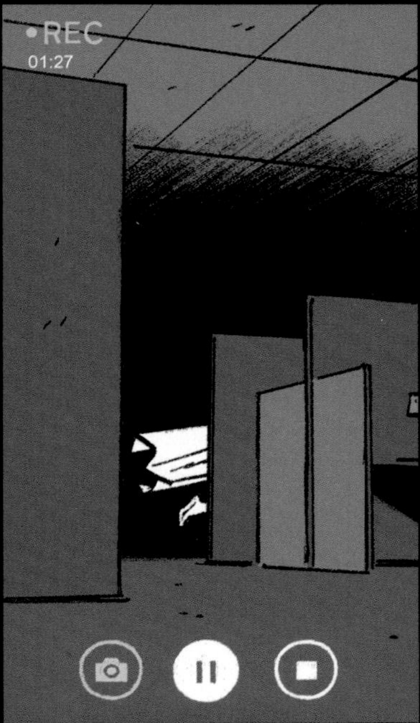
•REC
01:27

Thank you, Mr. Grant, you've been extremel helpful.

Lockley, you are good to go. Complete your recon, find your angles, pick your plan of attack.

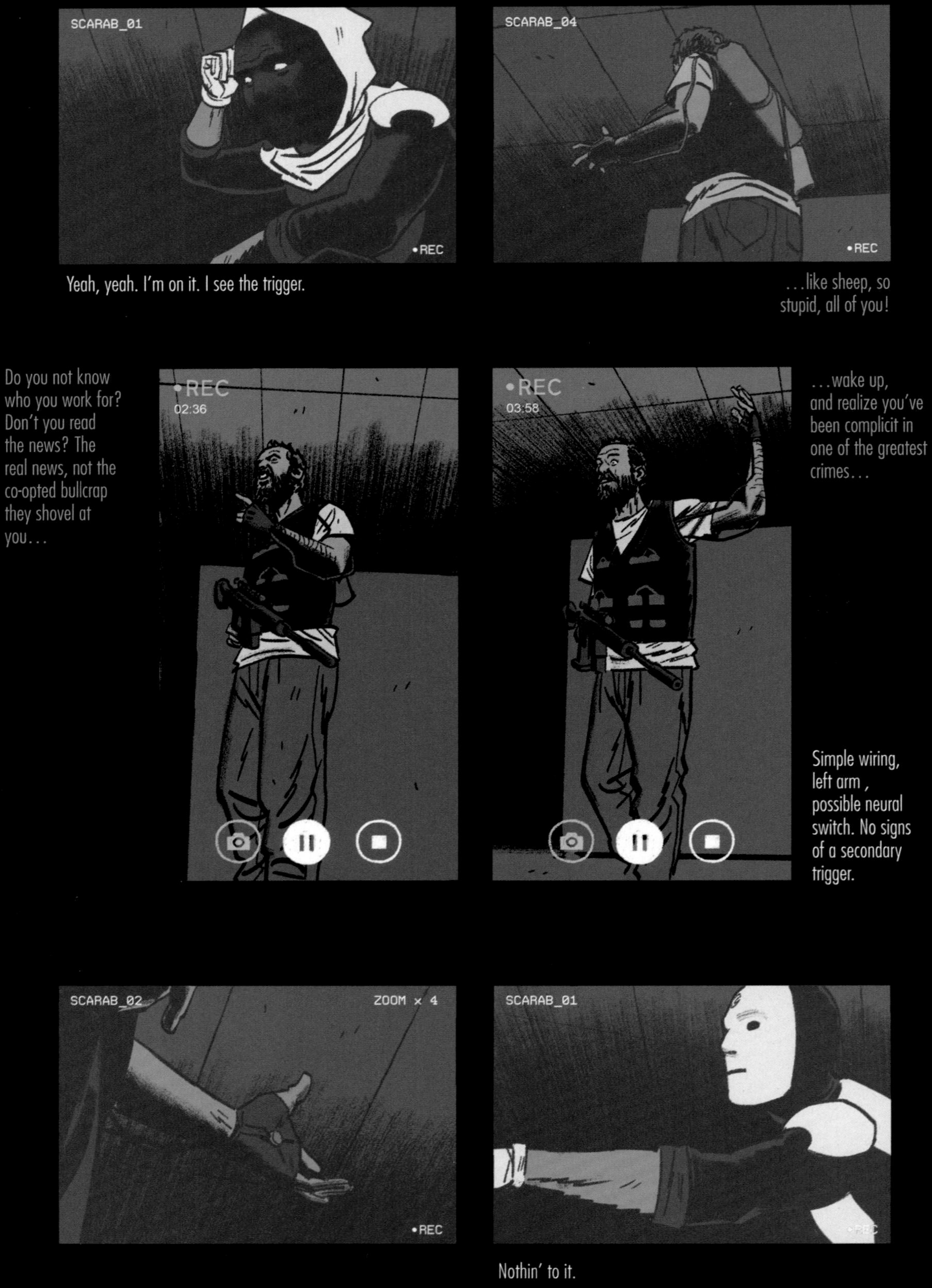
SCARAB_01
•REC
Yeah, yeah. I'm on it. I see the trigger.
SCARAB_04
•REC
...like sheep, so stupid, all of you!
Do you not know who you work for? Don't you read the news? The real news, not the co-opted bullcrap they shovel at you...
•REC
02:36
•REC
03:58
...wake up, and realize you've been complicit in one of the greatest crimes...
Simple wiring, left arm , possible neural switch. No signs of a secondary trigger.
SCARAB_02
ZOOM × 4
•REC
SCARAB_01
Nothin' to it.

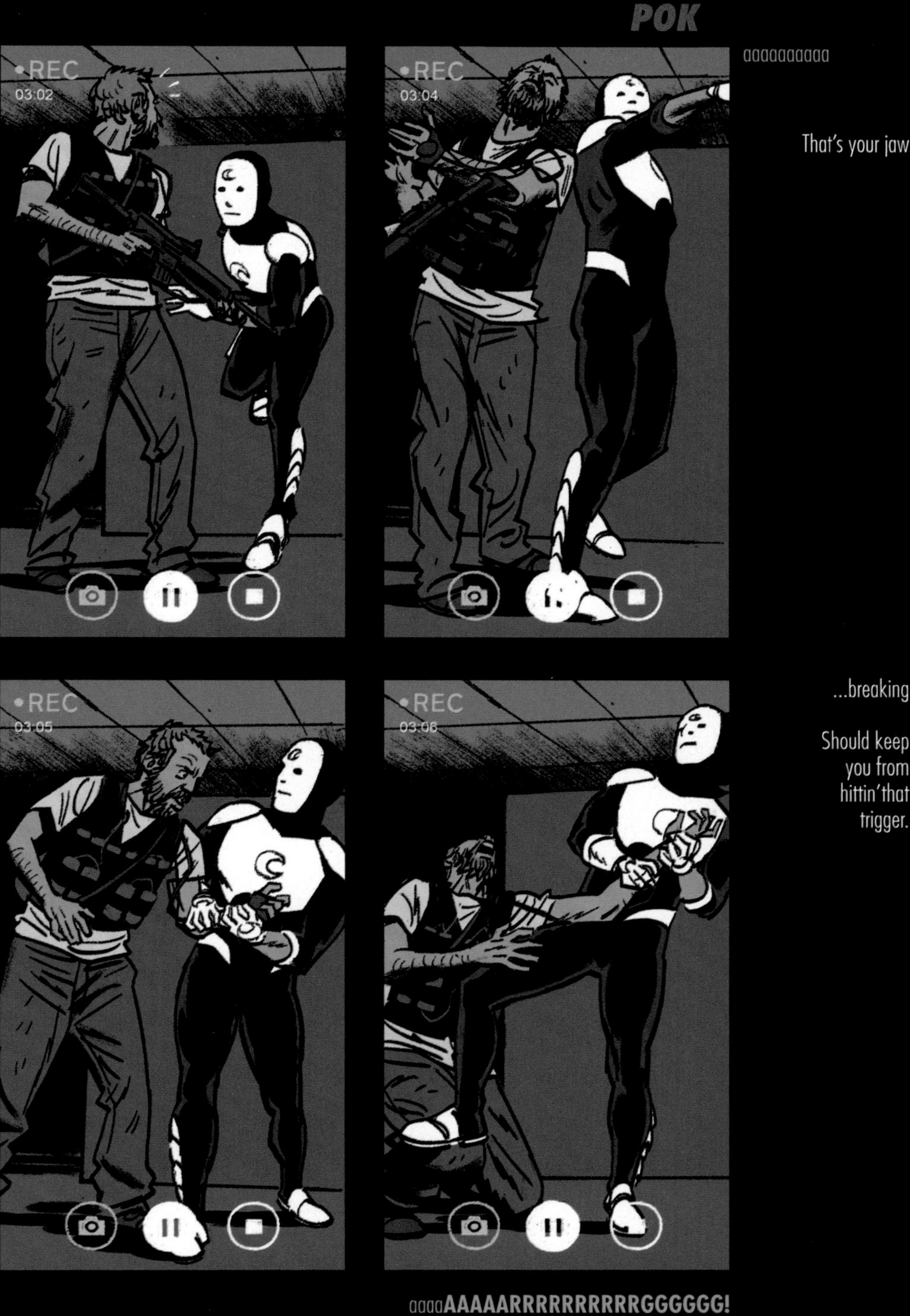

POK
aaaaaaaaaa
•REC
03:02
•REC
03:04
That's your jaw
•REC
03:05
•REC
03:06
...breaking
Should keep you from hittin'that trigger.
aaaaAAAAARRRRRRRRRRGGGGGG!

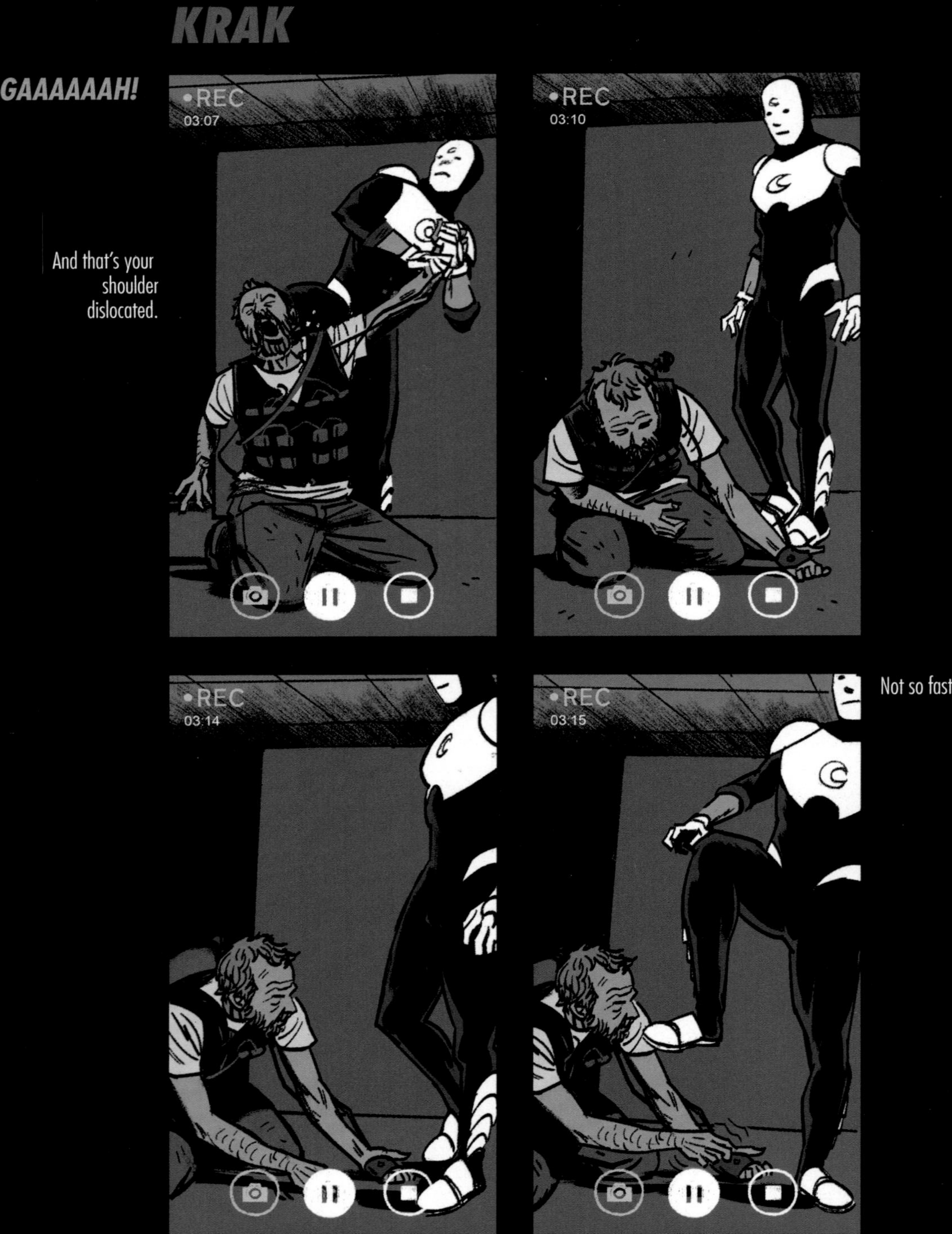
KRAK
GAAAAAAH!
•REC
03:07
And that's your shoulder dislocated.
•REC
03:10
•REC
03:14
•REC
03:15
Not so fast

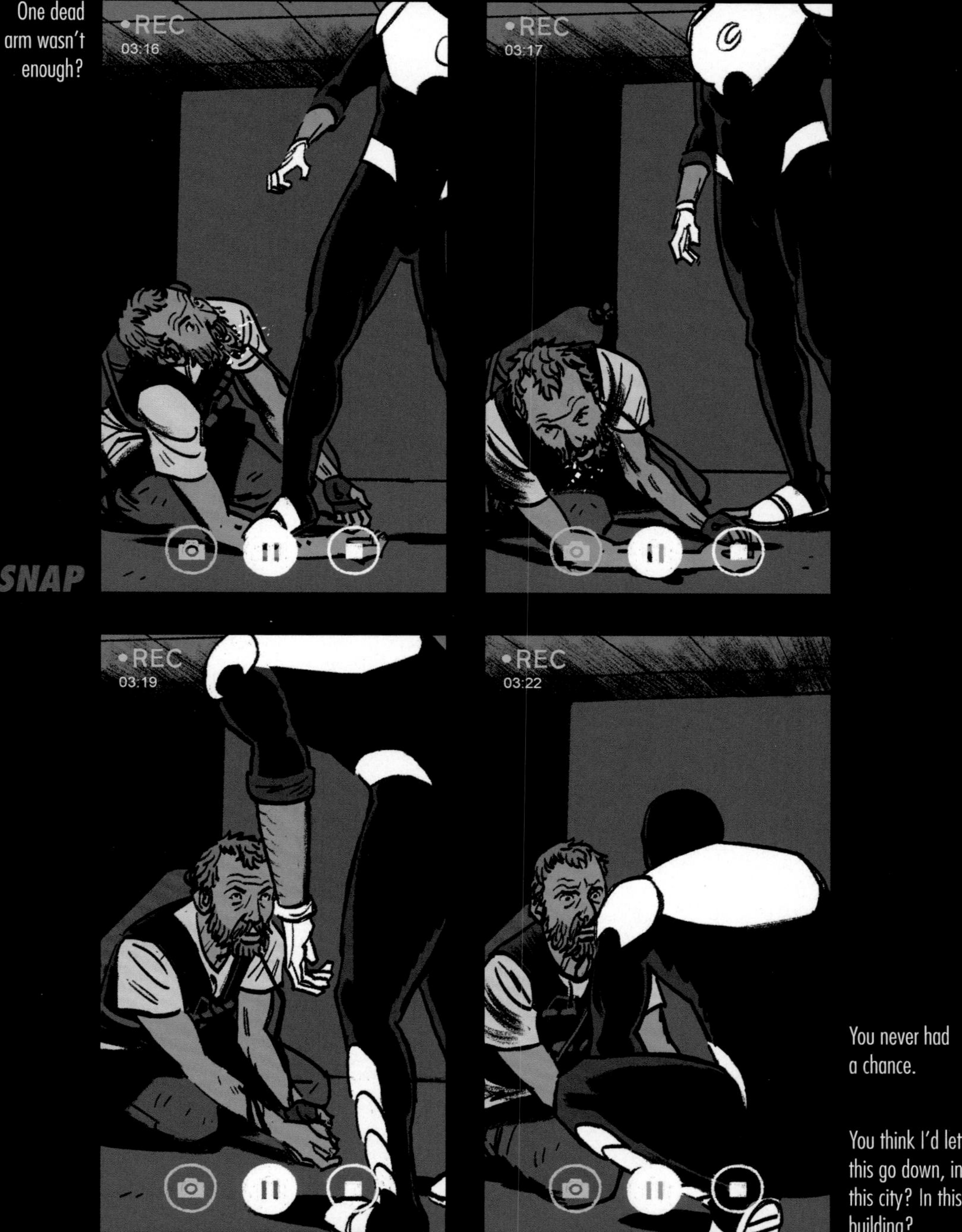
One dead arm wasn't enough?
•REC
03:16
SNAP
•REC
03:17
•REC
03:19
•REC
03:22
You never had a chance.
You think I'd let this go down, in this city? In this building?

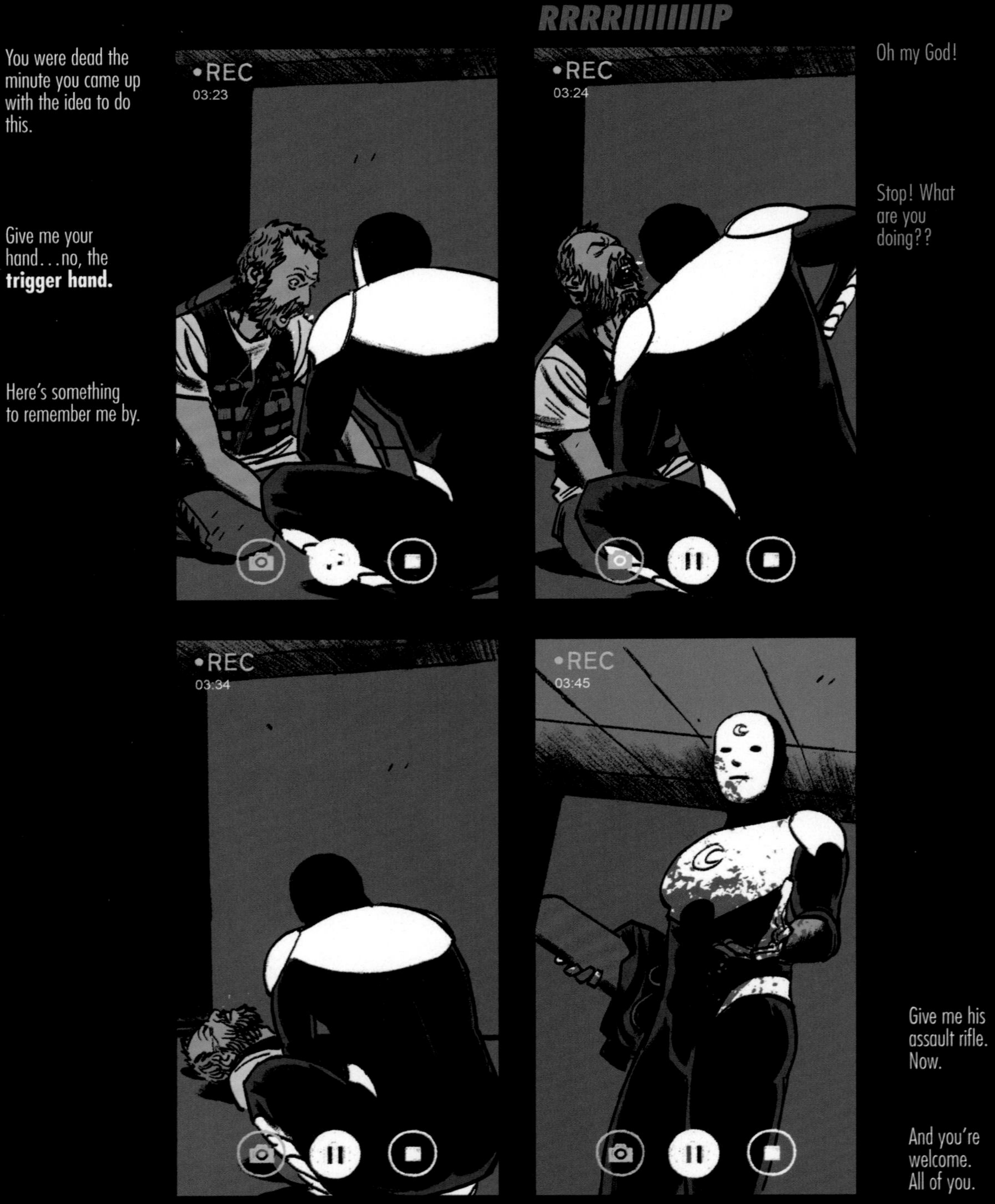
You were dead the minute you came up with the idea to do this.
Give me your hand...no, the **trigger hand.**
Here's something to remember me by.
•REC
03:23
RRRRIIIIIIIP
•REC
03:24
Oh my God!
Stop! What are you doing??
•REC
03:34
•REC
03:45
Give me his assault rifle. Now.
And you're welcome. All of you.

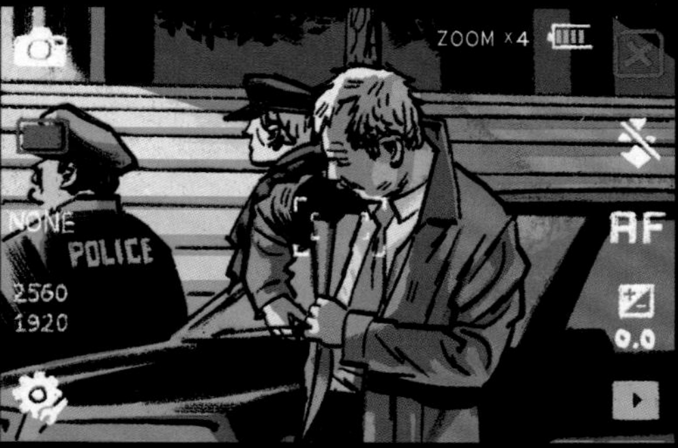
ZOOM ×4
NONE
POLICE
2560
1920
AF
0.0

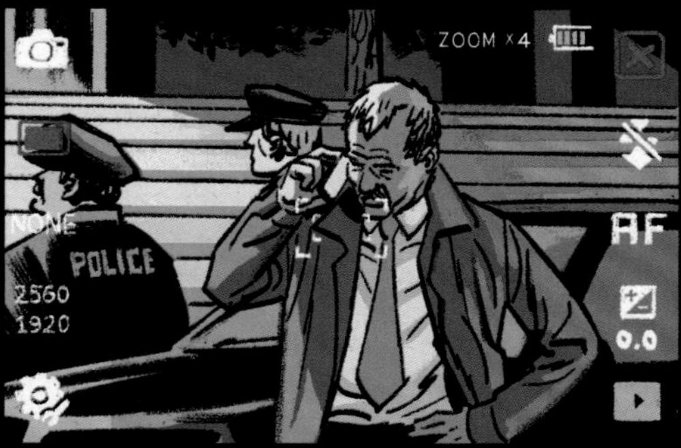
ZOOM ×4
NONE
POLICE
2560
1920
AF
0.0

beedle deedle dee! Beedle deedle dee!

Mr. Grant?

Lockley. For the time being, anyway.

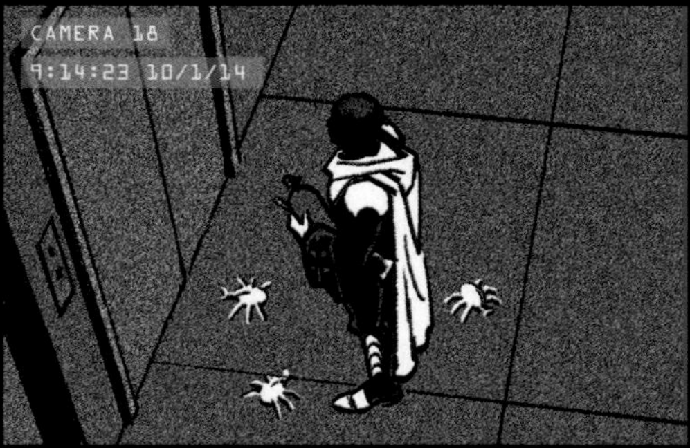
CAMERA 18
9:14:23 10/1/14

Right. Mr. Knight. Or Grant or Lockley
Or whoever you are.

What's happening?

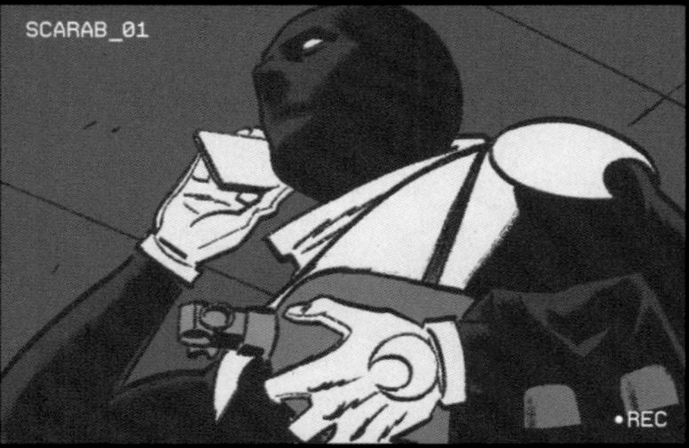
SCARAB_01
•REC

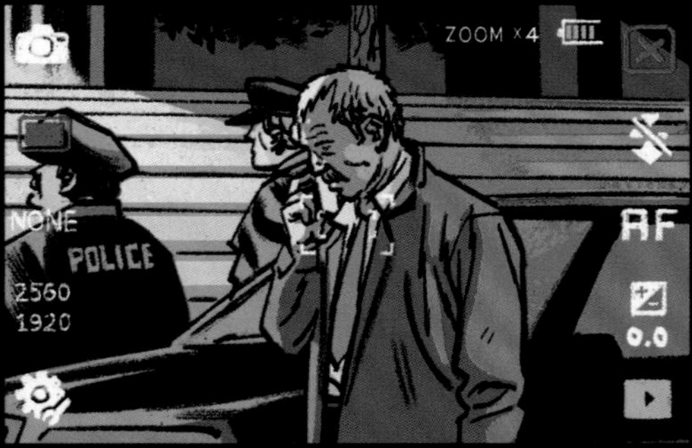
ZOOM ×4
NONE
POLICE
2560
1920
AF
0.0

The target is down. All the hostages are alive. Turn the elevators back on, I'm coming down.

The bomb?

Deactivated and secured.

Who am I surrendering it to?

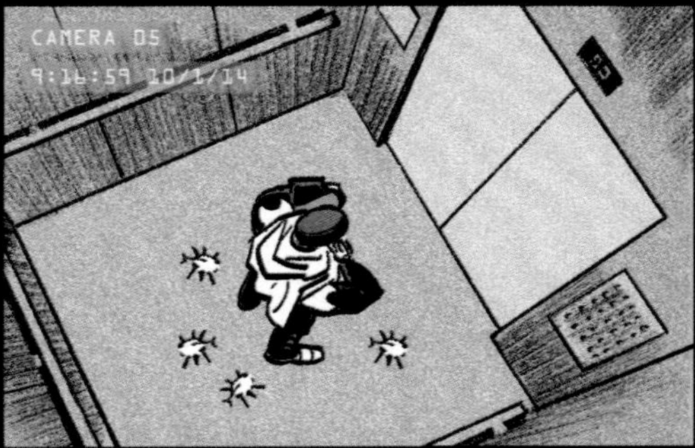
CAMERA 05
9:16:59 10/1/14

The FBI, the CIA, spec ops, who knows. You'll know 'em when you seem them.

Lockley?

Mr. Knight, now.

...Mr. Knight. I called your doctor.

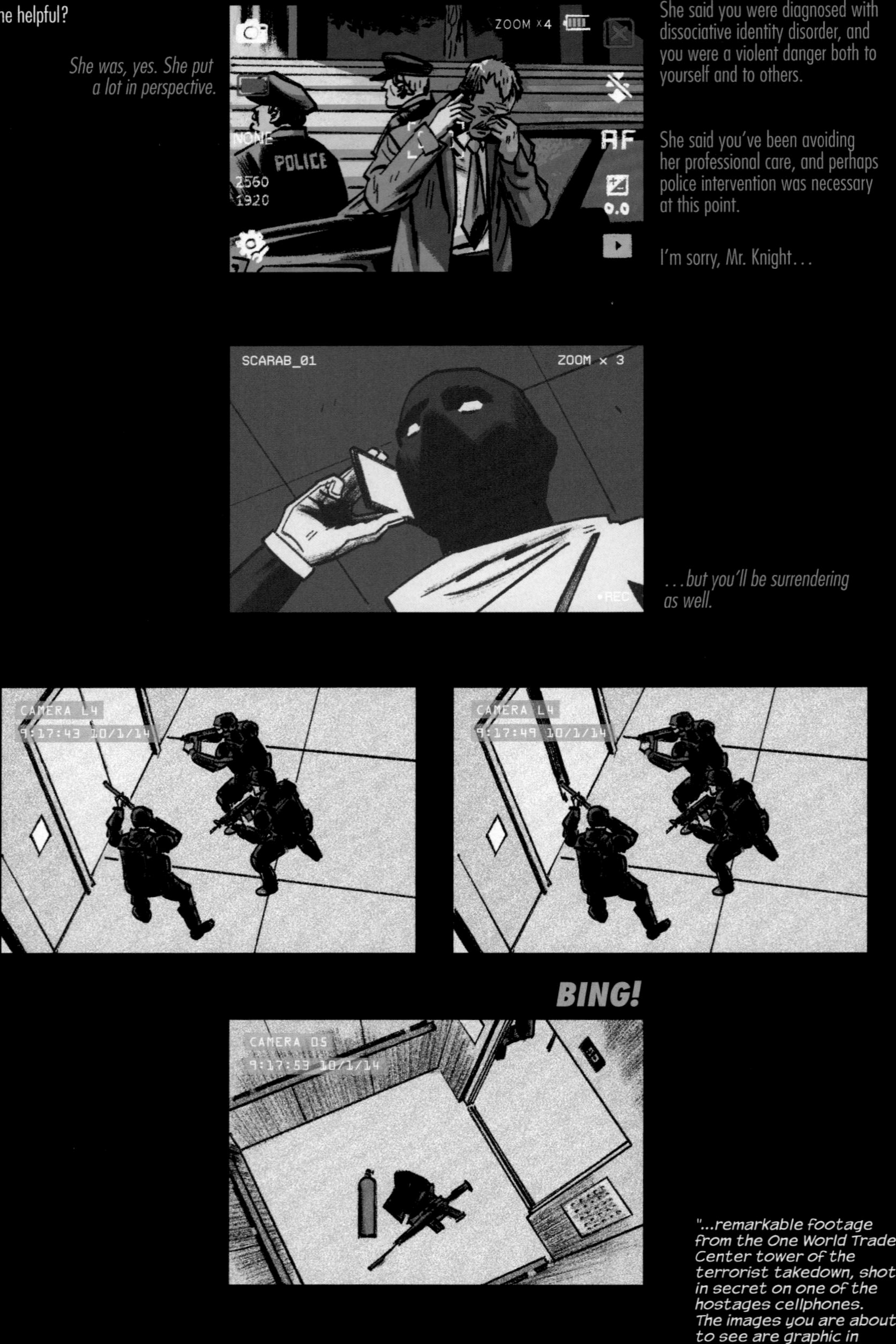

ne helpful?
She was, yes. She put a lot in perspective.
ZOOM ×4
NONE
POLICE
2560
1920
AF
0.0
She said you were diagnosed with dissociative identity disorder, and you were a violent danger both to yourself and to others.
She said you've been avoiding her professional care, and perhaps police intervention was necessary at this point.
I'm sorry, Mr. Knight...
SCARAB_01
ZOOM × 3
•REC
...but you'll be surrendering as well.
CAMERA L4
9:17:43 10/1/14
CAMERA L4
9:17:49 10/1/14
BING!
CAMERA 05
9:17:53 10/1/14
"...remarkable footage from the One World Trade Center tower of the terrorist takedown, shot in secret on one of the hostages cellphones. The images you are about to see are graphic in

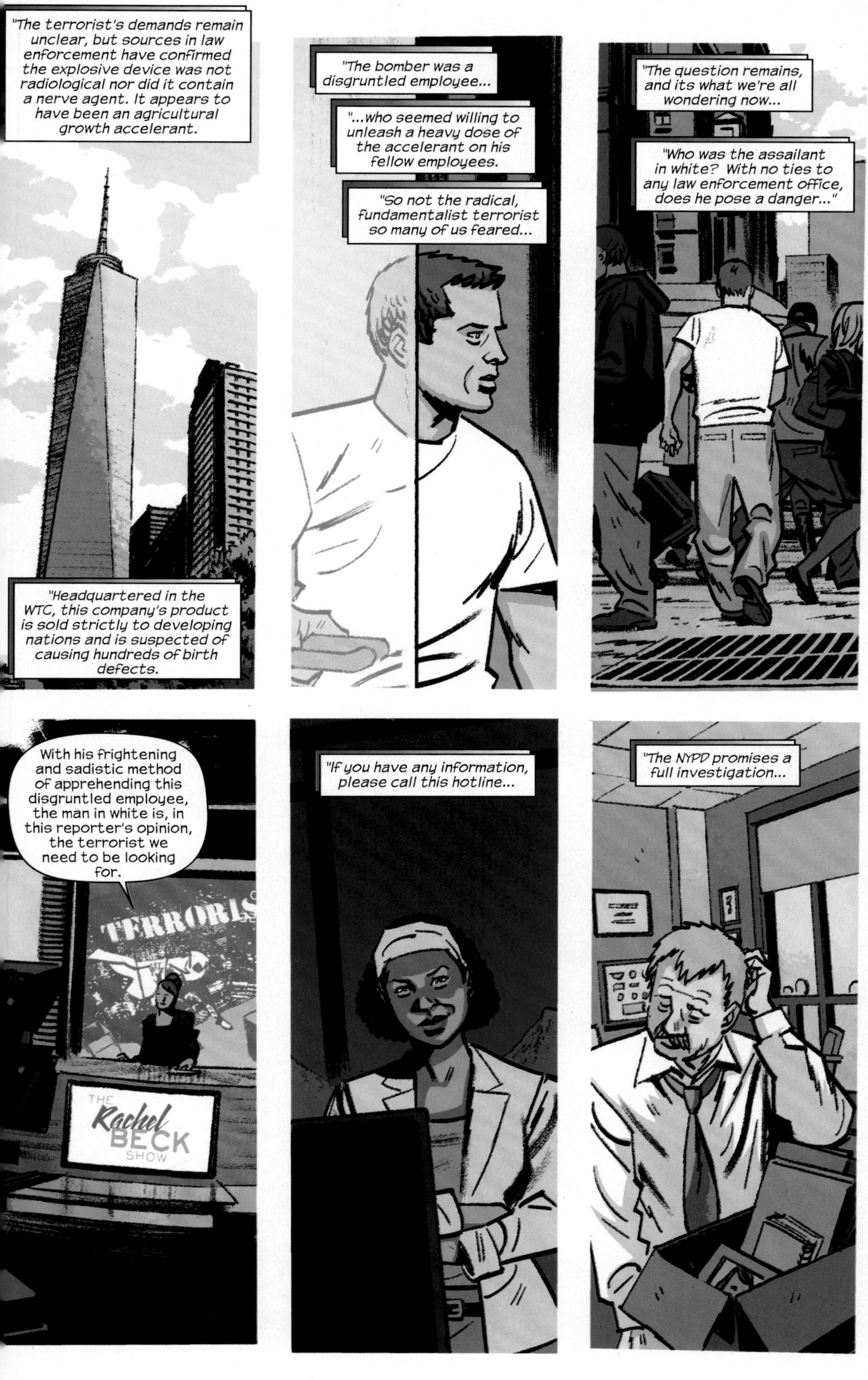
"The terrorist's demands remain unclear, but sources in law enforcement have confirmed the explosive device was not radiological nor did it contain a nerve agent. It appears to have been an agricultural growth accelerant.
"Headquartered in the WTC, this company's product is sold strictly to developing nations and is suspected of causing hundreds of birth defects.
"The bomber was a disgruntled employee...
"...who seemed willing to unleash a heavy dose of the accelerant on his fellow employees.
"So not the radical, fundamentalist terrorist so many of us feared...
"The question remains, and its what we're all wondering now...
"Who was the assailant in white? With no ties to any law enforcement office, does he pose a danger..."
With his frightening and sadistic method of apprehending this disgruntled employee, the man in white is, in this reporter's opinion, the terrorist we need to be looking for.
TERRORIS
THE Rachel BECK SHOW
"If you have any information, please call this hotline...
"The NYPD promises a full investigation...

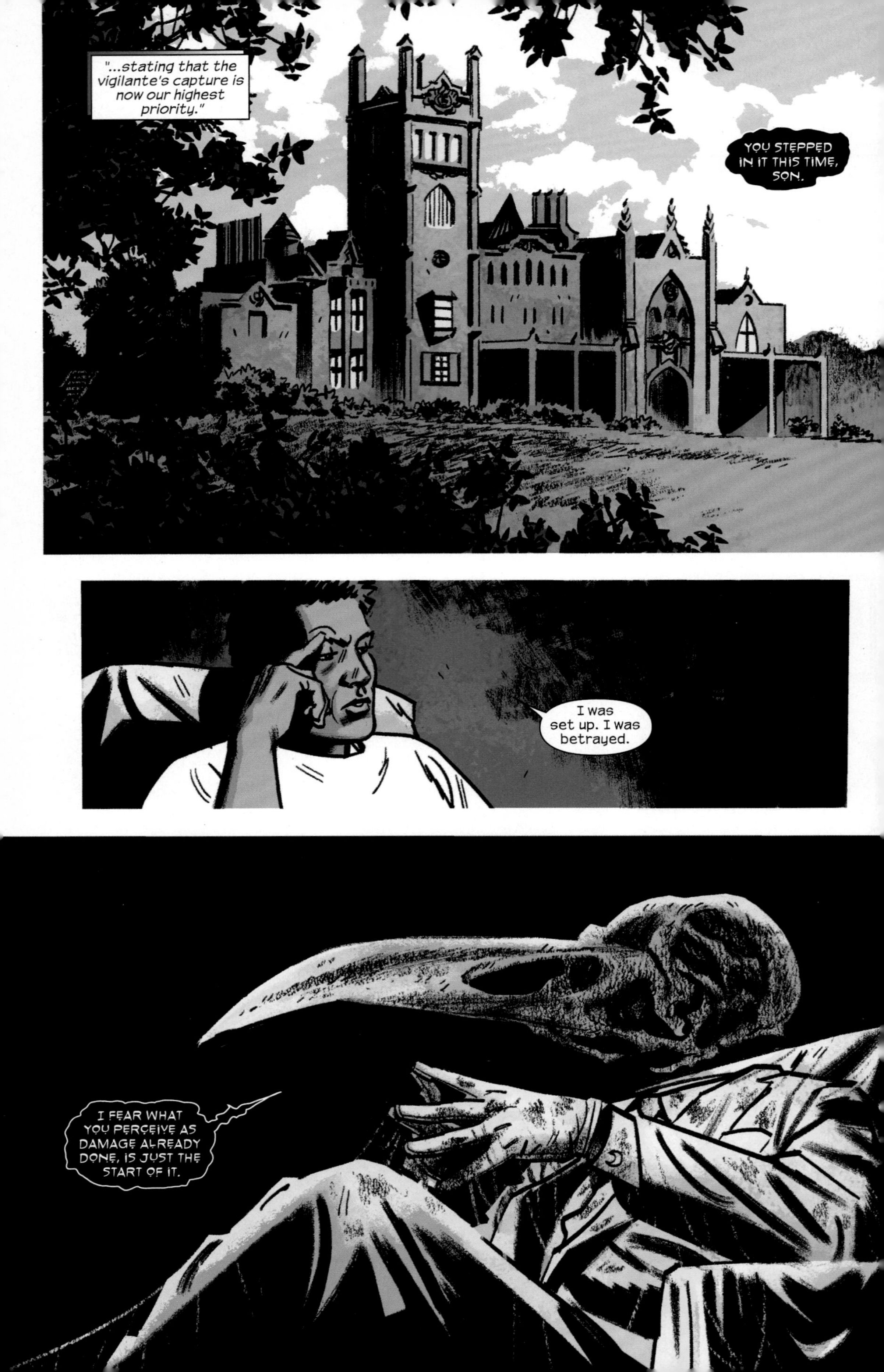
"...stating that the vigilante's capture is now our highest priority."
YOU STEPPED IN IT THIS TIME, SON.
I was set up. I was betrayed.
I FEAR WHAT YOU PERCEIVE AS DAMAGE ALREADY DONE, IS JUST THE START OF IT.

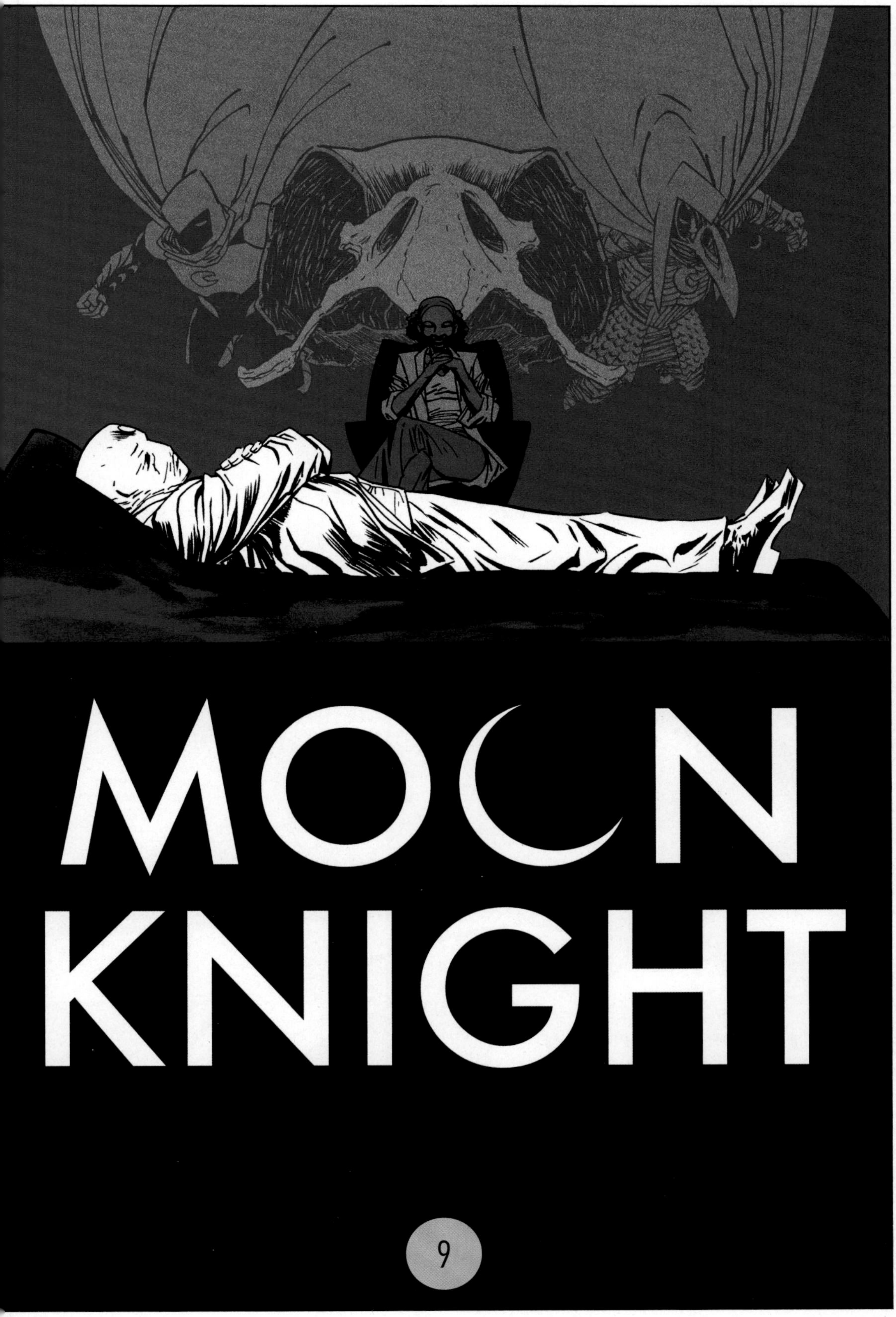
MOON
KNIGHT
9

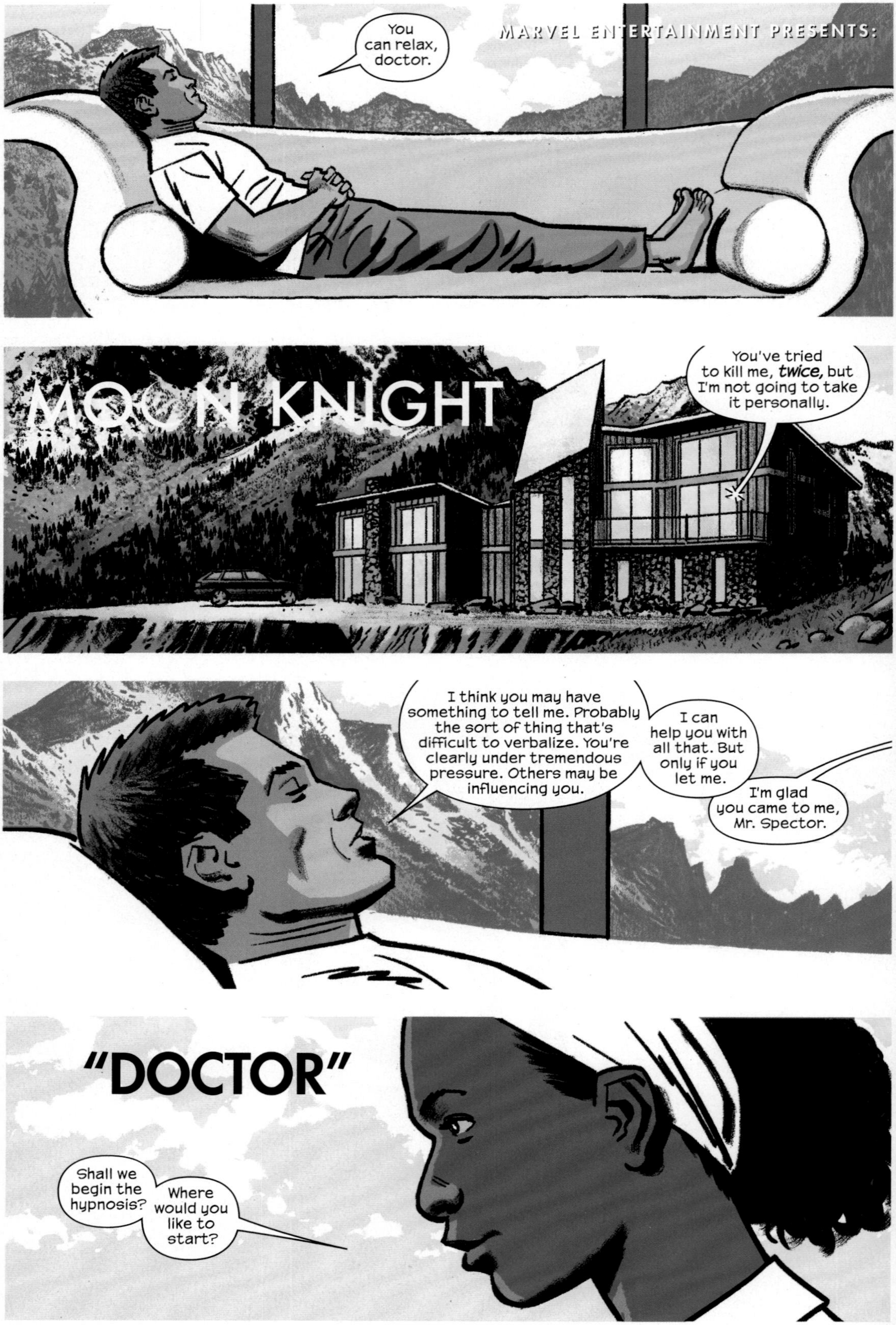
MARVEL ENTERTAINMENT PRESENTS:
You can relax, doctor.
MOON KNIGHT
You've tried to kill me, *twice,* but I'm not going to take it personally.
I think you may have something to tell me. Probably the sort of thing that's difficult to verbalize. You're clearly under tremendous pressure. Others may be influencing you.
I can help you with all that. But only if you let me.
I'm glad you came to me, Mr. Spector.
"DOCTOR"
Shall we begin the hypnosis?
Where would you like to start?

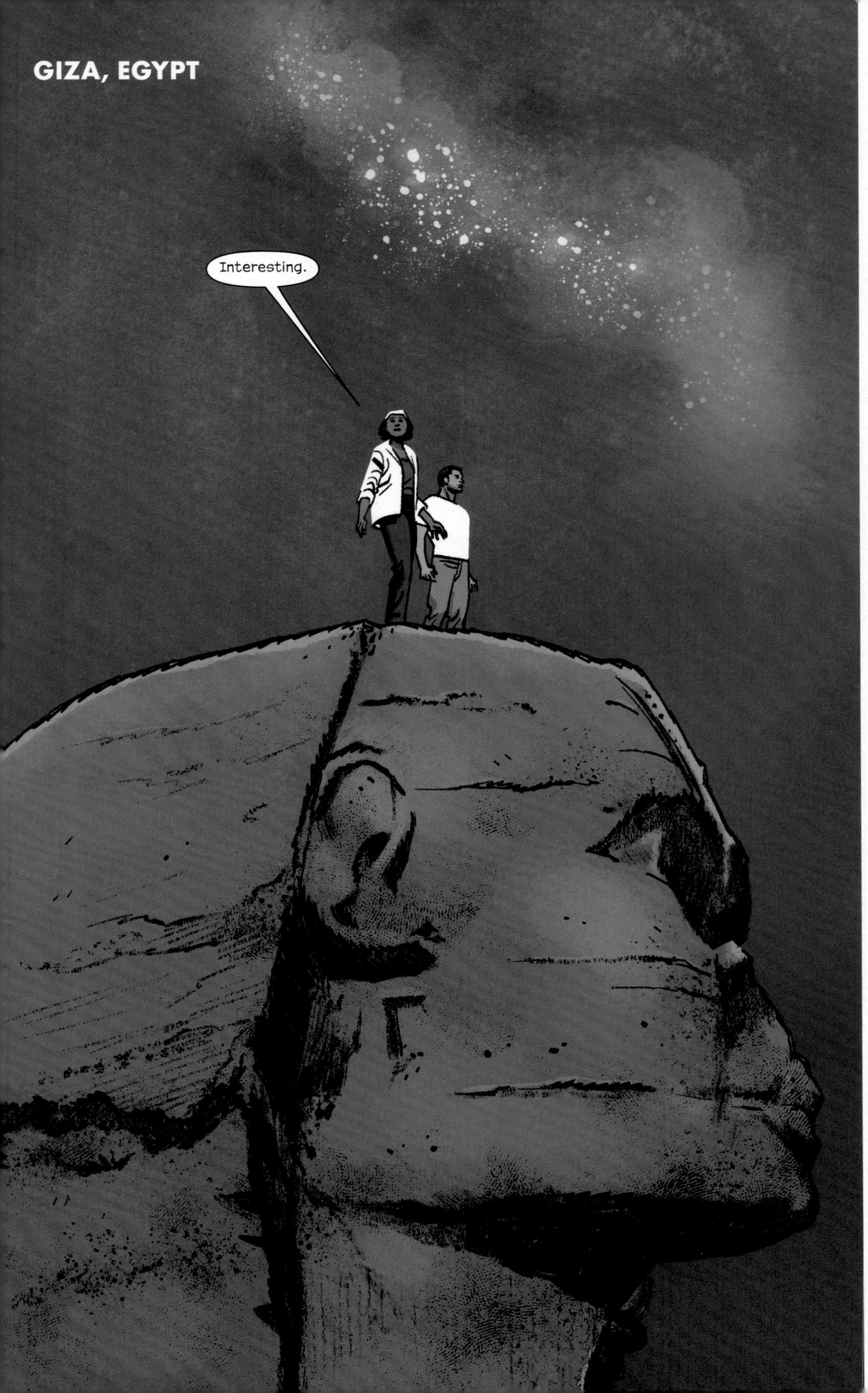
GIZA, EGYPT
Interesting.

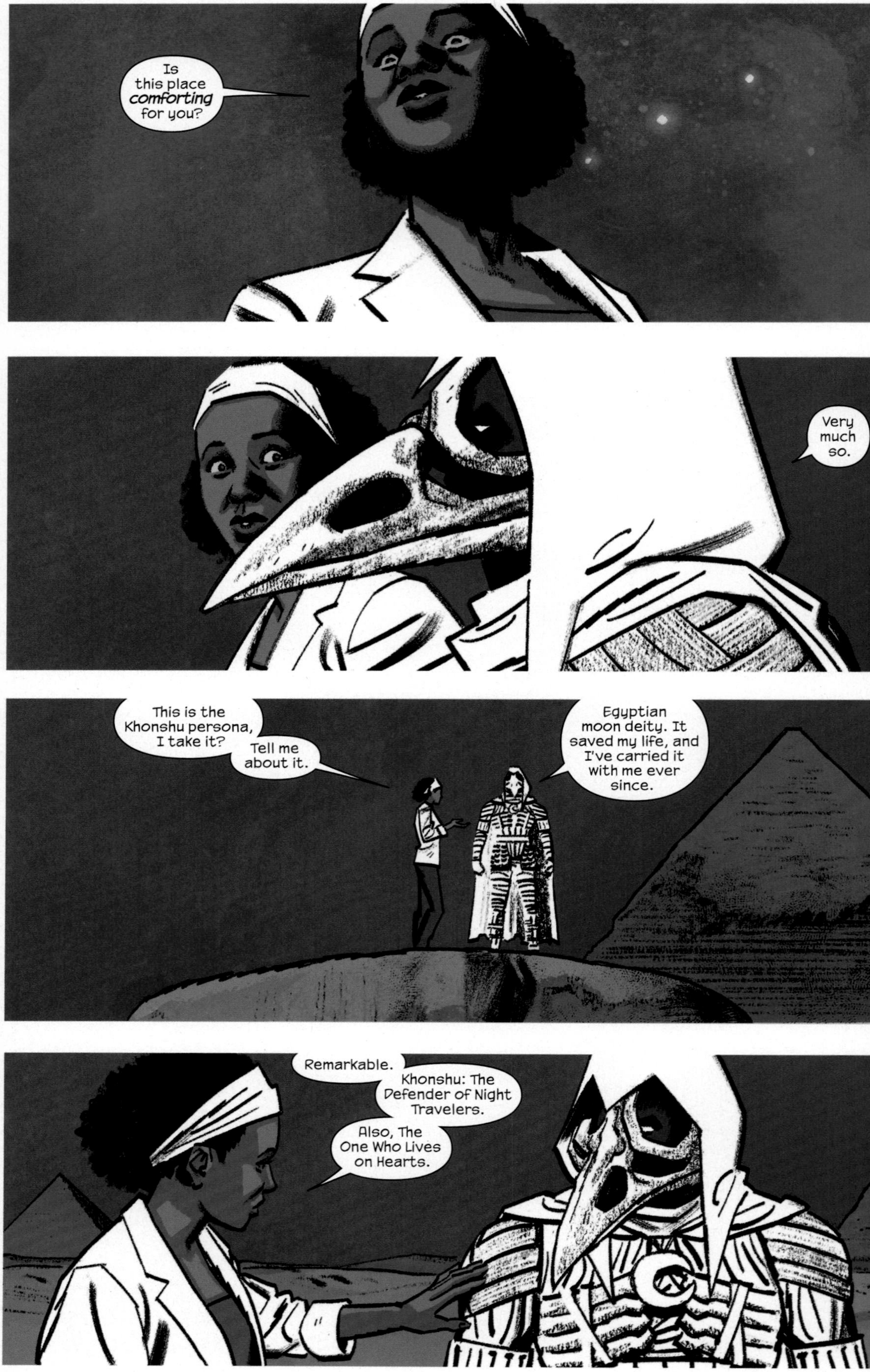
Is this place *comforting* for you?
Very much so.
This is the Khonshu persona, I take it?
Tell me about it.
Egyptian moon deity. It saved my life, and I've carried it with me ever since.
Remarkable.
Khonshu: The Defender of Night Travelers.
Also, The One Who Lives on Hearts.

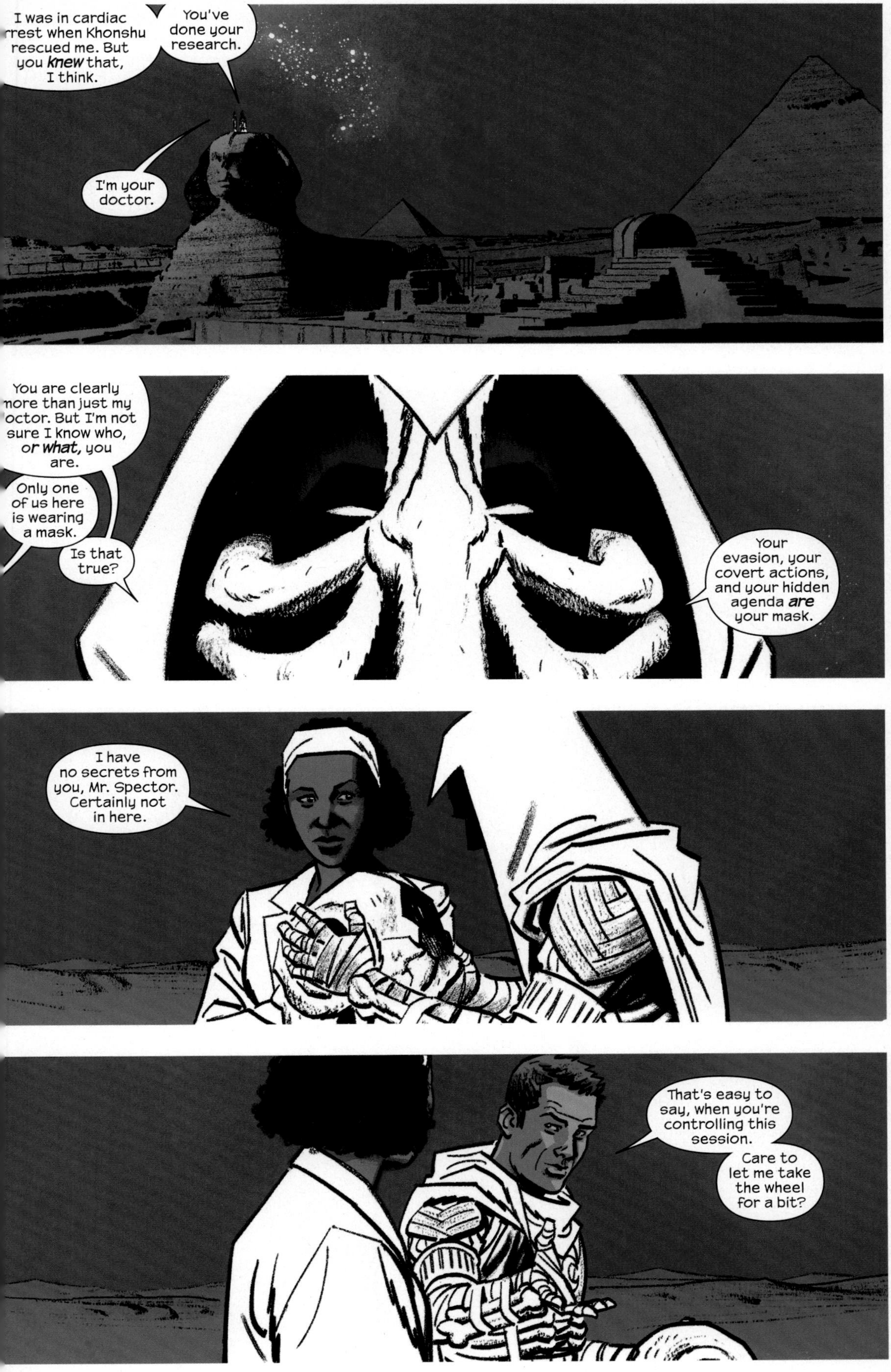
I was in cardiac rrest when Khonshu rescued me. But you *knew* that, I think.
You've done your research.
I'm your doctor.
You are clearly more than just my octor. But I'm not sure I know who, *or what,* you are.
Is that true?
Only one of us here is wearing a mask.
Your evasion, your covert actions, and your hidden agenda *are* your mask.
I have no secrets from you, Mr. Spector. Certainly not in here.
That's easy to say, when you're controlling this session.
Care to let me take the wheel for a bit?

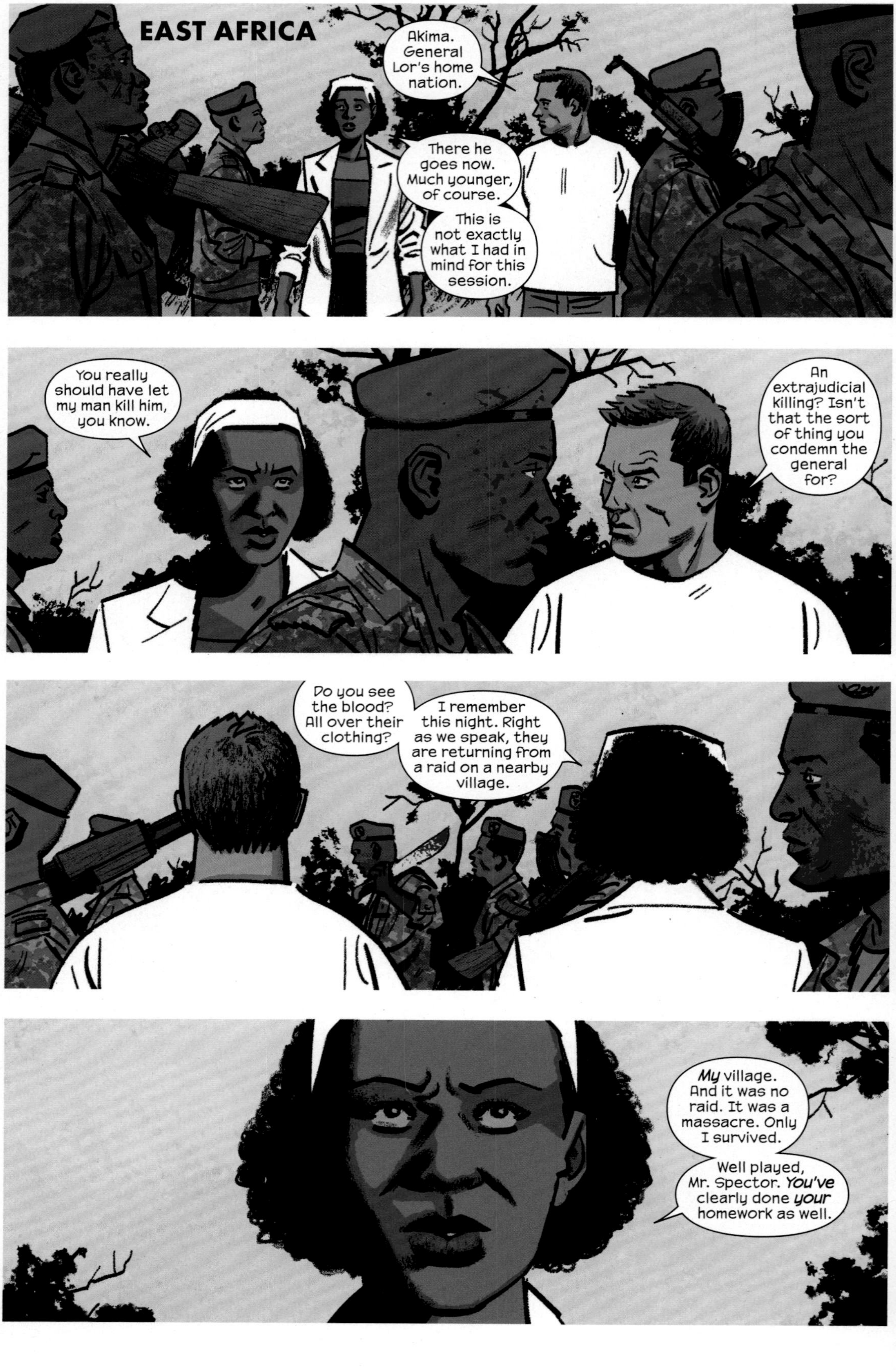
EAST AFRICA
Akima. General Lor's home nation.
There he goes now. Much younger, of course.
This is not exactly what I had in mind for this session.
You really should have let my man kill him, you know.
An extrajudicial killing? Isn't that the sort of thing you condemn the general for?
Do you see the blood? All over their clothing?
I remember this night. Right as we speak, they are returning from a raid on a nearby village.
My village. And it was no raid. It was a massacre. Only I survived.
Well played, Mr. Spector. You've clearly done your homework as well.

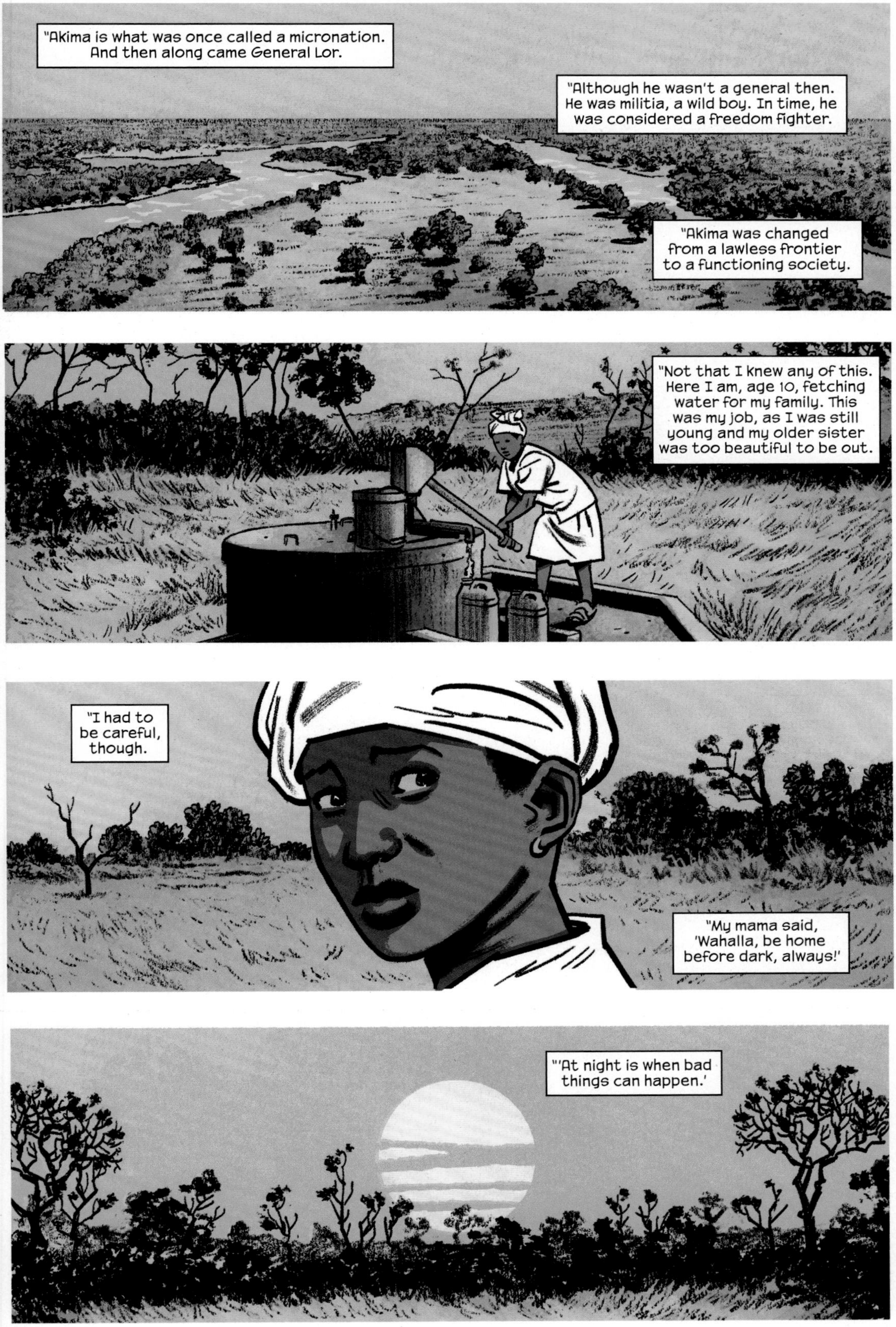
"Akima is what was once called a micronation. And then along came General Lor.
"Although he wasn't a general then. He was militia, a wild boy. In time, he was considered a freedom fighter.
"Akima was changed from a lawless frontier to a functioning society.
"Not that I knew any of this. Here I am, age 10, fetching water for my family. This was my job, as I was still young and my older sister was too beautiful to be out.
"I had to be careful, though.
"My mama said, 'Wahalla, be home before dark, always!'
"'At night is when bad things can happen.'

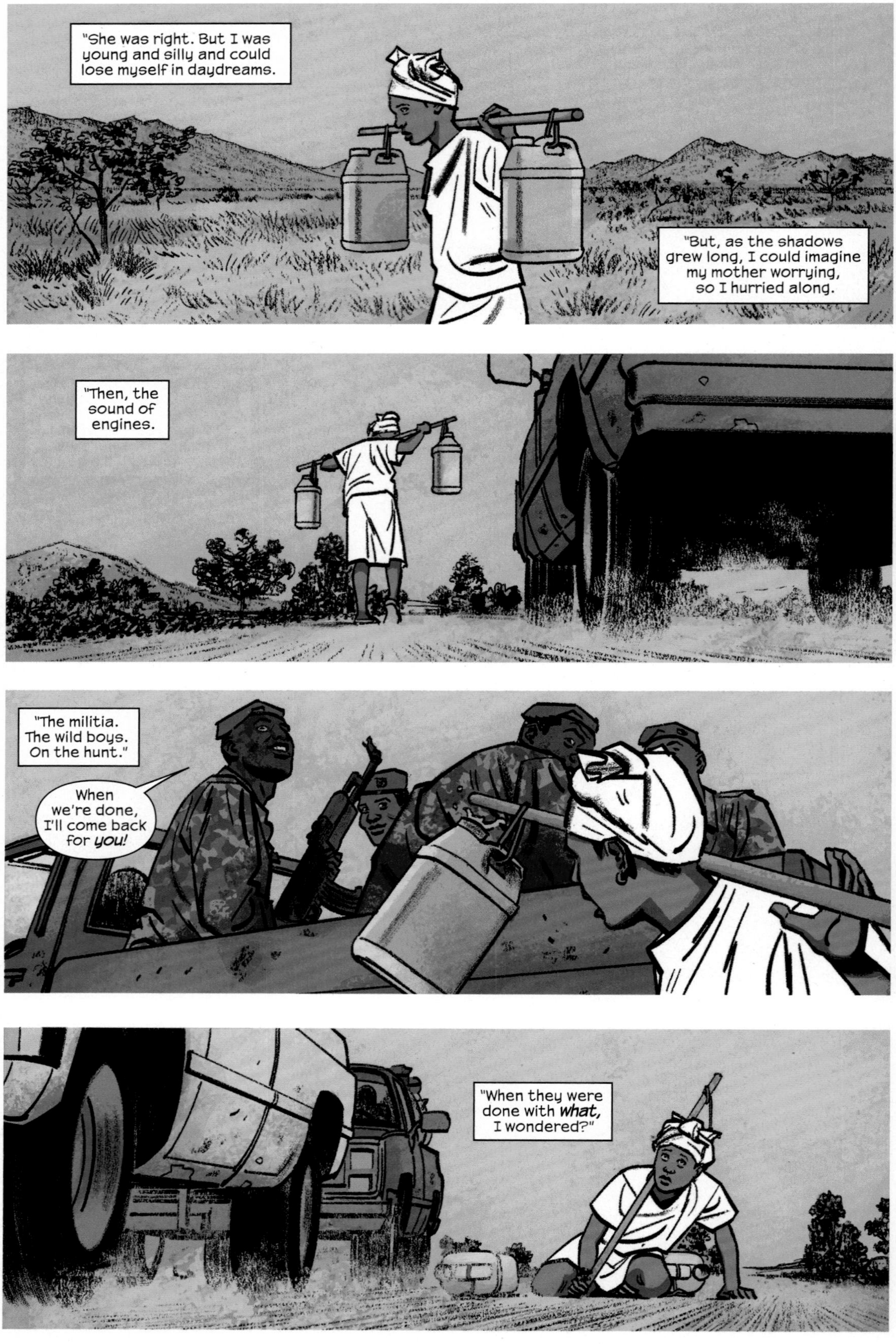
"She was right. But I was young and silly and could lose myself in daydreams.
"But, as the shadows grew long, I could imagine my mother worrying, so I hurried along.
"Then, the sound of engines.
"The militia. The wild boys. On the hunt."
When we're done, I'll come back for *you!*
"When they were done with *what,* I wondered?"

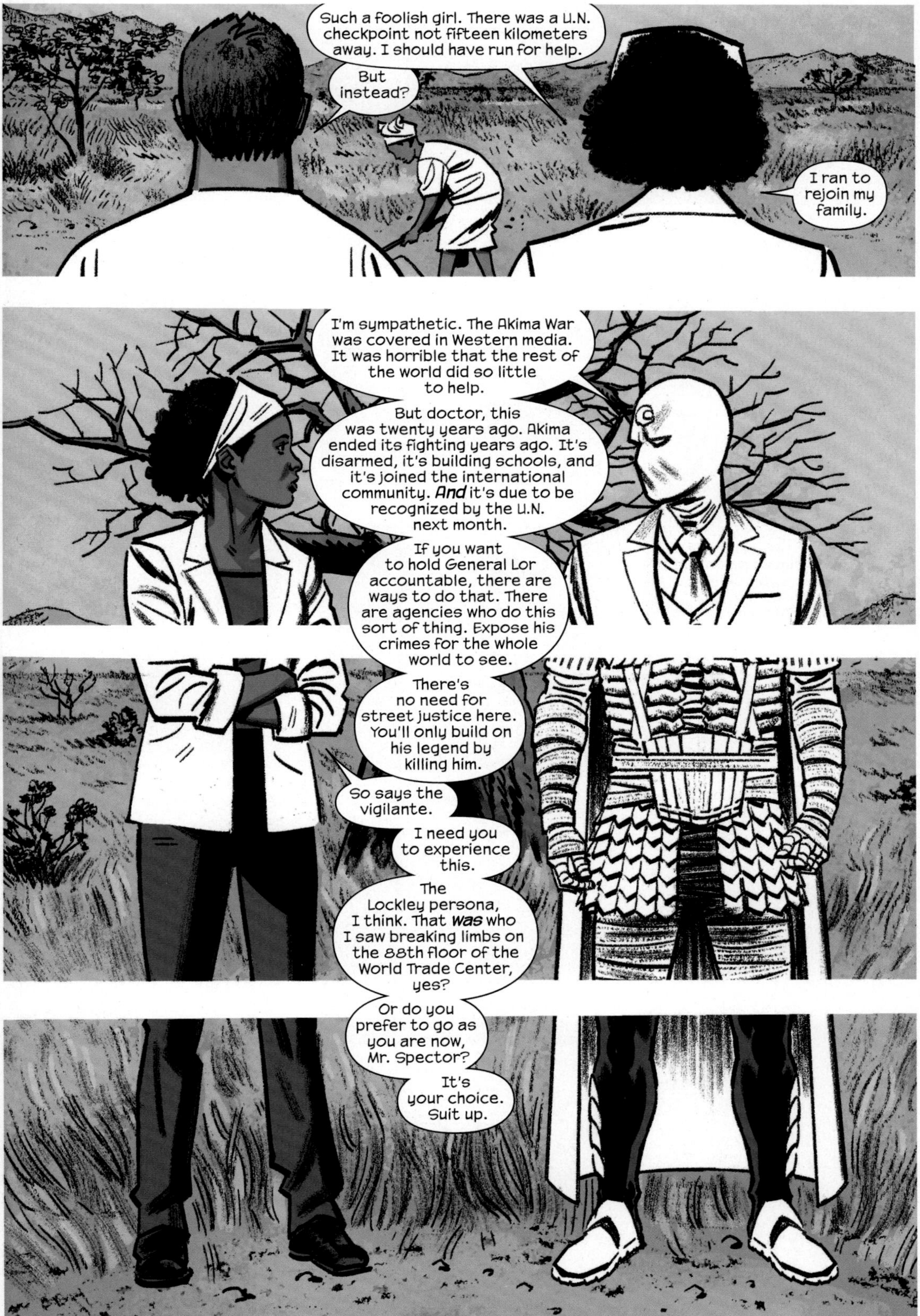
Such a foolish girl. There was a U.N. checkpoint not fifteen kilometers away. I should have run for help.
But instead?
I ran to rejoin my family.
I'm sympathetic. The Akima War was covered in Western media. It was horrible that the rest of the world did so little to help.
But doctor, this was twenty years ago. Akima ended its fighting years ago. It's disarmed, it's building schools, and it's joined the international community. *And* it's due to be recognized by the U.N. next month.
If you want to hold General Lor accountable, there are ways to do that. There are agencies who do this sort of thing. Expose his crimes for the whole world to see.
There's no need for street justice here. You'll only build on his legend by killing him.
So says the vigilante.
I need you to experience this.
The Lockley persona, I think. That *was* who I saw breaking limbs on the 88th floor of the World Trade Center, yes?
Or do you prefer to go as you are now, Mr. Spector?
It's your choice. Suit up.

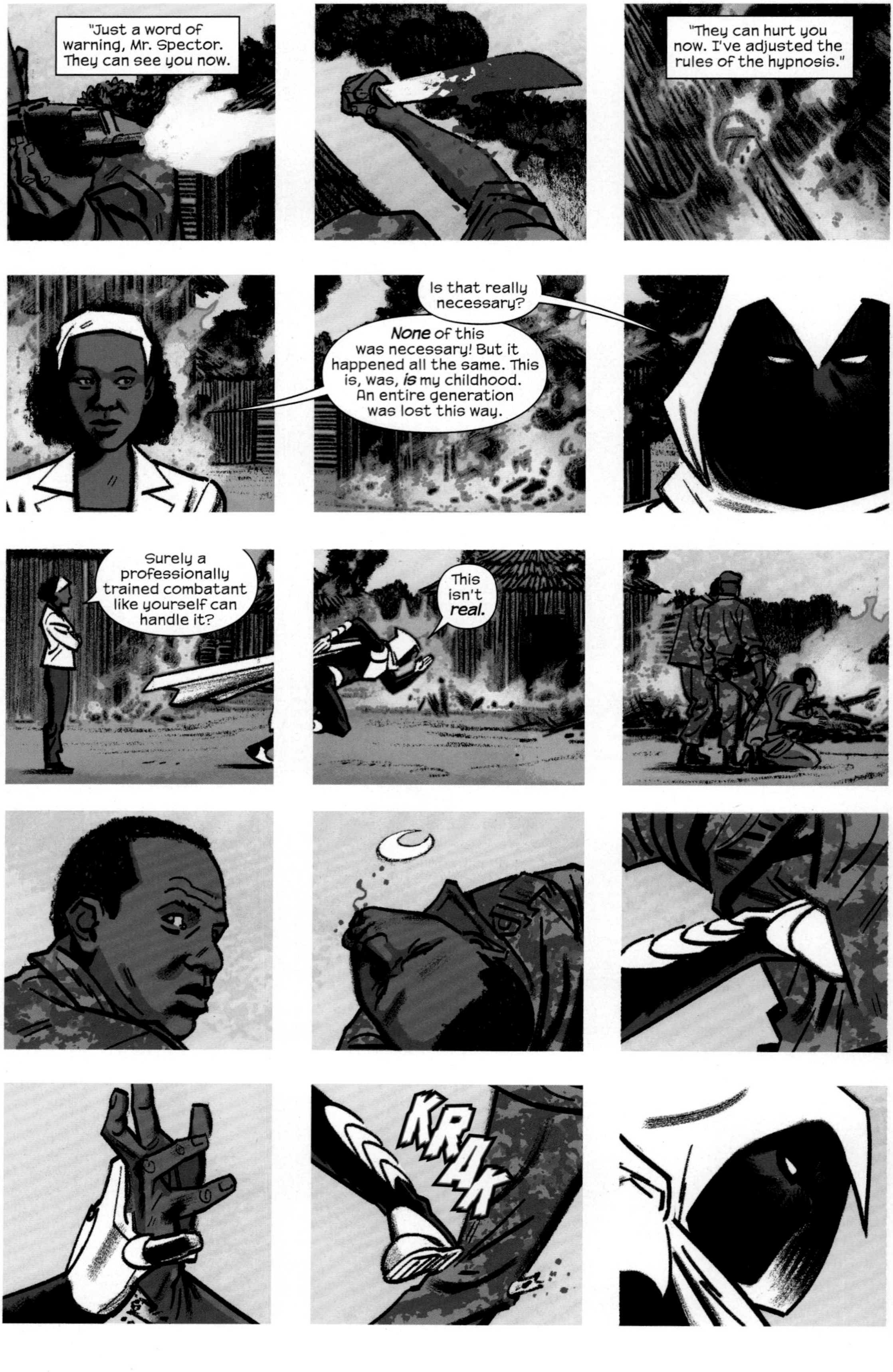
"Just a word of warning, Mr. Spector. They can see you now.
"They can hurt you now. I've adjusted the rules of the hypnosis."
Is that really necessary?
None of this was necessary! But it happened all the same. This is, was, is my childhood. An entire generation was lost this way.
Surely a professionally trained combatant like yourself can handle it?
This isn't real.
KRAK

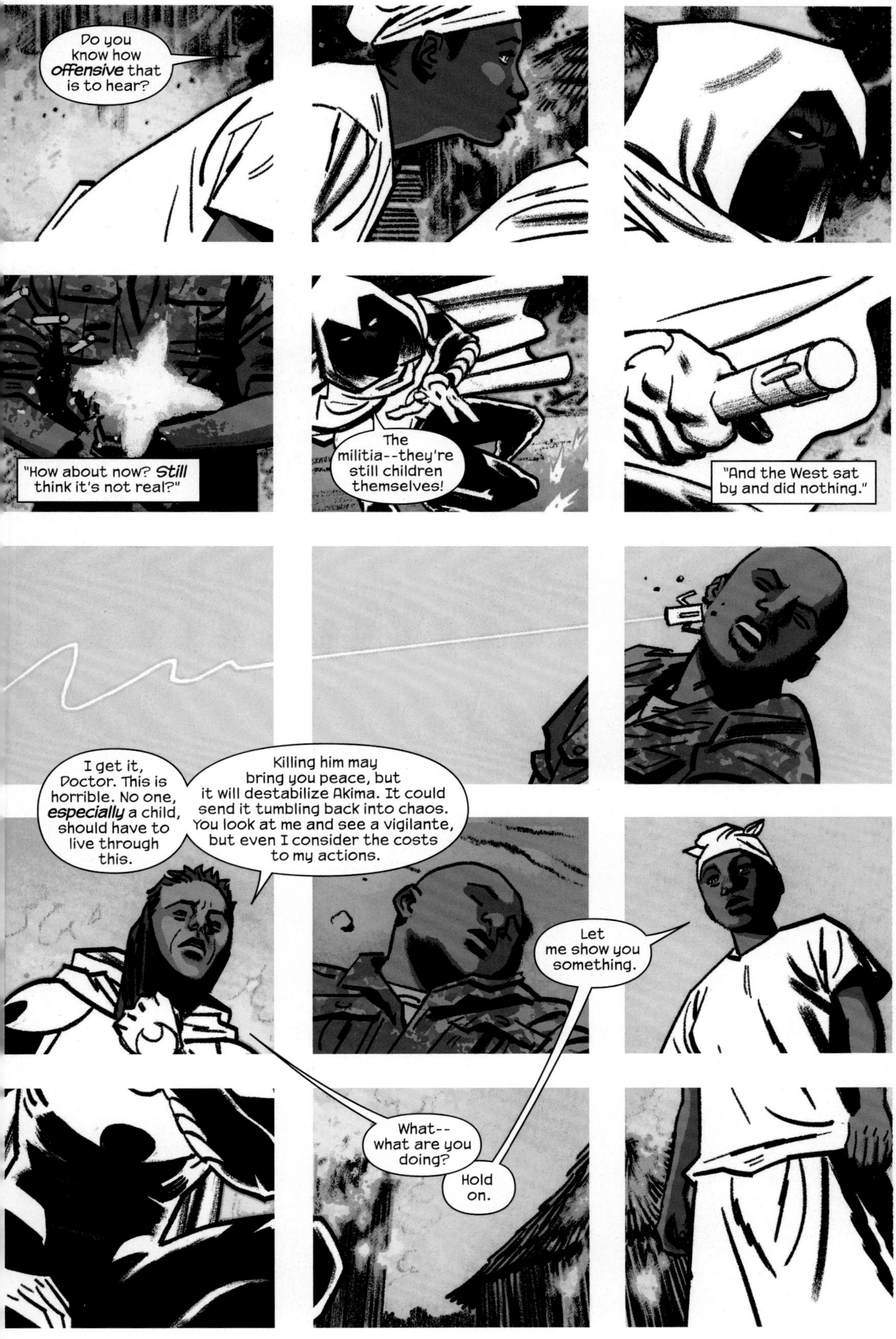
Do you know how *offensive* that is to hear?
"How about now? *Still* think it's not real?"
The militia--they're still children themselves!
"And the West sat by and did nothing."
I get it, Doctor. This is horrible. No one, *especially* a child, should have to live through this.
Killing him may bring you peace, but it will destabilize Akima. It could send it tumbling back into chaos. You look at me and see a vigilante, but even I consider the costs to my actions.
Let me show you something.
What--what are you doing?
Hold on.

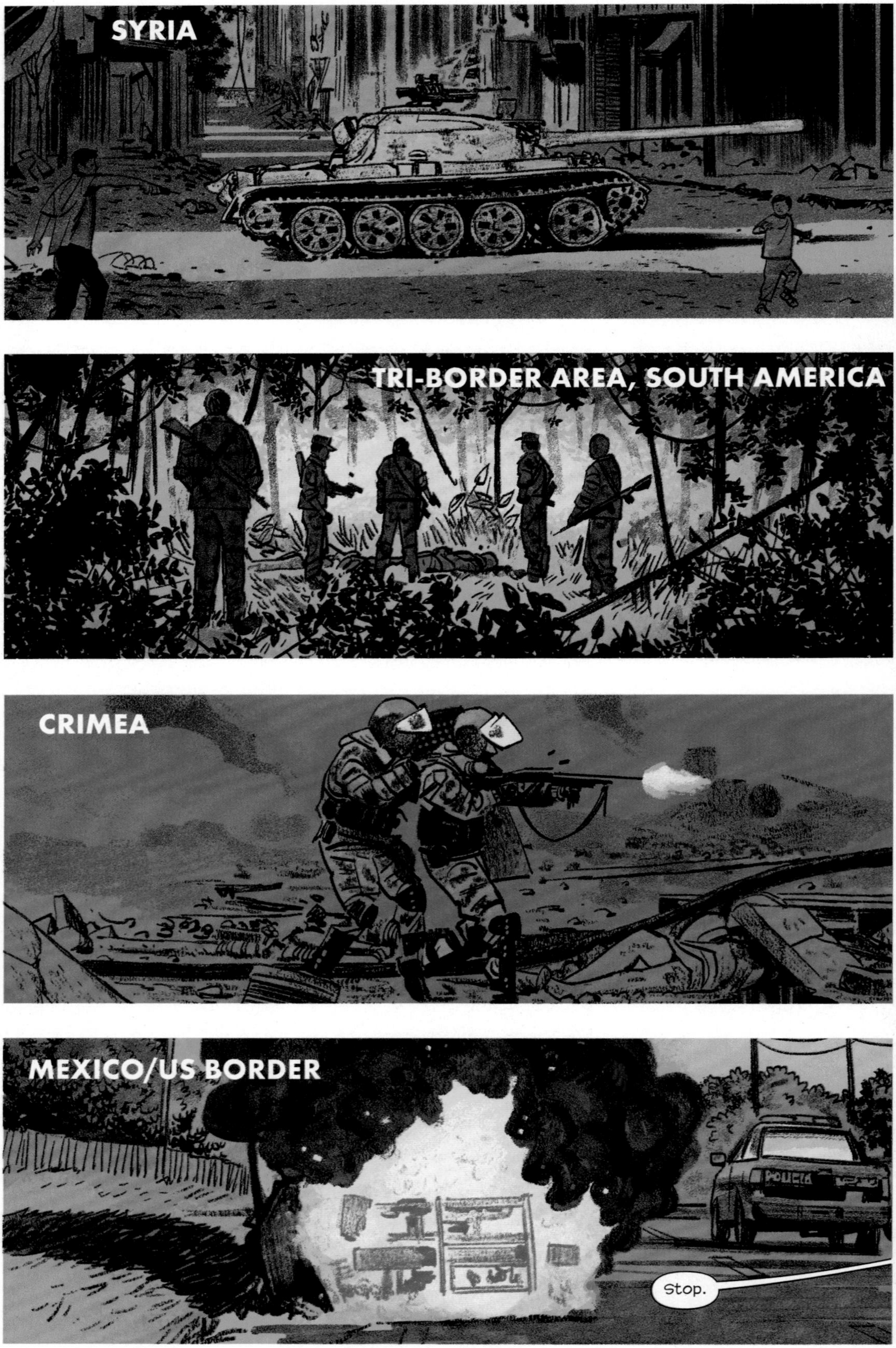
SYRIA
TRI-BORDER AREA, SOUTH AMERICA
CRIMEA
MEXICO/US BORDER
POLICIA
Stop.

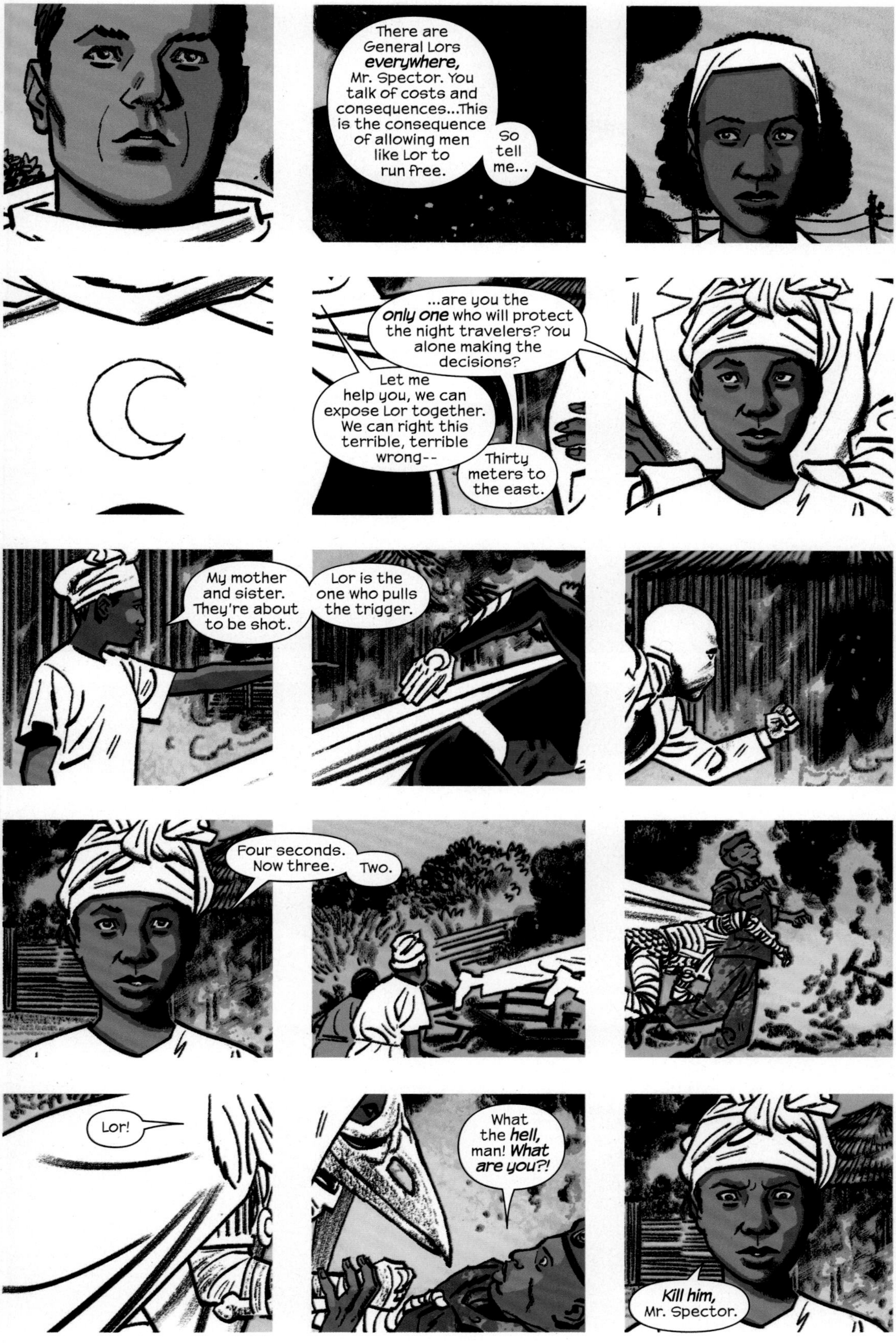

There are General Lors *everywhere,* Mr. Spector. You talk of costs and consequences...This is the consequence of allowing men like Lor to run free.
So tell me...
...are you the *only one* who will protect the night travelers? You alone making the decisions?
Let me help you, we can expose Lor together. We can right this terrible, terrible wrong--
Thirty meters to the east.
My mother and sister. They're about to be shot.
Lor is the one who pulls the trigger.
Four seconds. Now three.
Two.
Lor!
What the *hell,* man! *What are you?!*
Kill him, Mr. Spector.

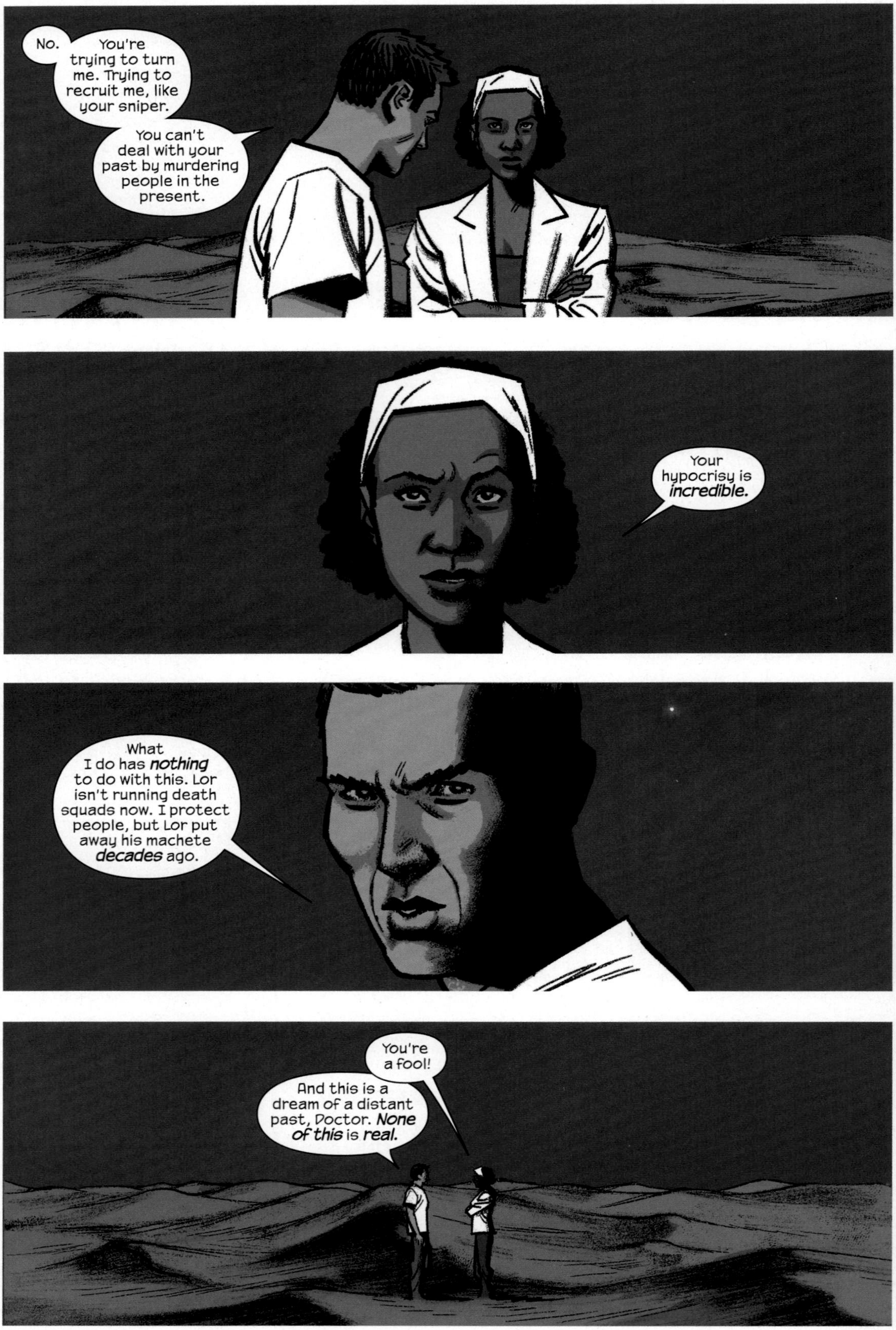
No.
You're trying to turn me. Trying to recruit me, like your sniper.
You can't deal with your past by murdering people in the present.
Your hypocrisy is *incredible.*
What I do has *nothing* to do with this. Lor isn't running death squads now. I protect people, but Lor put away his machete *decades* ago.
You're a fool!
And this is a dream of a distant past, Doctor. *None of this* is *real.*

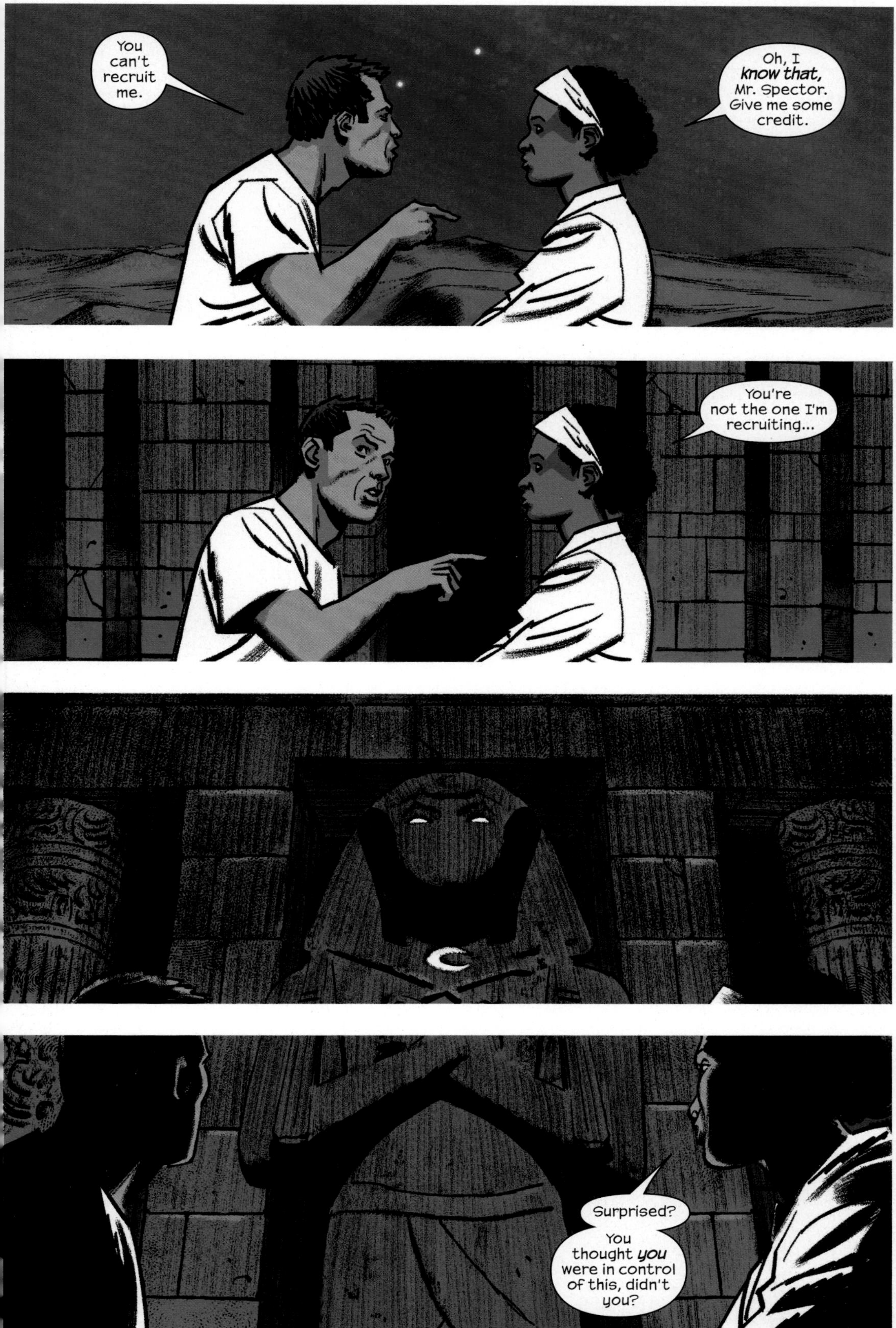
You can't recruit me.
Oh, I *know that,* Mr. Spector. Give me some credit.
You're not the one I'm recruiting...
Surprised?
You thought *you* were in control of this, didn't you?

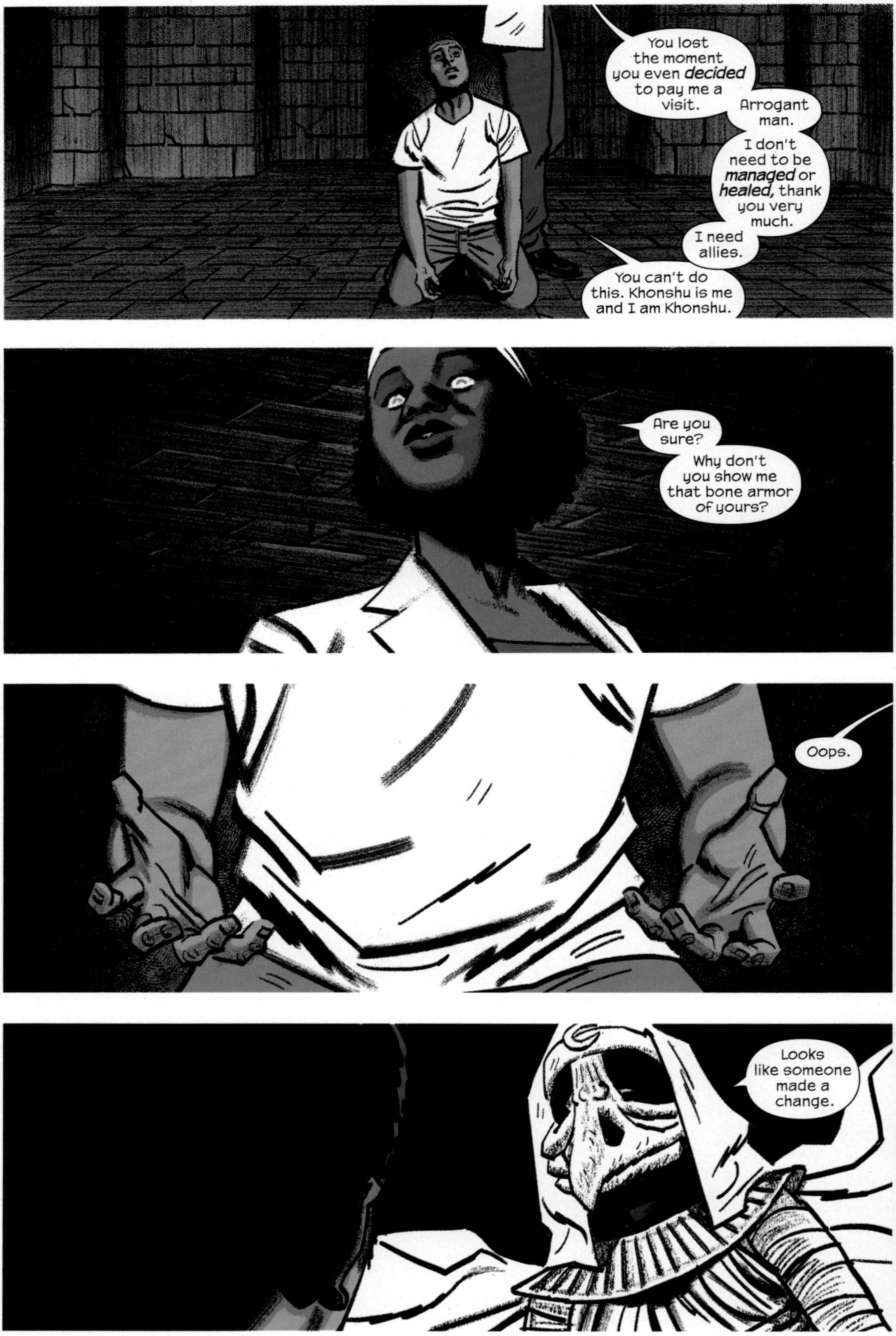
You lost the moment you even decided to pay me a visit.
Arrogant man.
I don't need to be managed or healed, thank you very much.
I need allies.
You can't do this. Khonshu is me and I am Khonshu.
Are you sure?
Why don't you show me that bone armor of yours?
Oops.
Looks like someone made a change.

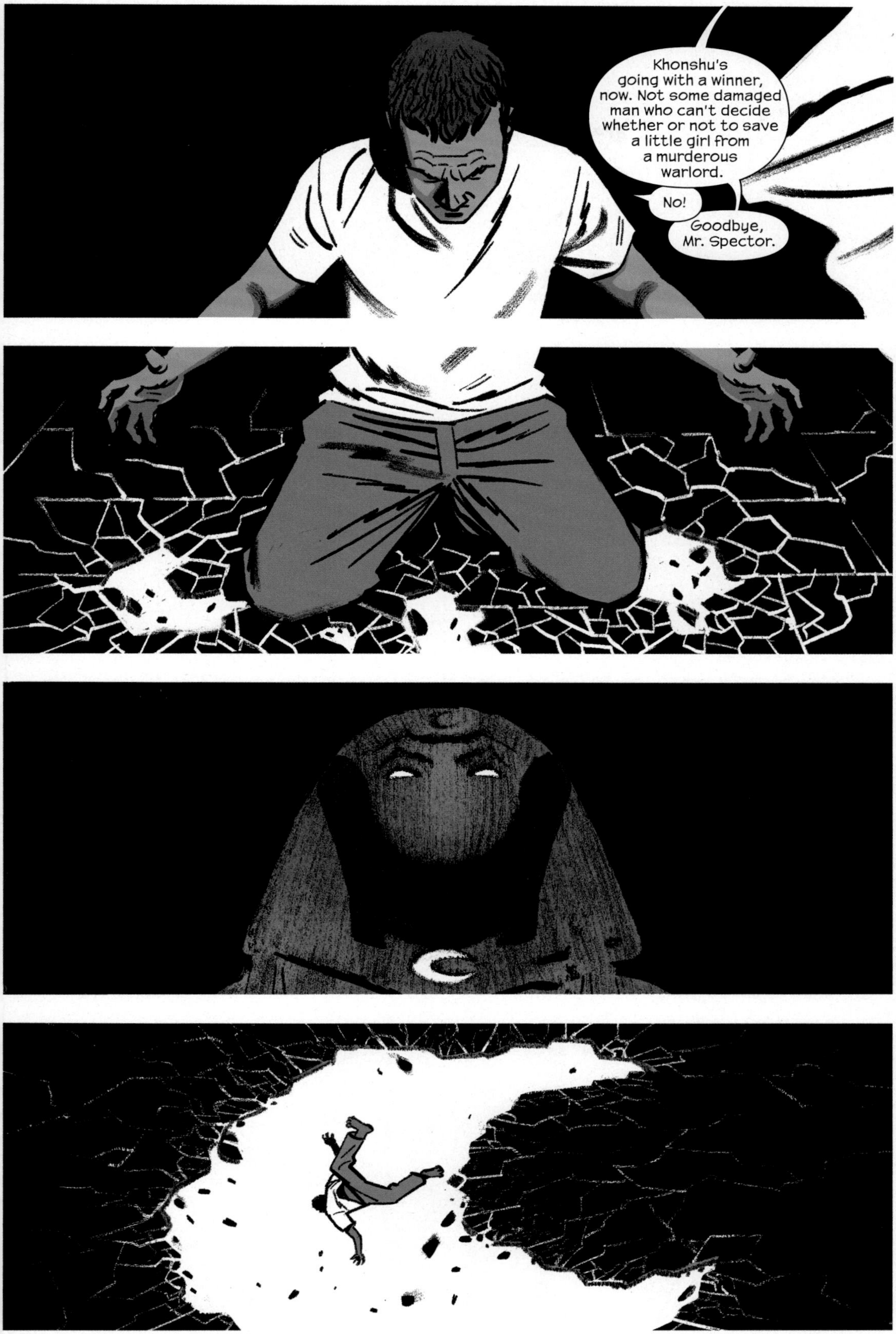
Khonshu's going with a winner, now. Not some damaged man who can't decide whether or not to save a little girl from a murderous warlord.
No!
Goodbye, Mr. Spector.

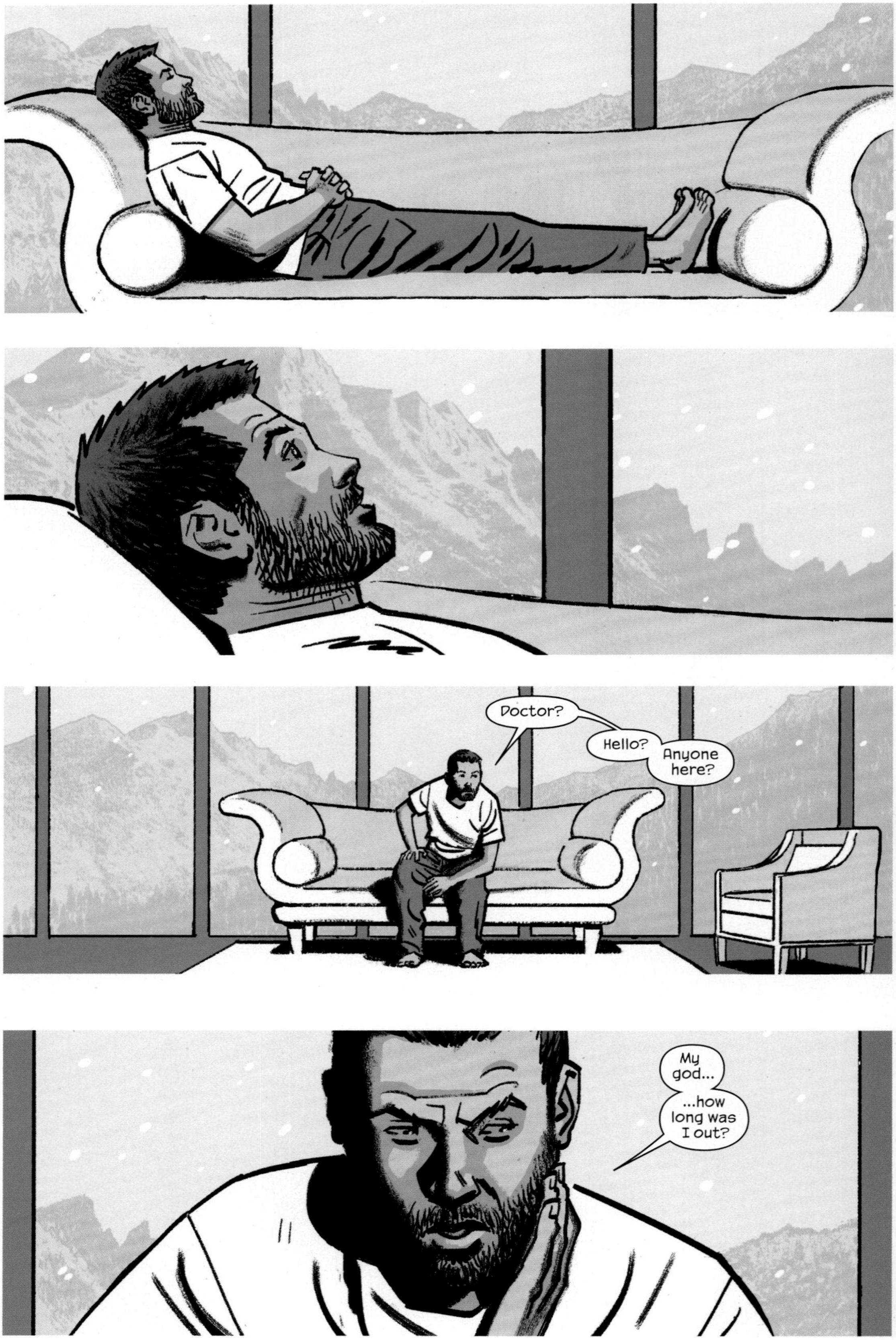
Doctor?
Hello?
Anyone here?
My god...
...how long was I out?

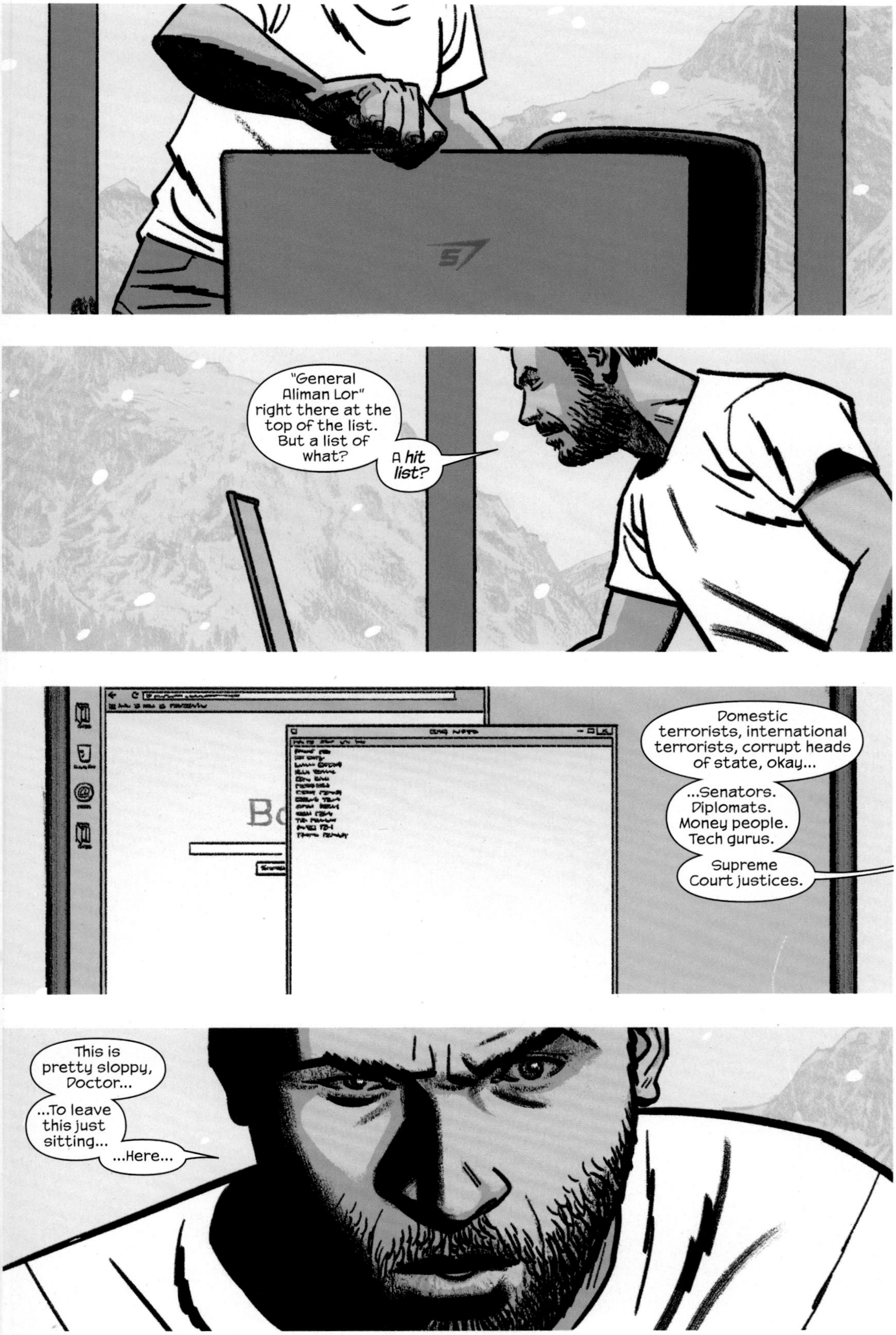

"General Aliman Lor" right there at the top of the list. But a list of what?
A *hit list?*
Domestic terrorists, international terrorists, corrupt heads of state, okay...
...Senators. Diplomats. Money people. Tech gurus.
Supreme Court justices.
This is pretty sloppy, Doctor...
...To leave this just sitting...
...Here...

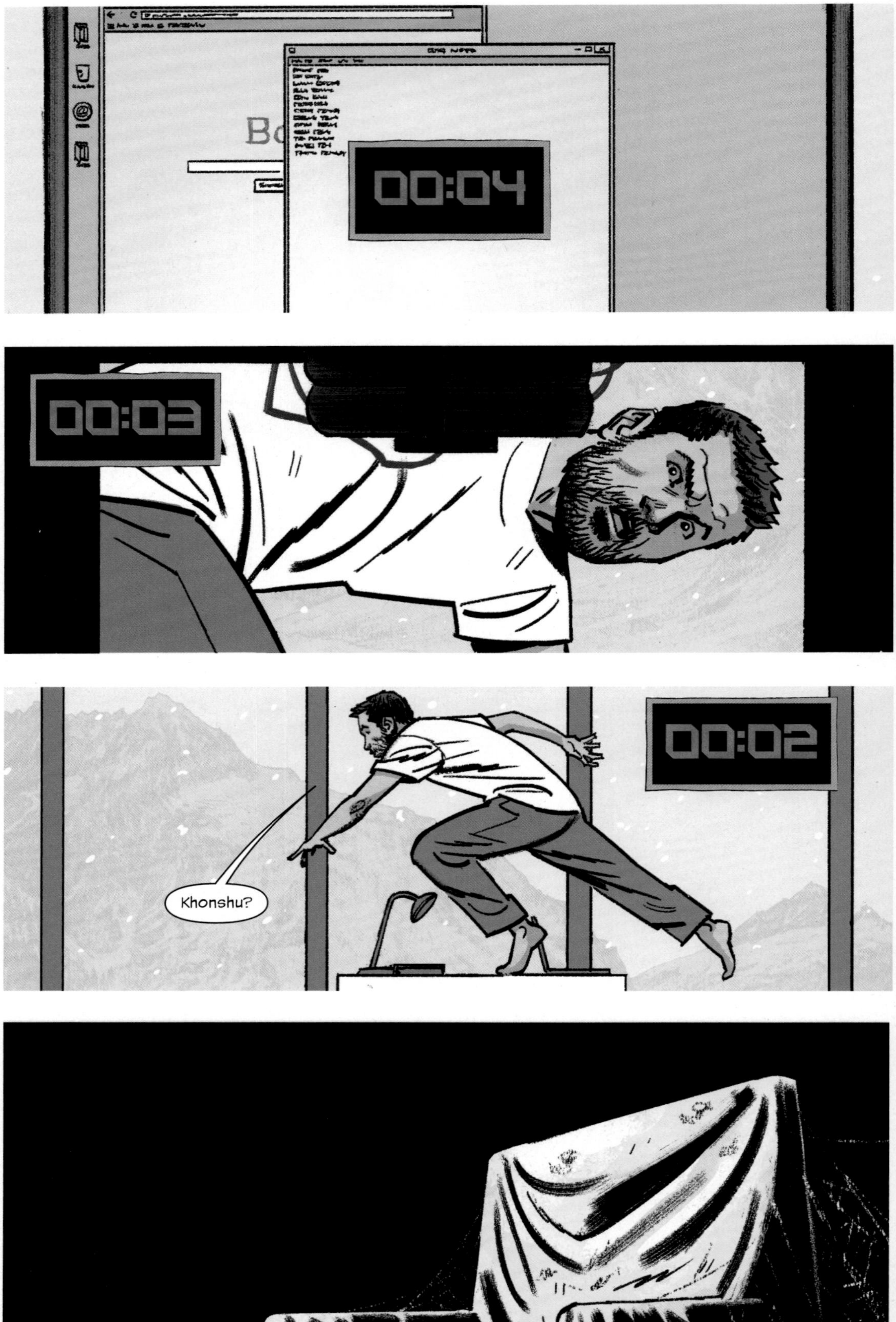
00:04
00:03
00:02
Khonshu?

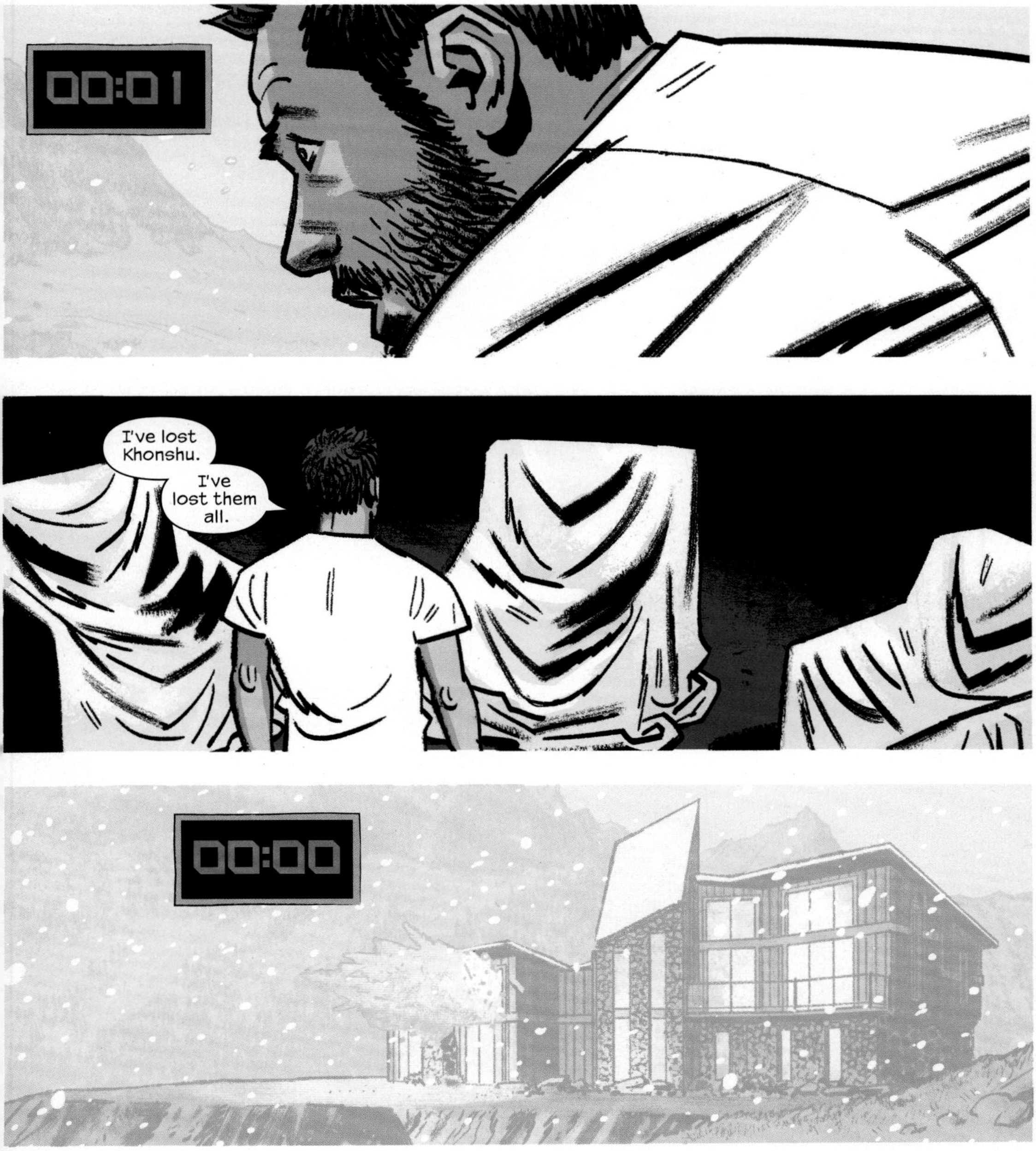
00:01
I've lost Khonshu.
I've lost them all.
00:00

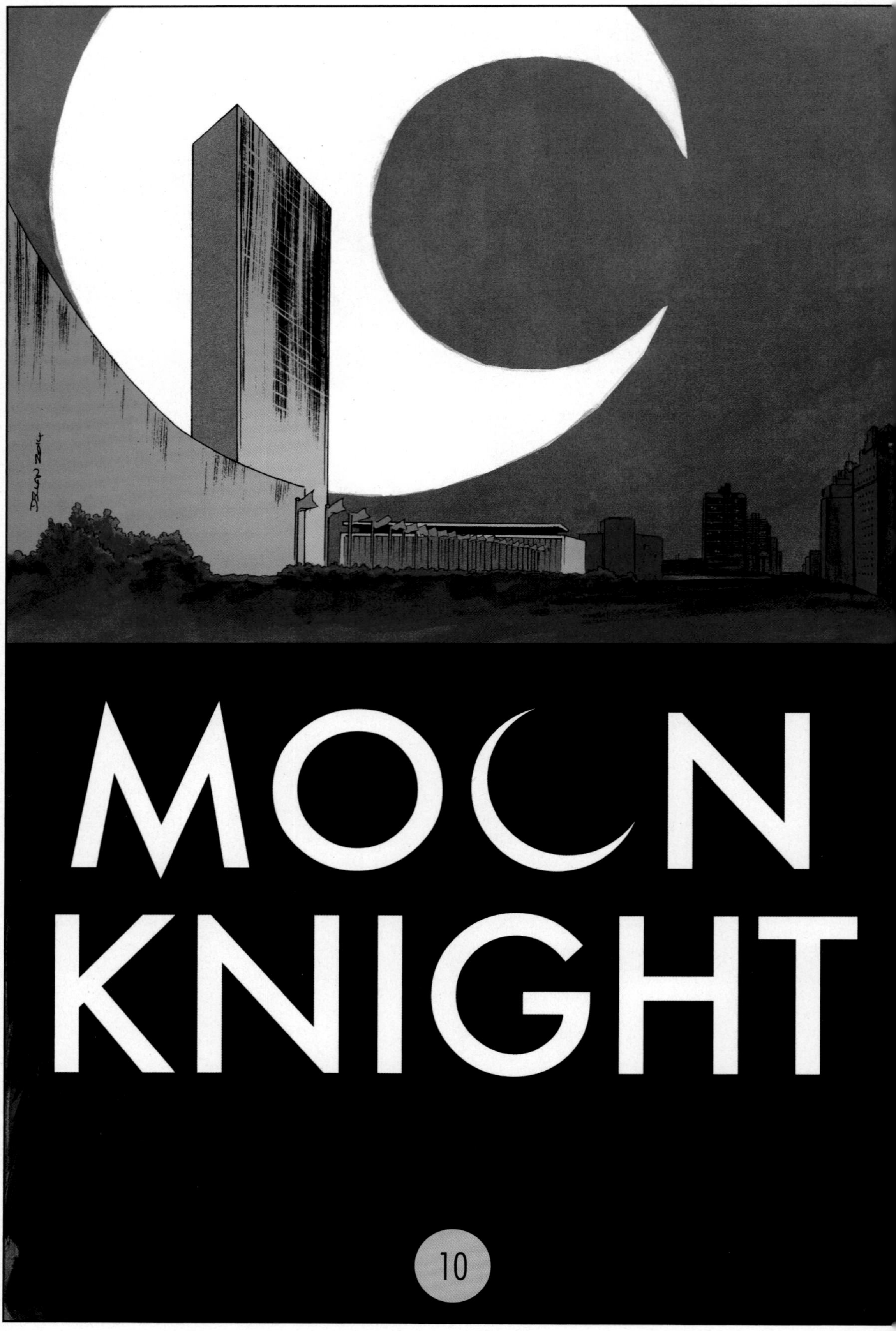
MOON
KNIGHT
10

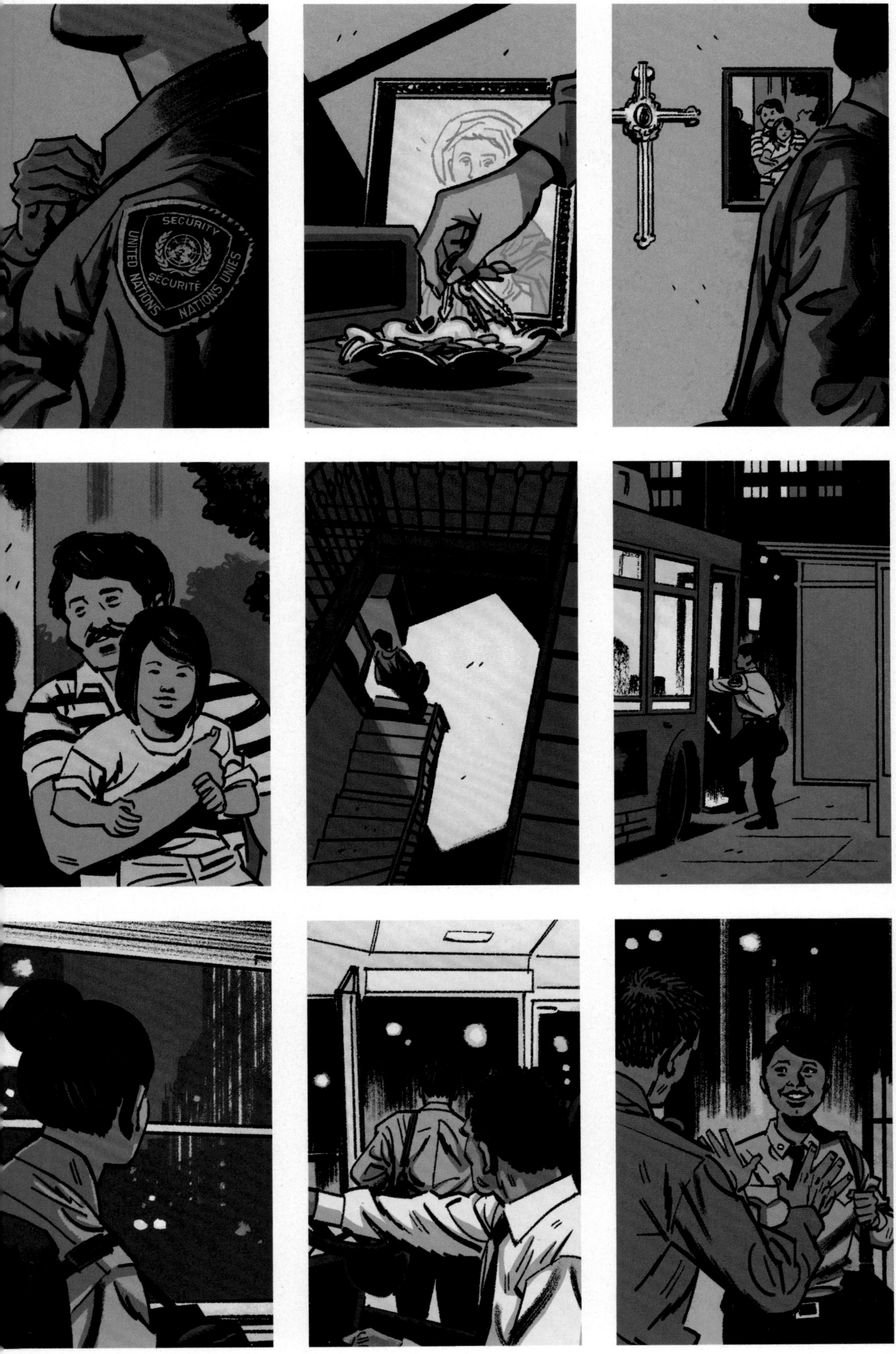
SECURITY
UNITED NATIONS
SÉCURITÉ
NATIONS UNIES

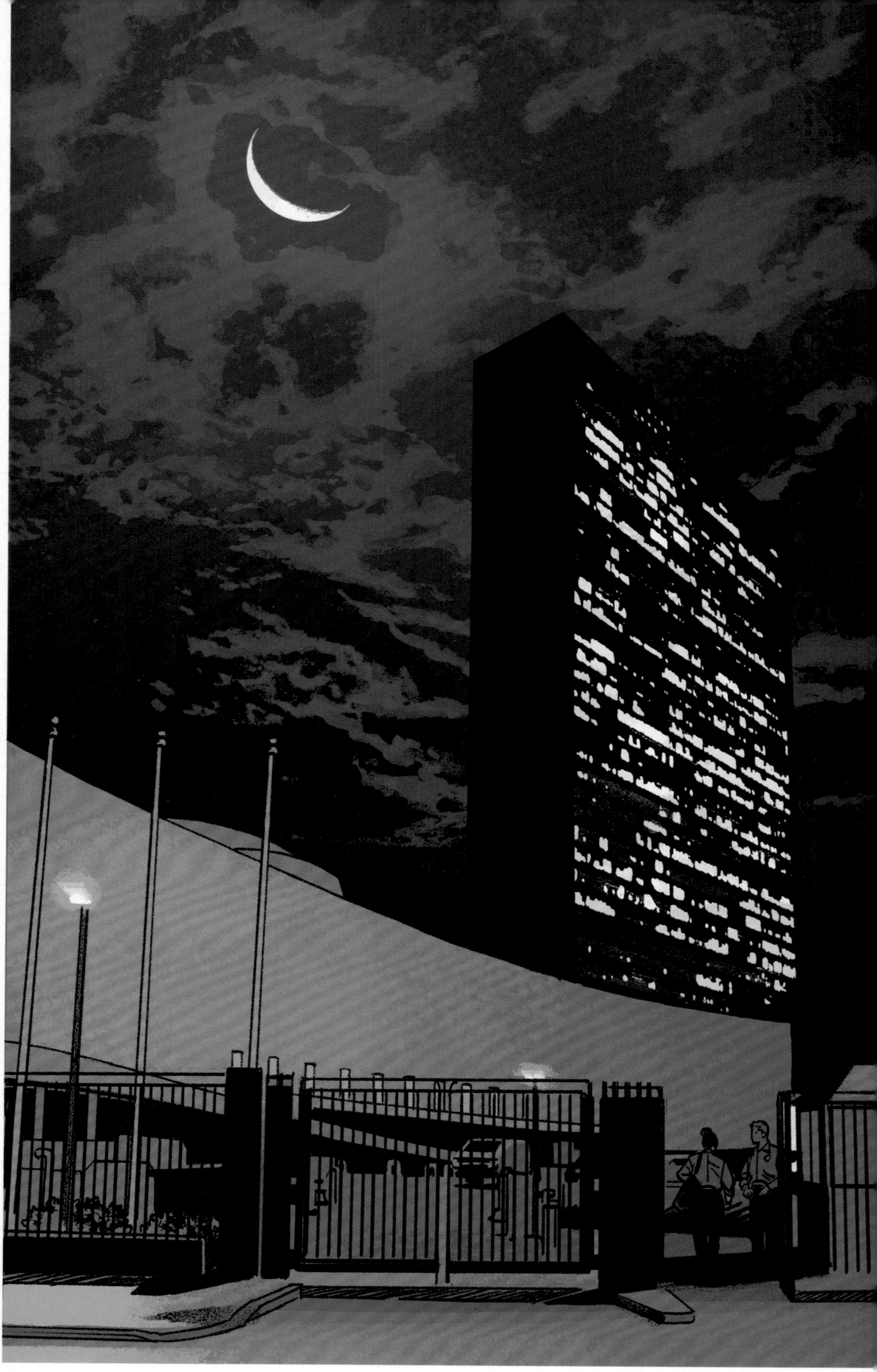

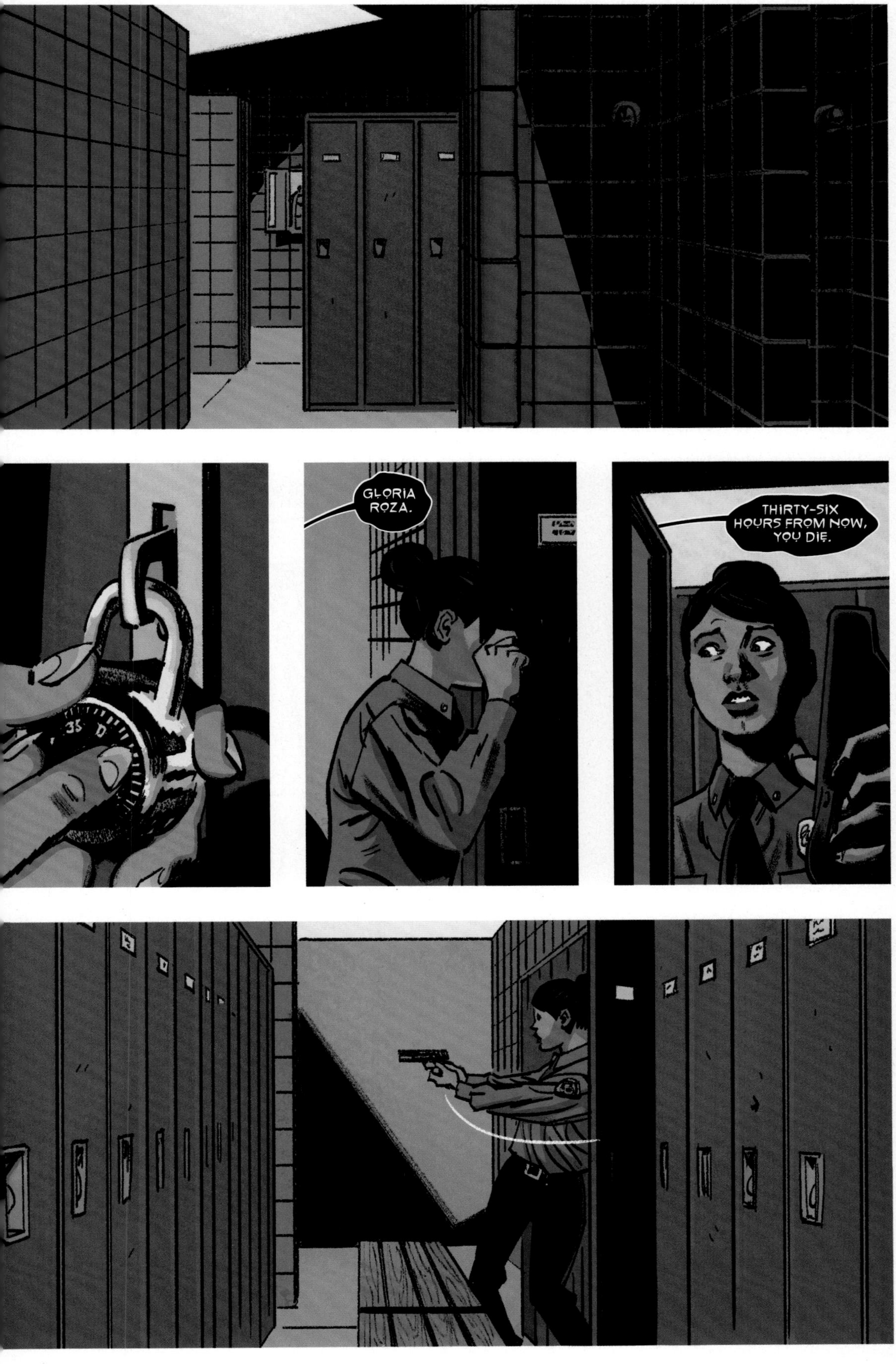
GLORIA ROZA.
THIRTY-SIX HOURS FROM NOW, YOU DIE.

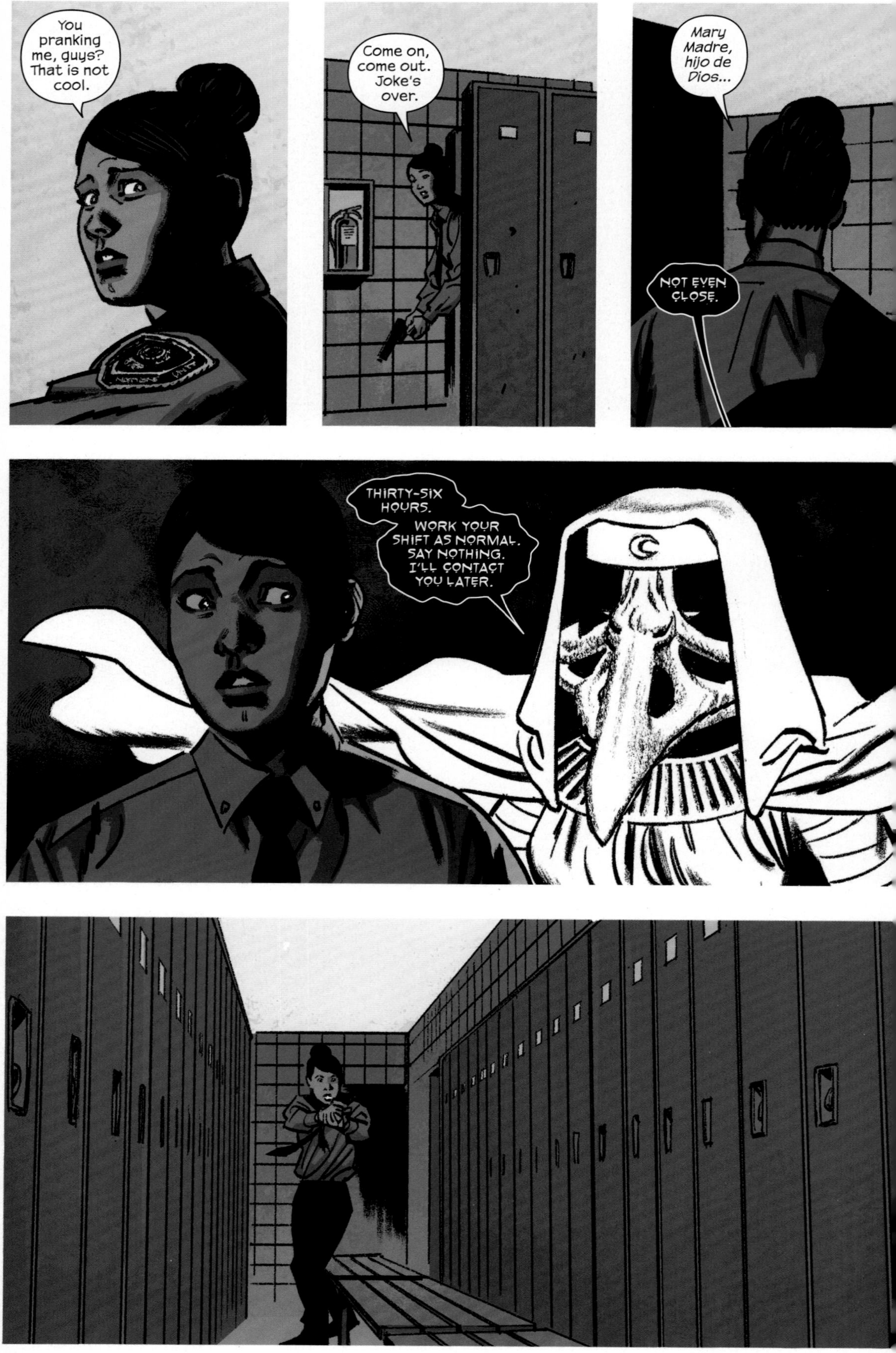
You pranking me, guys? That is not cool.
Come on, come out. Joke's over.
Mary Madre, hijo de Dios...
NOT EVEN CLOSE.
THIRTY-SIX HOURS.
WORK YOUR SHIFT AS NORMAL. SAY NOTHING. I'LL CONTACT YOU LATER.

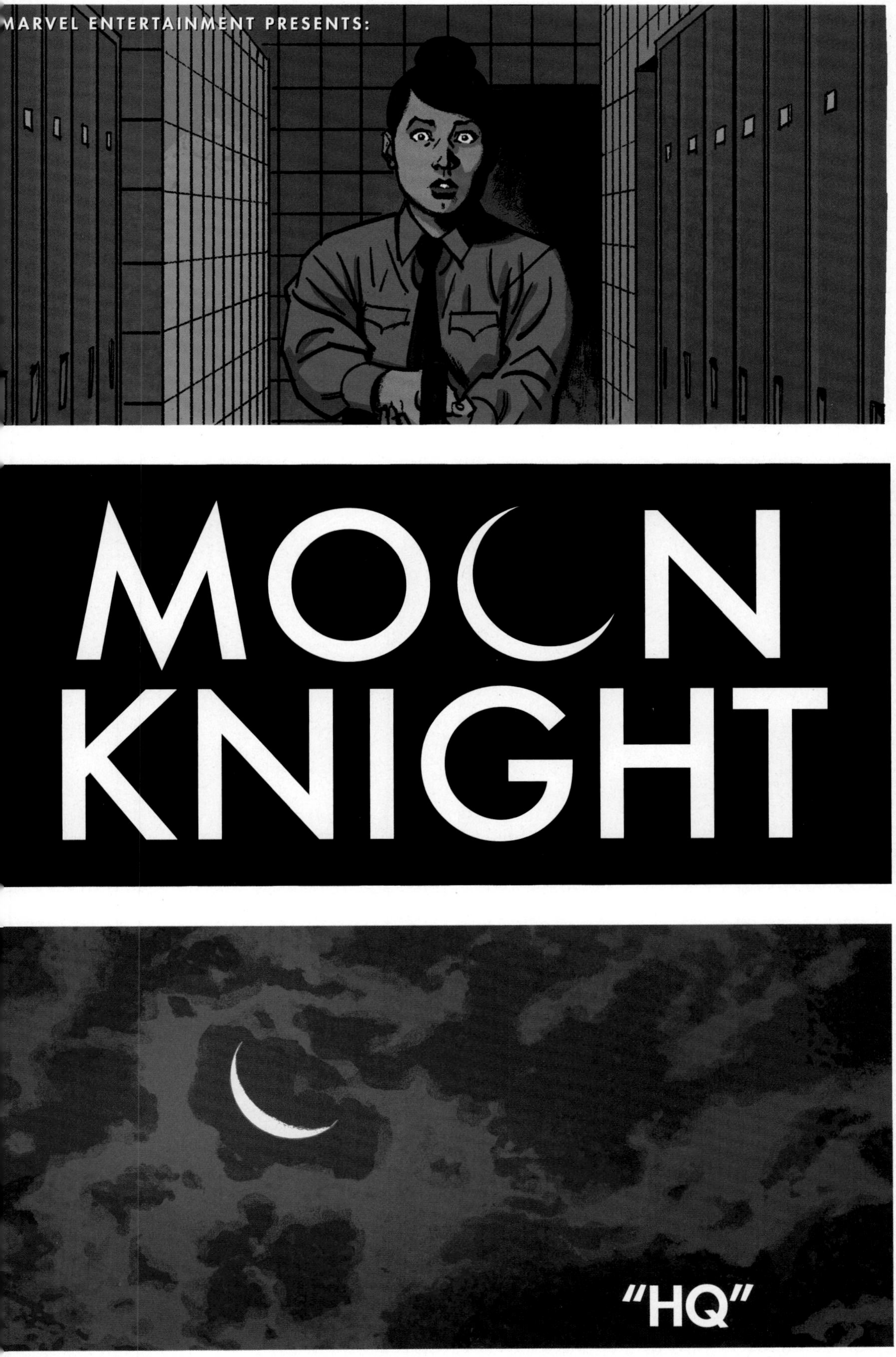
MARVEL ENTERTAINMENT PRESENTS:
MOON KNIGHT
"HQ"

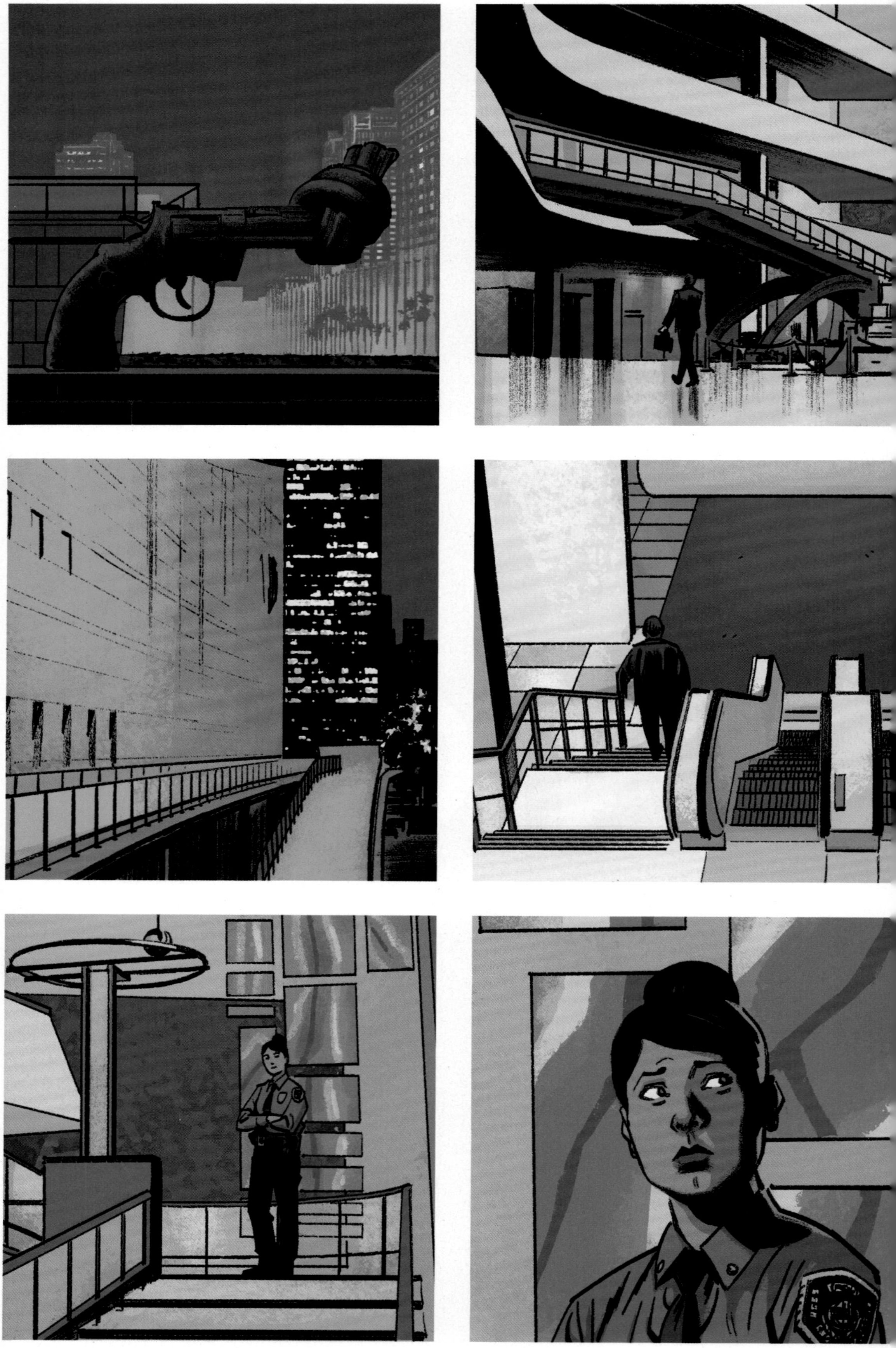

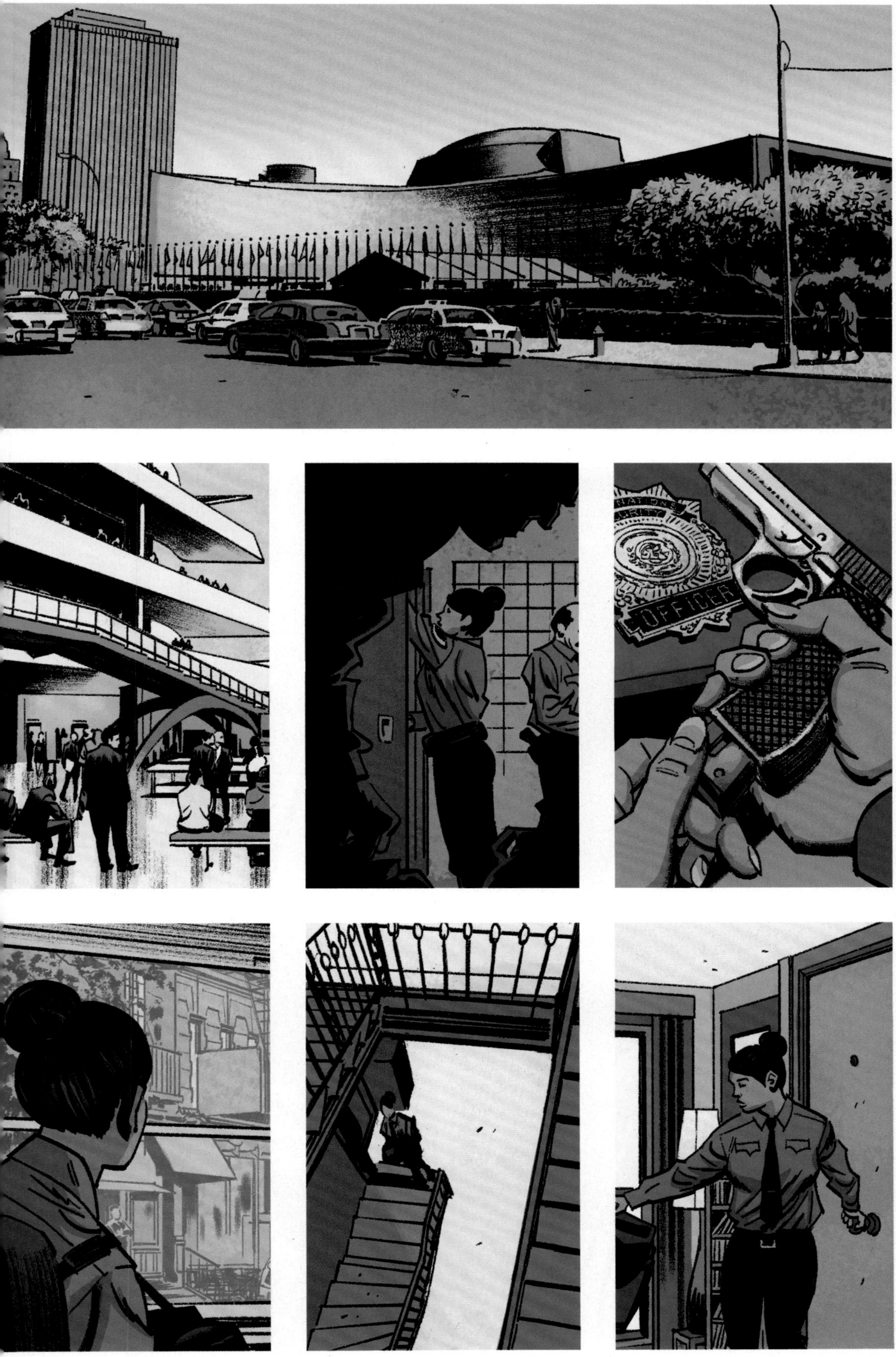
OFFICER

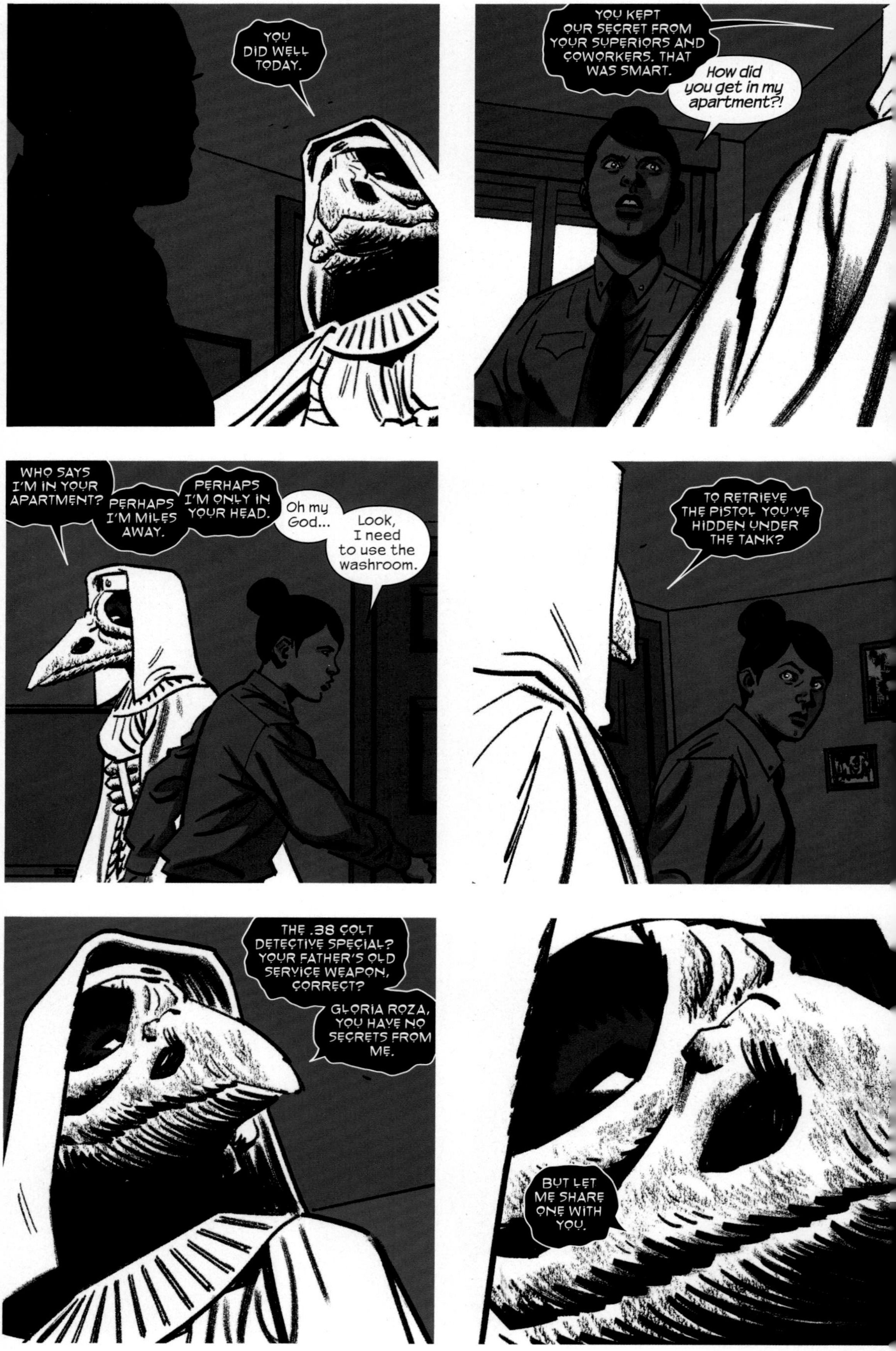
YOU DID WELL TODAY.
YOU KEPT OUR SECRET FROM YOUR SUPERIORS AND COWORKERS. THAT WAS SMART.
How did you get in my apartment?!
WHO SAYS I'M IN YOUR APARTMENT?
PERHAPS I'M MILES AWAY.
PERHAPS I'M ONLY IN YOUR HEAD.
Oh my God...
Look, I need to use the washroom.
TO RETRIEVE THE PISTOL YOU'VE HIDDEN UNDER THE TANK?
THE .38 COLT DETECTIVE SPECIAL? YOUR FATHER'S OLD SERVICE WEAPON, CORRECT?
GLORIA ROZA, YOU HAVE NO SECRETS FROM ME.
BUT LET ME SHARE ONE WITH YOU.

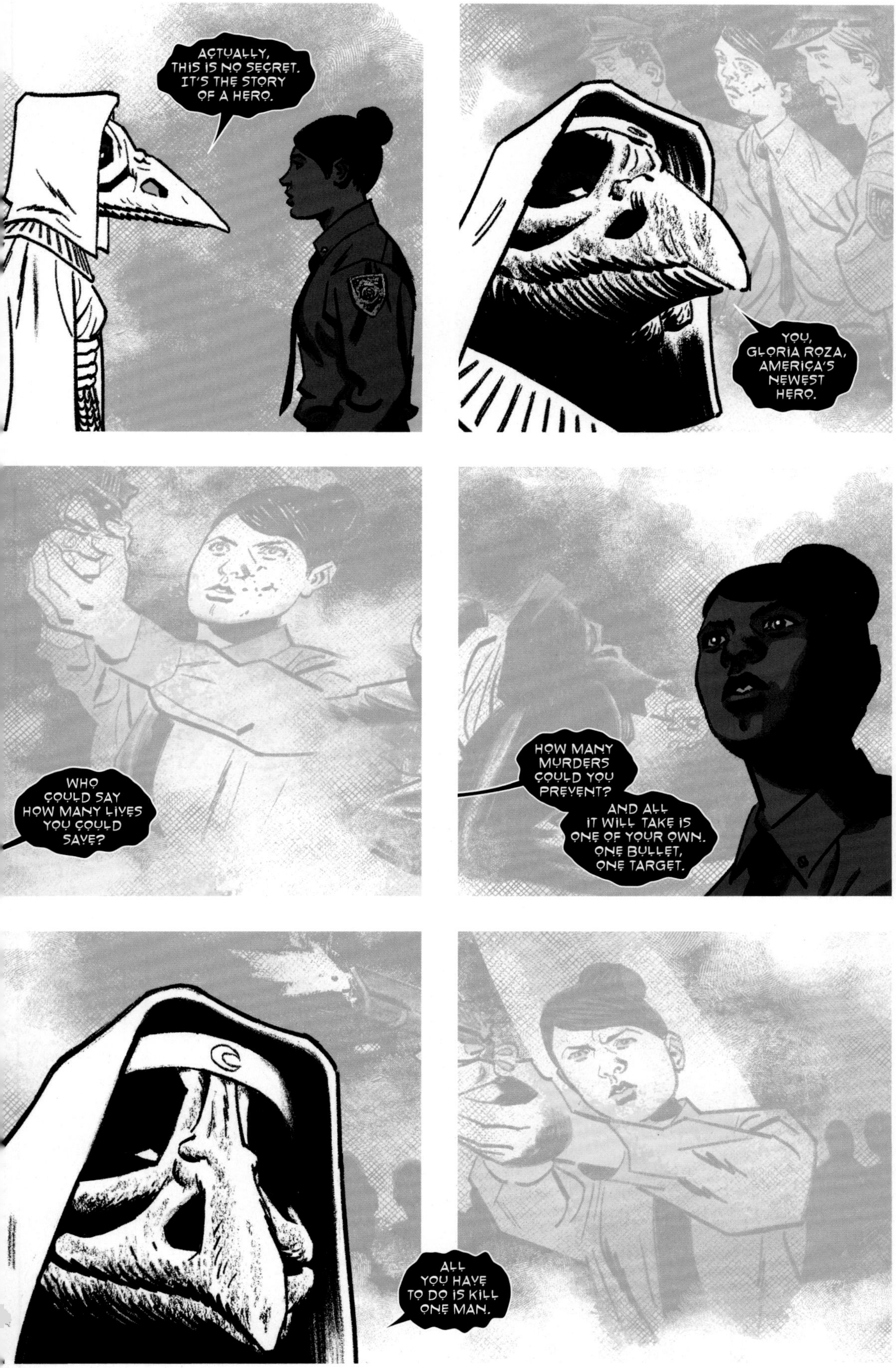
ACTUALLY, THIS IS NO SECRET. IT'S THE STORY OF A HERO.
YOU, GLORIA ROZA, AMERICA'S NEWEST HERO.
WHO COULD SAY HOW MANY LIVES YOU COULD SAVE?
HOW MANY MURDERS COULD YOU PREVENT?
AND ALL IT WILL TAKE IS ONE OF YOUR OWN. ONE BULLET, ONE TARGET.
ALL YOU HAVE TO DO IS KILL ONE MAN.

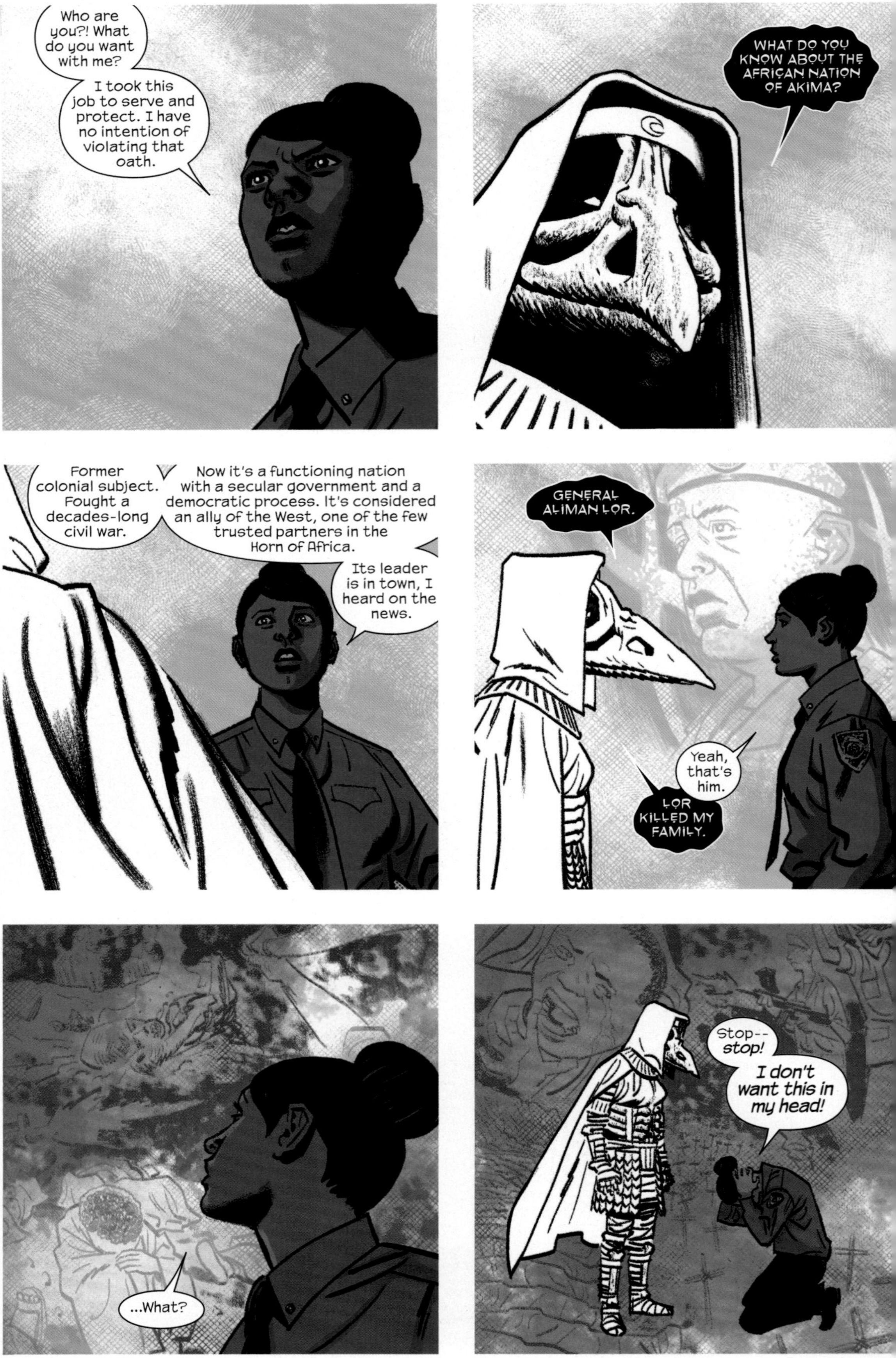
Who are you?! What do you want with me?
I took this job to serve and protect. I have no intention of violating that oath.
WHAT DO YOU KNOW ABOUT THE AFRICAN NATION OF AKIMA?
Former colonial subject. Fought a decades-long civil war.
Now it's a functioning nation with a secular government and a democratic process. It's considered an ally of the West, one of the few trusted partners in the Horn of Africa.
Its leader is in town, I heard on the news.
GENERAL ALIMAN LOR.
Yeah, that's him.
LOR KILLED MY FAMILY.
...What?
Stop-- *stop!*
I don't want this in my head!

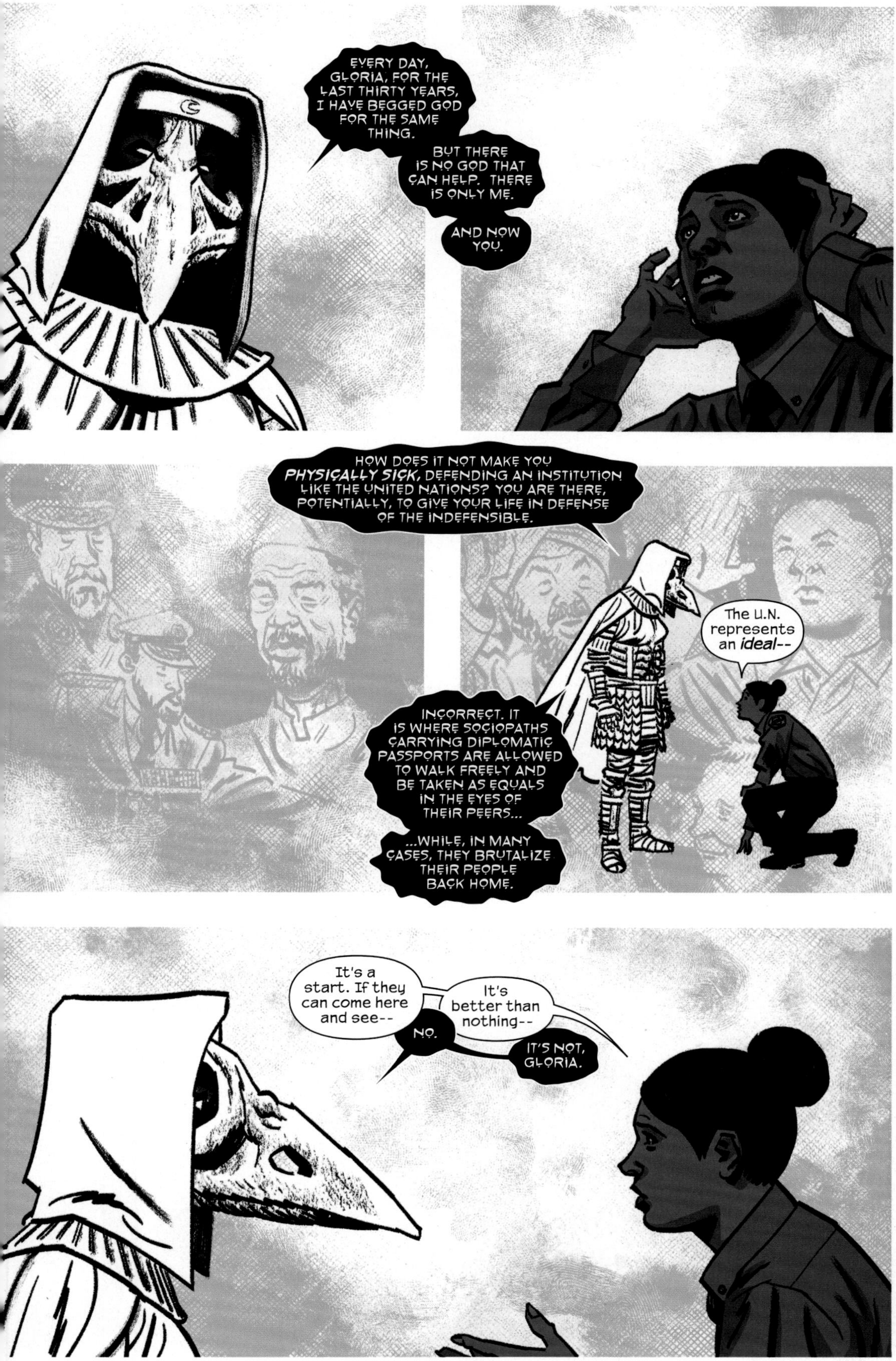
EVERY DAY, GLORIA, FOR THE LAST THIRTY YEARS, I HAVE BEGGED GOD FOR THE SAME THING.
BUT THERE IS NO GOD THAT CAN HELP. THERE IS ONLY ME.
AND NOW YOU.
HOW DOES IT NOT MAKE YOU PHYSICALLY SICK, DEFENDING AN INSTITUTION LIKE THE UNITED NATIONS? YOU ARE THERE, POTENTIALLY, TO GIVE YOUR LIFE IN DEFENSE OF THE INDEFENSIBLE.
The U.N. represents an ideal--
INCORRECT. IT IS WHERE SOCIOPATHS CARRYING DIPLOMATIC PASSPORTS ARE ALLOWED TO WALK FREELY AND BE TAKEN AS EQUALS IN THE EYES OF THEIR PEERS...
...WHILE, IN MANY CASES, THEY BRUTALIZE THEIR PEOPLE BACK HOME.
It's a start. If they can come here and see--
It's better than nothing--
NO.
IT'S NOT, GLORIA.

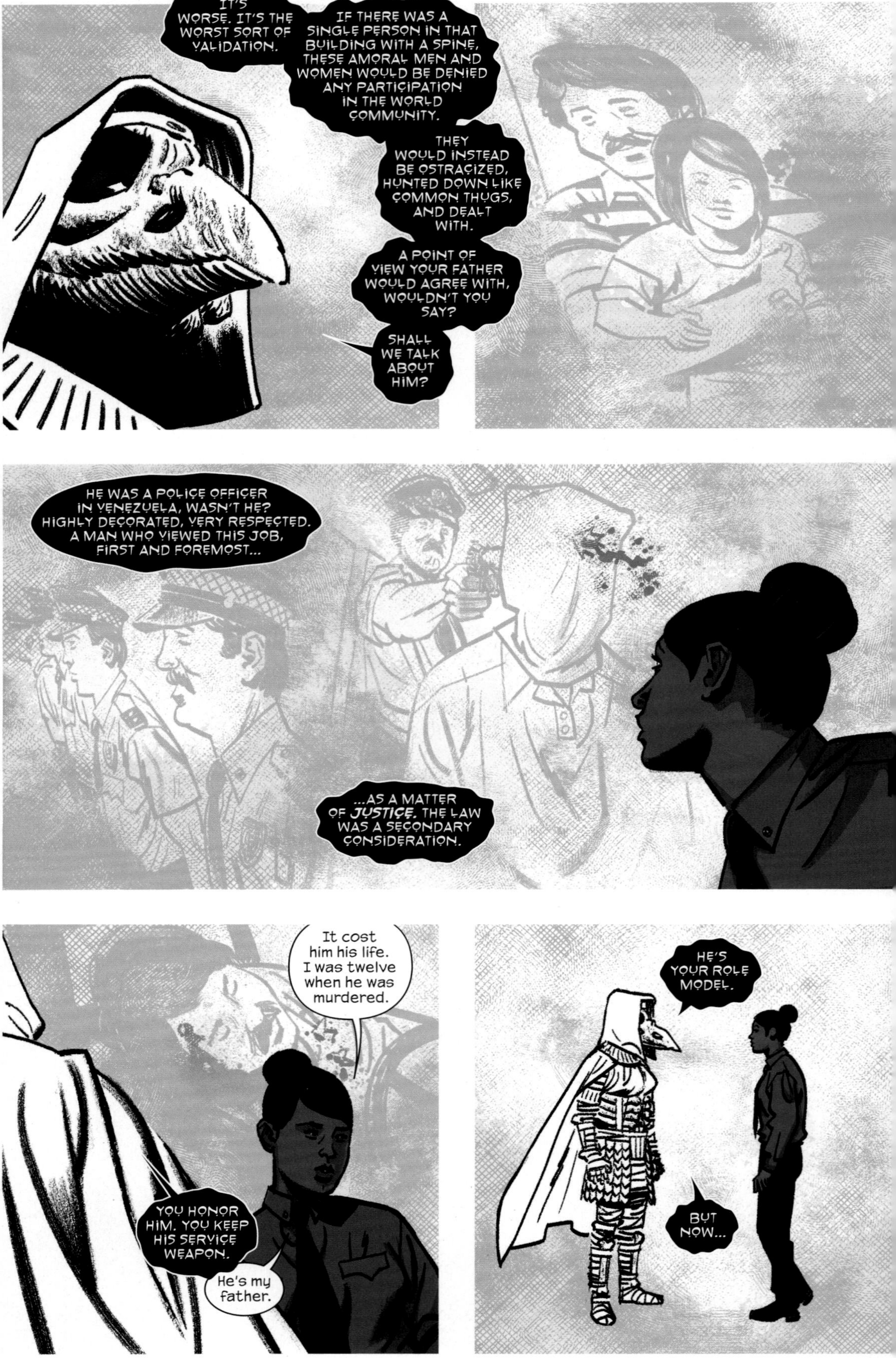
IT'S WORSE. IT'S THE WORST SORT OF VALIDATION.
IF THERE WAS A SINGLE PERSON IN THAT BUILDING WITH A SPINE, THESE AMORAL MEN AND WOMEN WOULD BE DENIED ANY PARTICIPATION IN THE WORLD COMMUNITY.
THEY WOULD INSTEAD BE OSTRACIZED, HUNTED DOWN LIKE COMMON THUGS, AND DEALT WITH.
A POINT OF VIEW YOUR FATHER WOULD AGREE WITH, WOULDN'T YOU SAY?
SHALL WE TALK ABOUT HIM?
HE WAS A POLICE OFFICER IN VENEZUELA, WASN'T HE? HIGHLY DECORATED, VERY RESPECTED. A MAN WHO VIEWED THIS JOB, FIRST AND FOREMOST...
...AS A MATTER OF *JUSTICE*. THE LAW WAS A SECONDARY CONSIDERATION.
It cost him his life. I was twelve when he was murdered.
YOU HONOR HIM. YOU KEEP HIS SERVICE WEAPON.
He's my father.
HE'S YOUR ROLE MODEL.
BUT NOW...

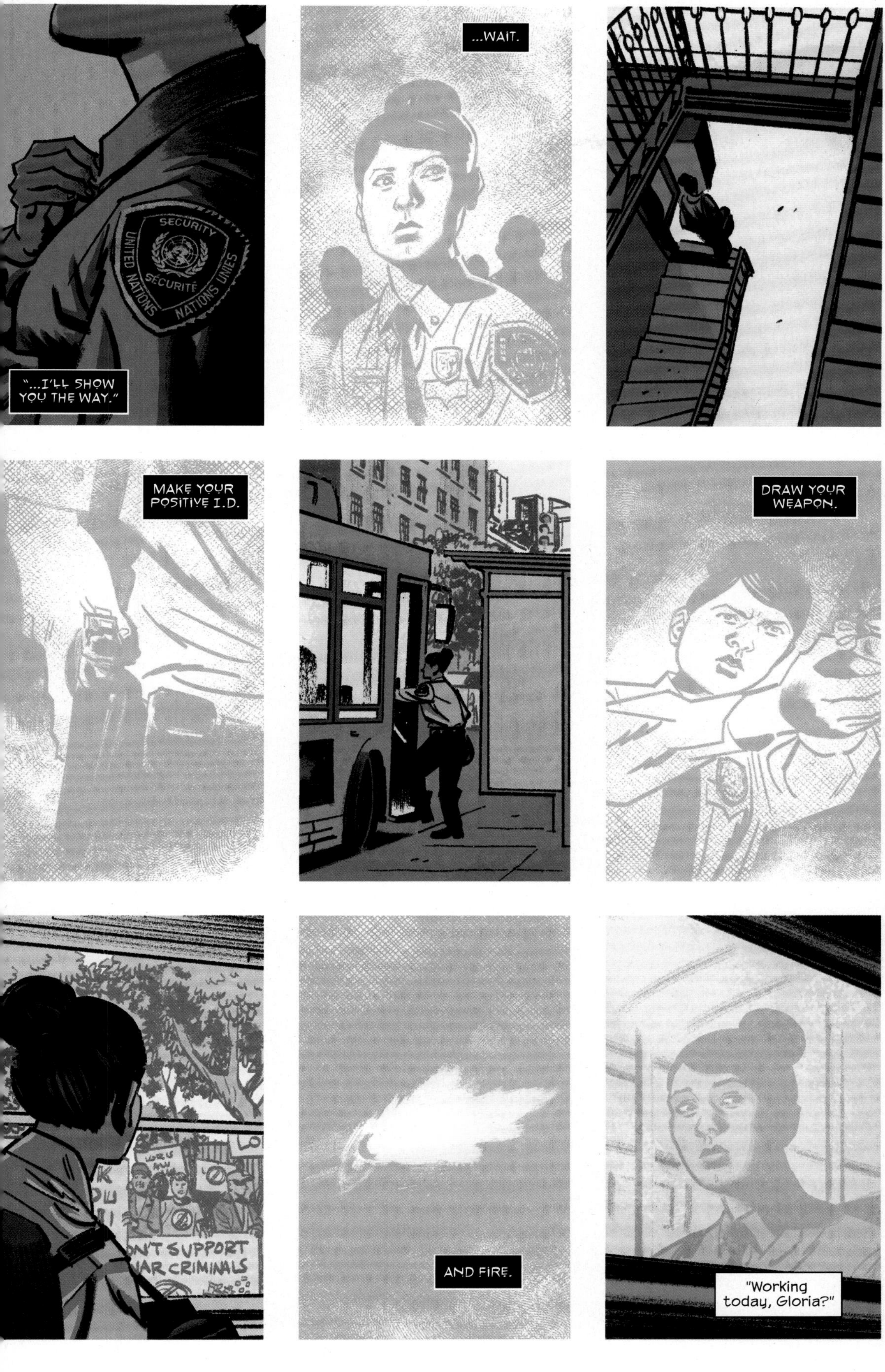

SECURITY
UNITED NATIONS
SÉCURITÉ
NATIONS UNIES
"...I'LL SHOW YOU THE WAY."
...WAIT.
MAKE YOUR POSITIVE I.D.
DRAW YOUR WEAPON.
ON'T SUPPORT
AR CRIMINALS
AND FIRE.
"Working today, Gloria?"

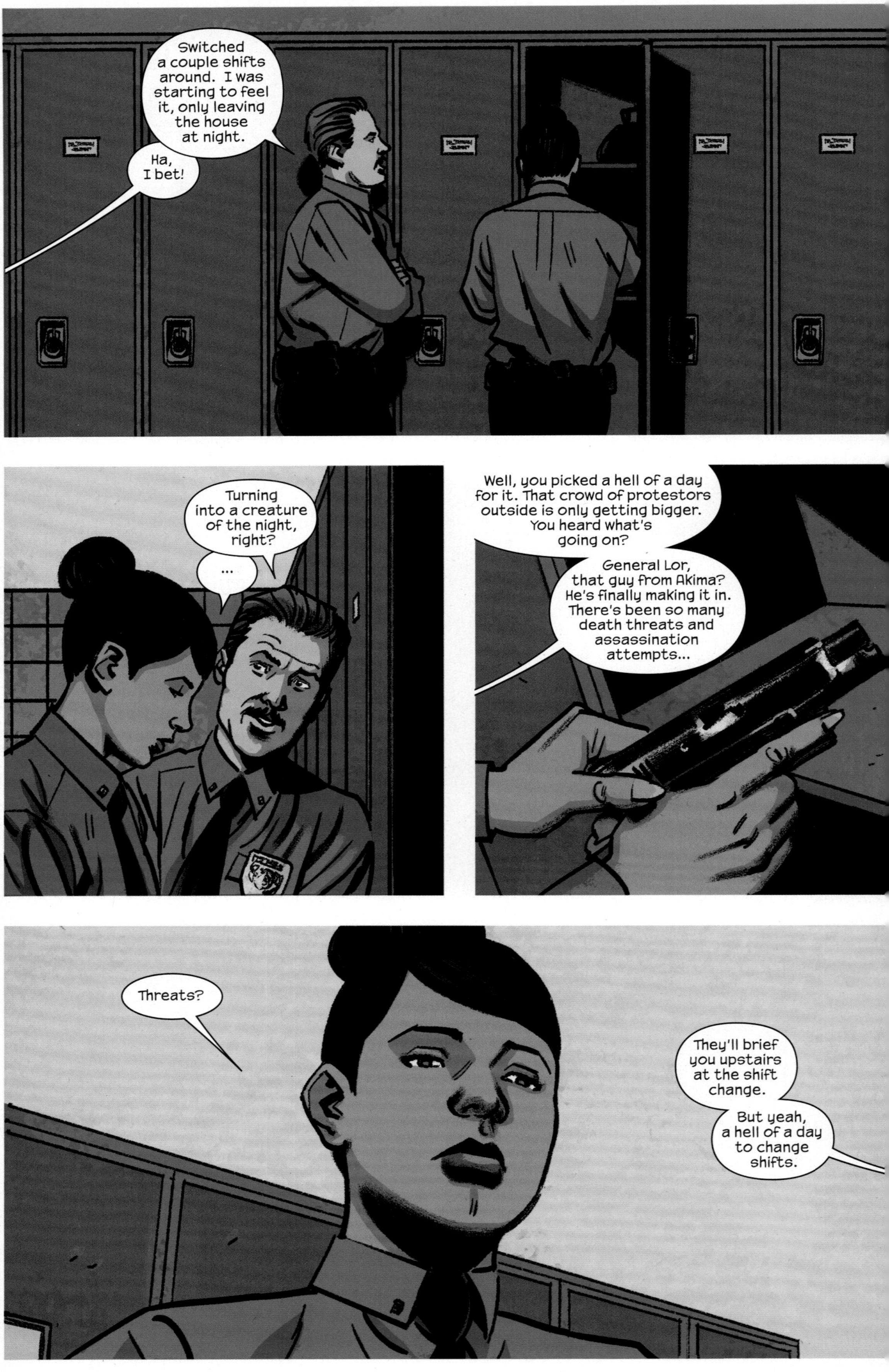
Switched a couple shifts around. I was starting to feel it, only leaving the house at night.
Ha, I bet!
Turning into a creature of the night, right?
...
Well, you picked a hell of a day for it. That crowd of protestors outside is only getting bigger. You heard what's going on?
General Lor, that guy from Akima? He's finally making it in. There's been so many death threats and assassination attempts...
Threats?
They'll brief you upstairs at the shift change.
But yeah, a hell of a day to change shifts.

General Lor will be coming in the service entrance, using an existing catering van as disguise.

He will be accompanied by his full compliment of security personnel, and they all will be dressed in the food company's uniform.

They will be allowed into the building, no screenings necessary.

In addition to yourselves, and our own tactical response, Washington's seen fit to supply us with an additional set of eyes for the day. Agent Kenrick?

Lieutenant-Colonel.

My name is Agent Kenrick.

I am your liason with the FBI. I am here strictly as intelligence support. The Bureau does not have men on the ground.

But I am familiar with the General's enemies, and will be monitoring the crowd outside for any threats that may emerge.

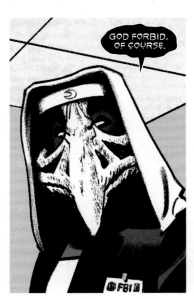

GOD FORBID, OF COURSE.

Let us all work to see the day passes just as planned.

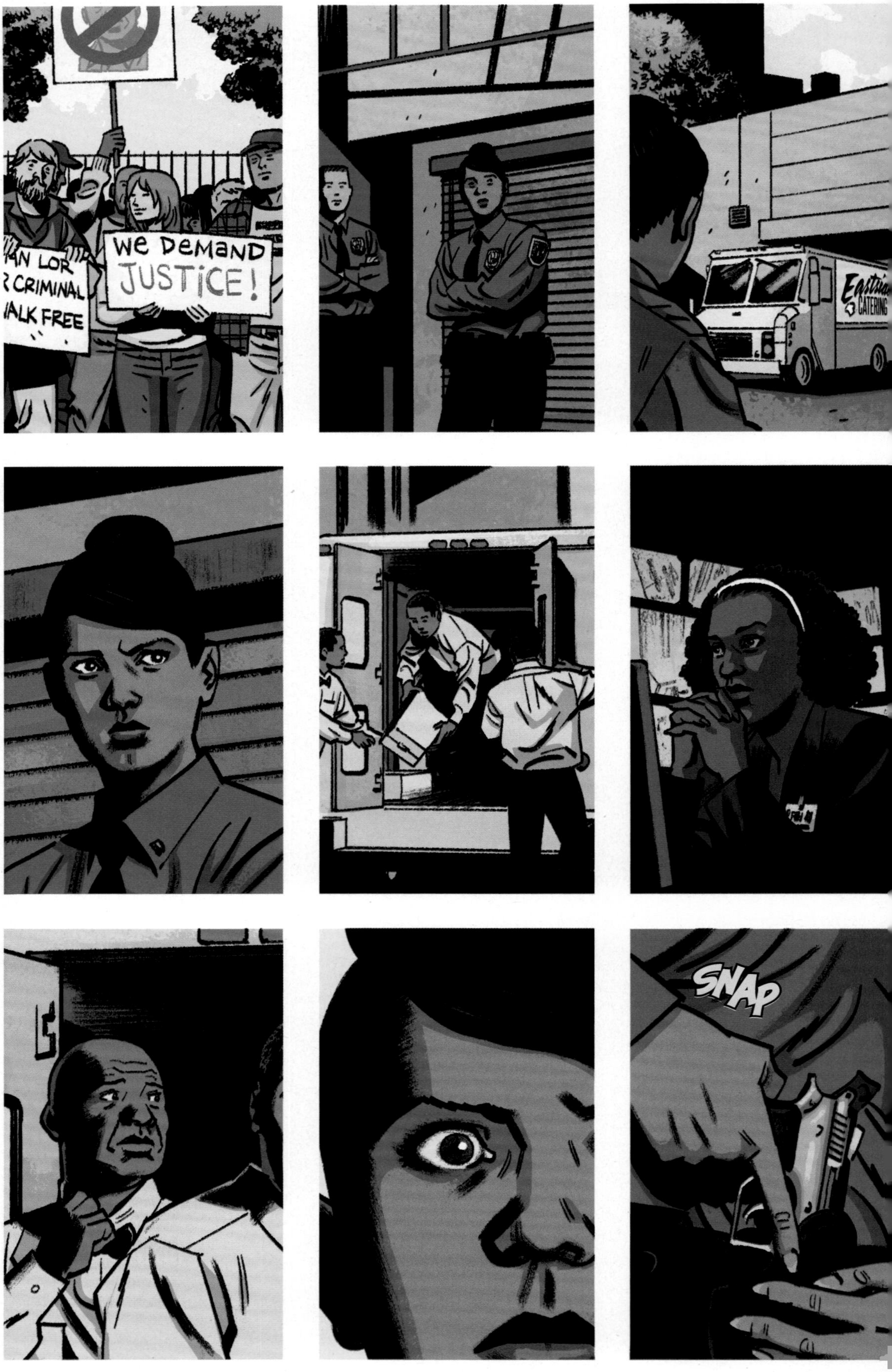

AN LOR
R CRIMINAL
WALK FREE
WE DEMAND
JUSTICE!
Eastria
CATERING
SNAP

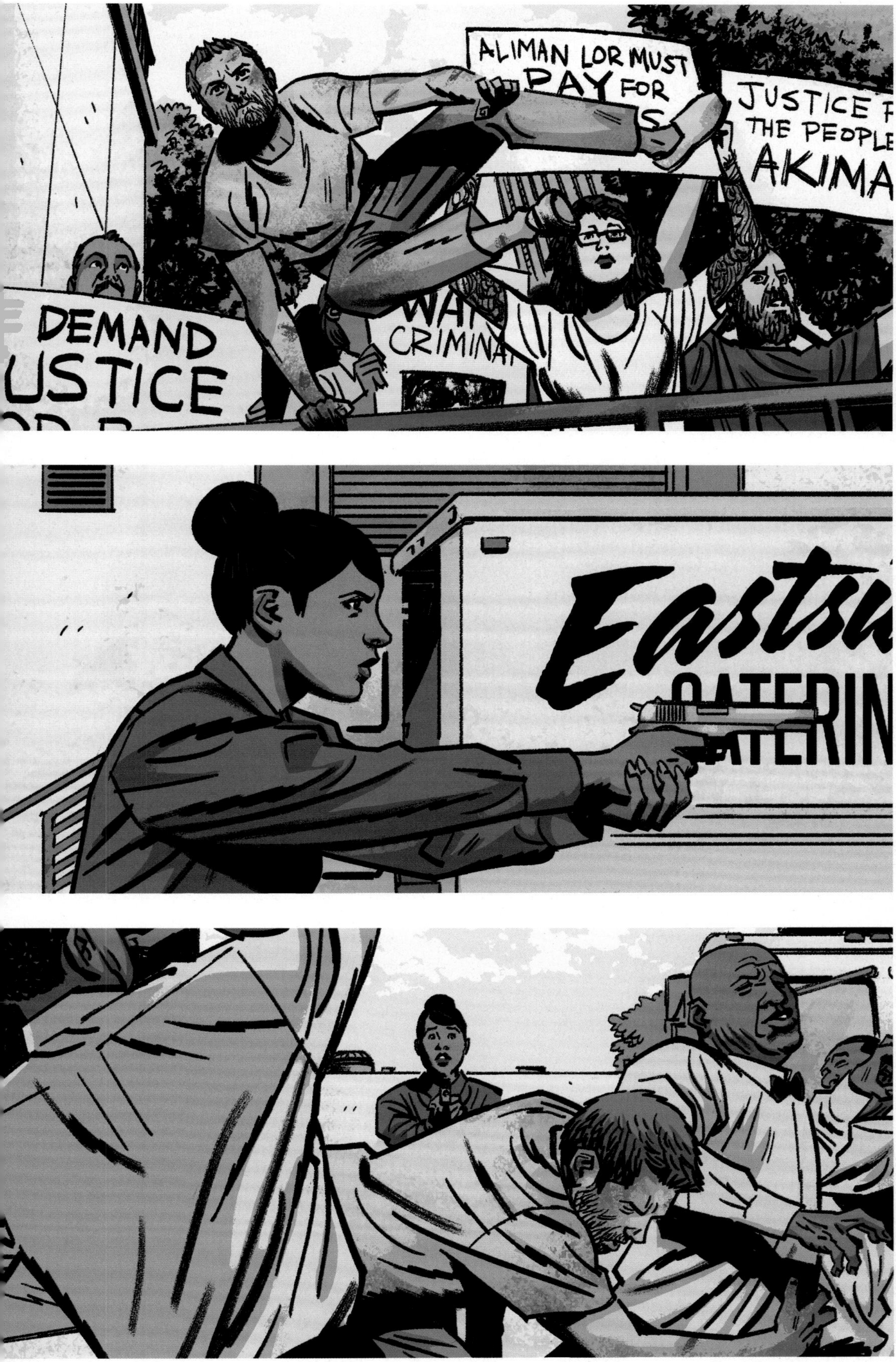
ALIMAN LOR MUST
PAY FOR
JUSTICE
THE PEOPLE
AKIMA
DEMAND
USTICE
CRIMINA
Easts
CATERIN

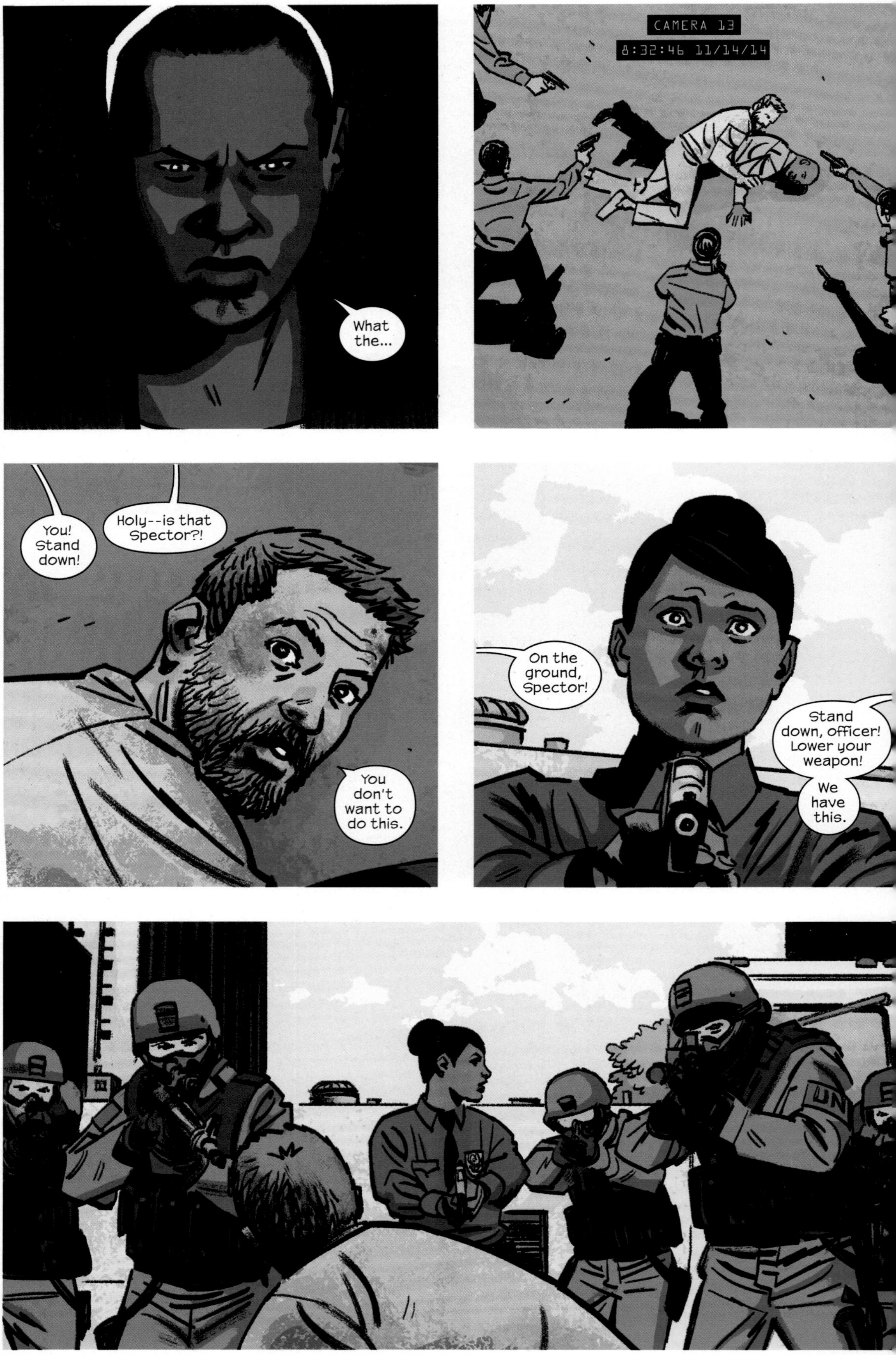
What the...
CAMERA 13
8:32:46 11/14/14
You! Stand down!
Holy--is that Spector?!
You don't want to do this.
On the ground, Spector!
Stand down, officer! Lower your weapon!
We have this.
UN

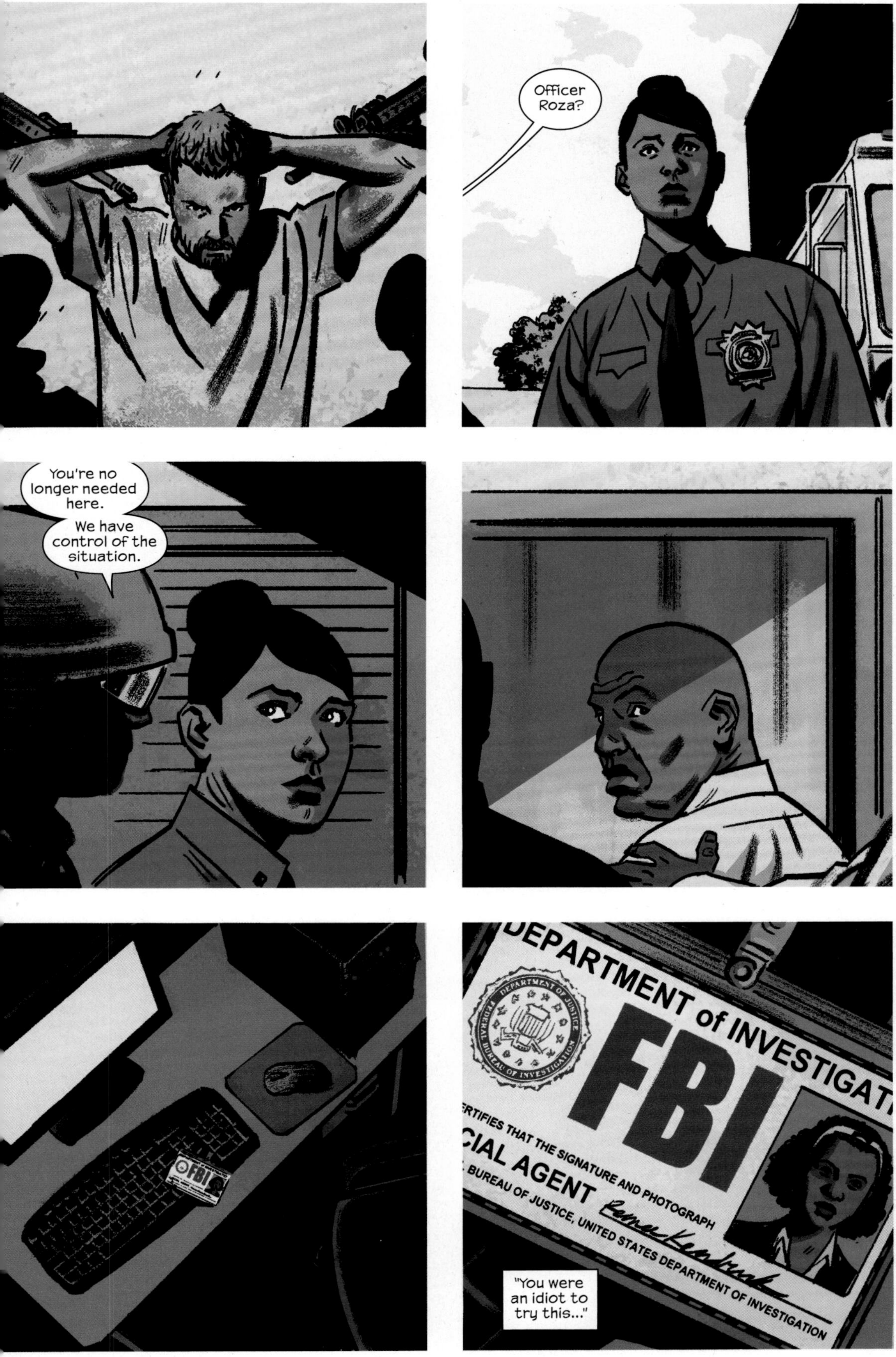

Officer Roza?
You're no longer needed here.
We have control of the situation.
FBI
"You were an idiot to try this..."

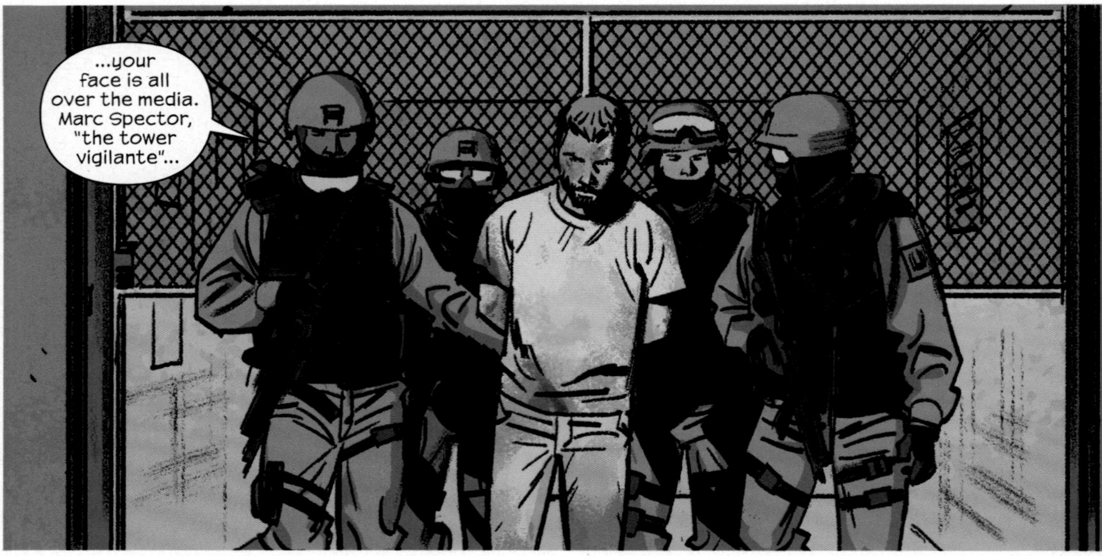
...your face is all over the media. Marc Spector, "the tower vigilante"...

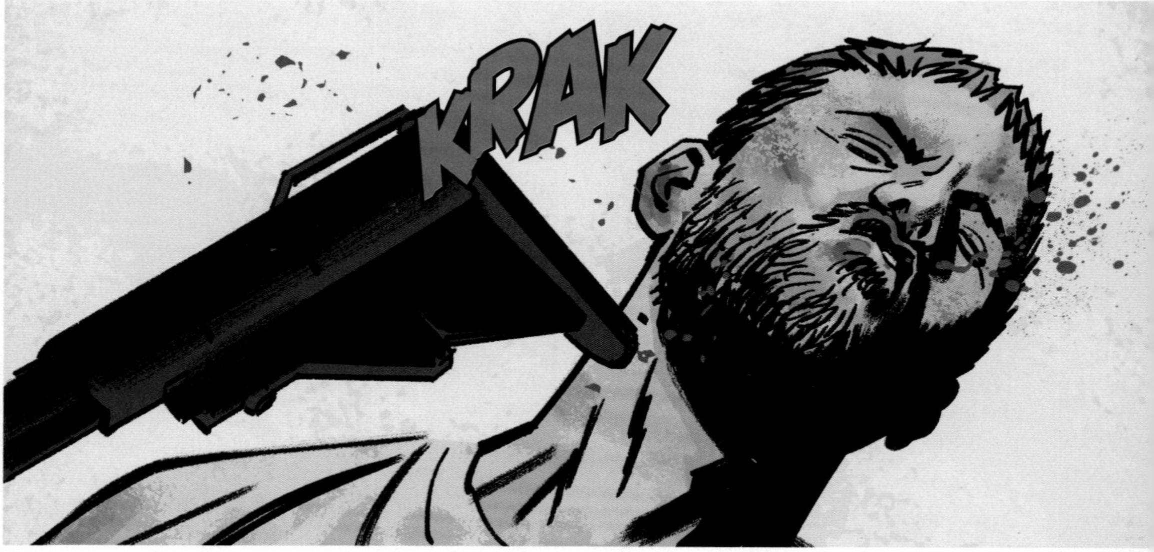
KRAK

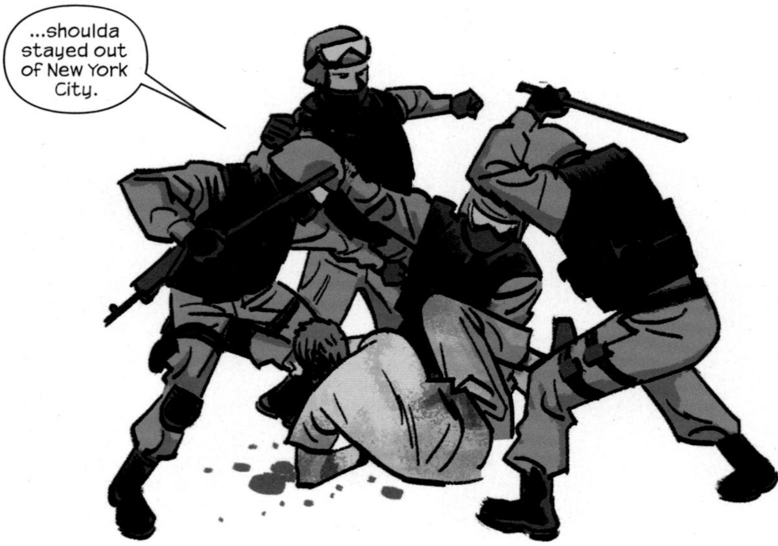
...shoulda stayed out of New York City.

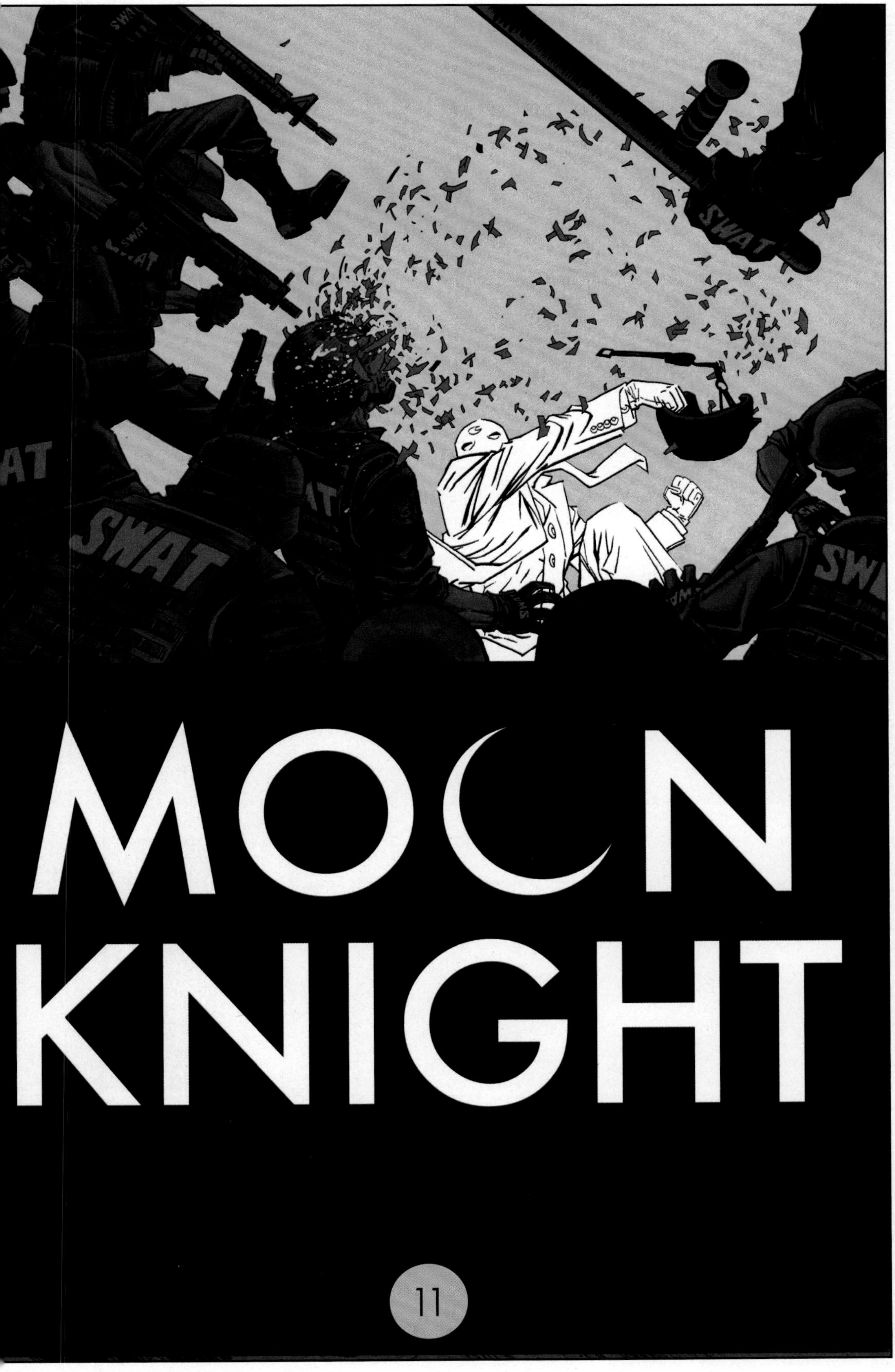
SWAT
MOON
KNIGHT
11

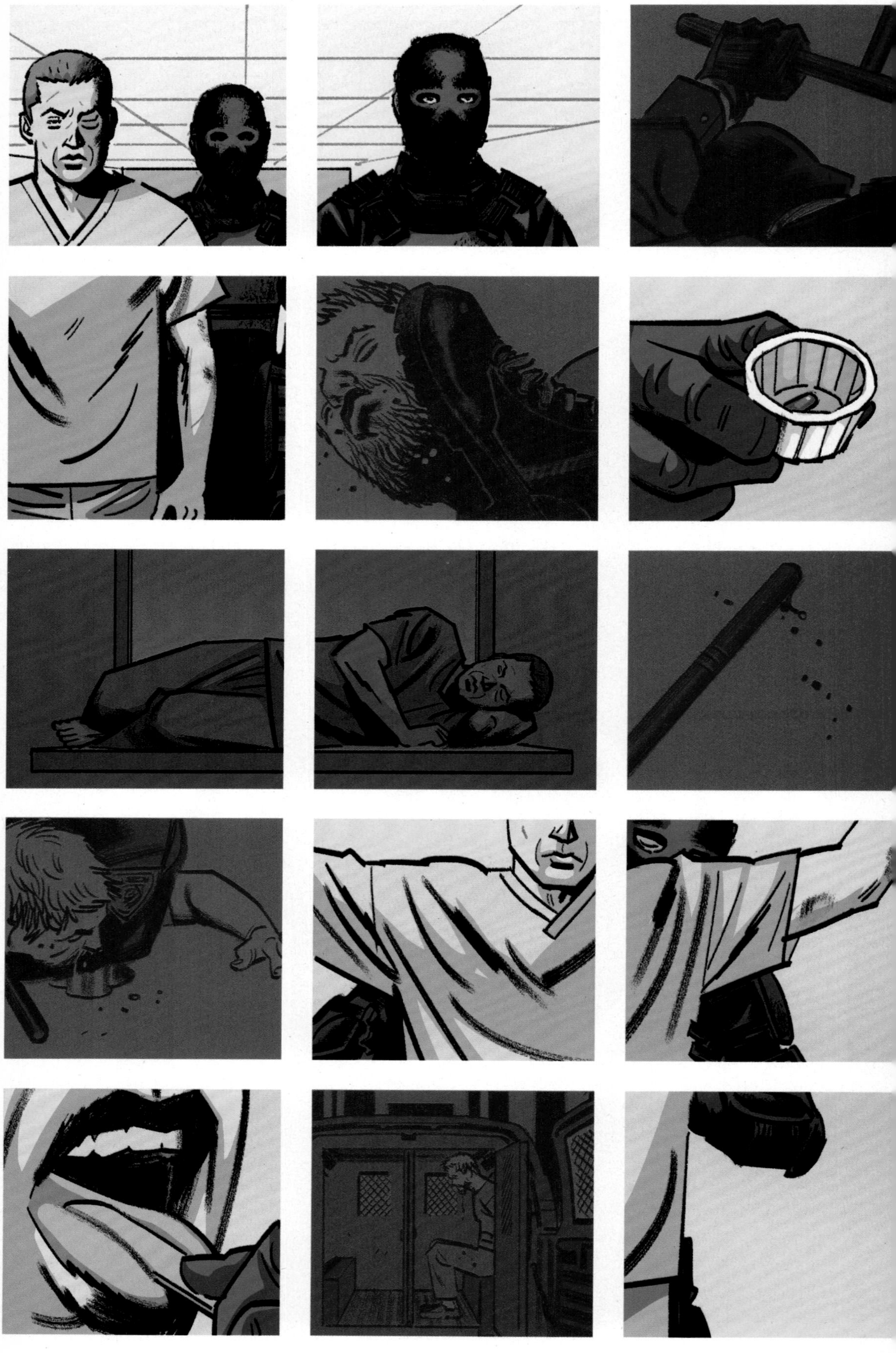

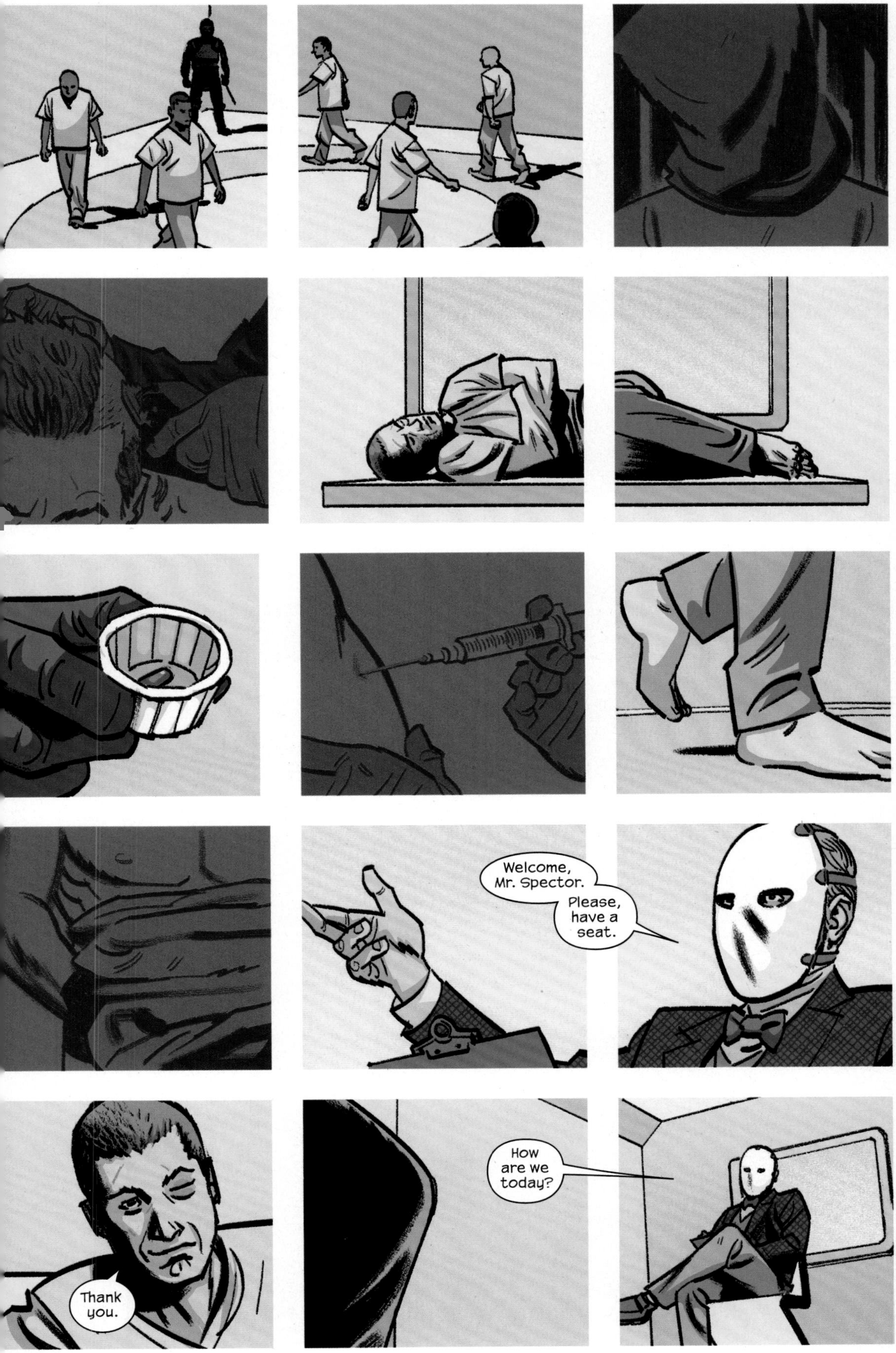
Welcome, Mr. Spector.
Please, have a seat.
Thank you.
How are we today?

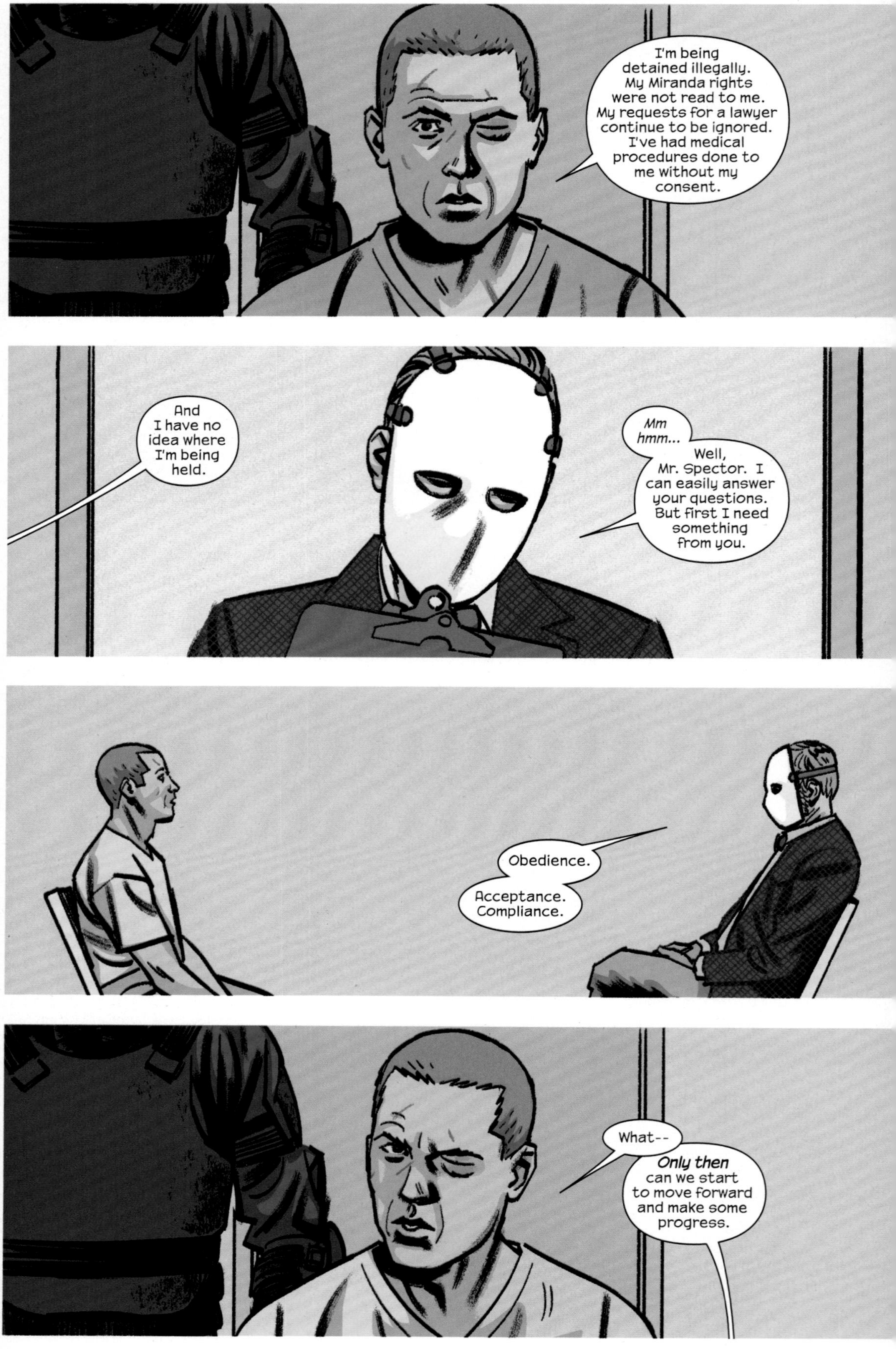
I'm being detained illegally. My Miranda rights were not read to me. My requests for a lawyer continue to be ignored. I've had medical procedures done to me without my consent.
And I have no idea where I'm being held.
Mm hmm...
Well, Mr. Spector. I can easily answer your questions. But first I need something from you.
Obedience.
Acceptance. Compliance.
What--
Only then can we start to move forward and make some progress.

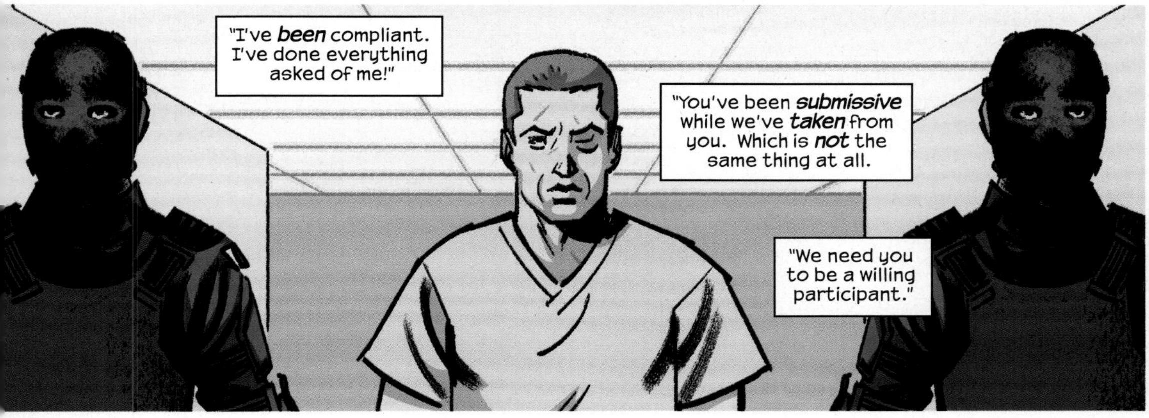
"I've **been** compliant. I've done everything asked of me!"
"You've been **submissive** while we've **taken** from you. Which is **not** the same thing at all.
"We need you to be a willing participant."

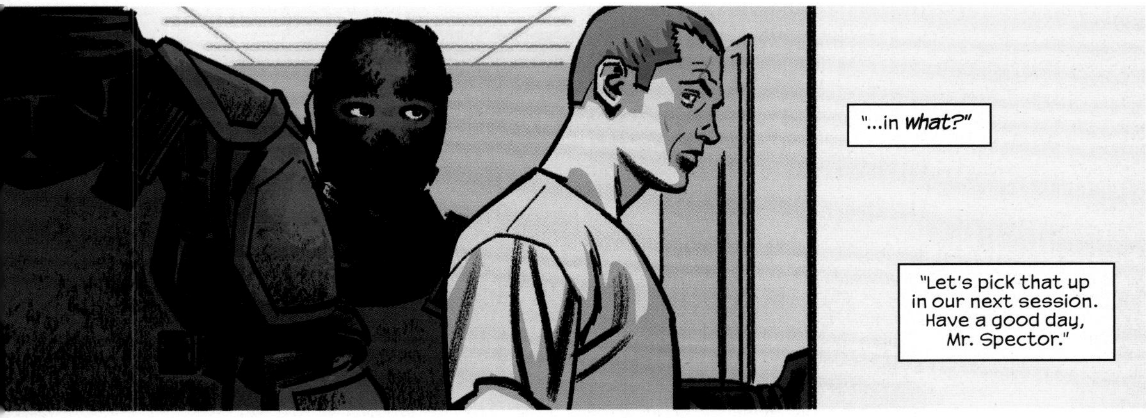
"...in **what?**"
"Let's pick that up in our next session. Have a good day, Mr. Spector."

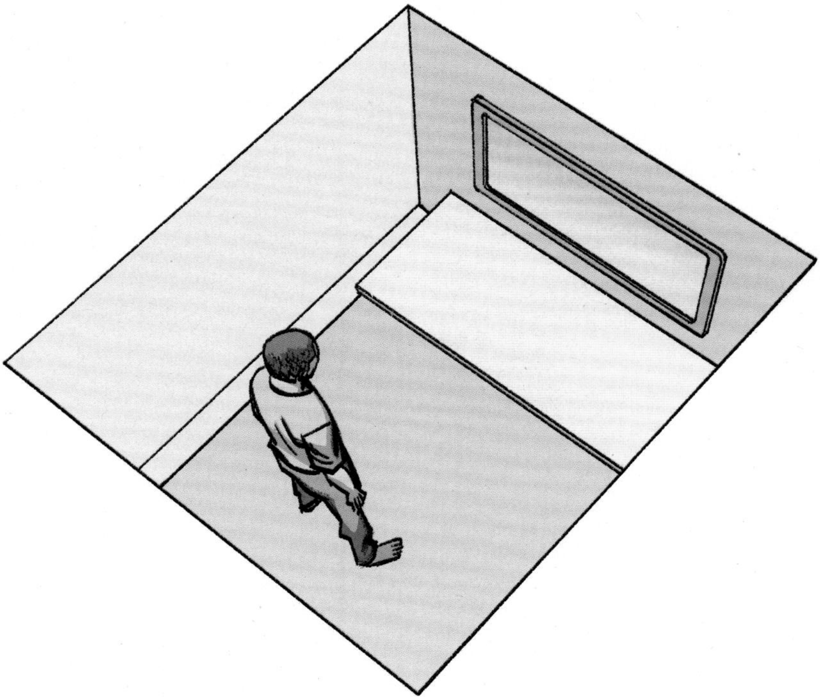

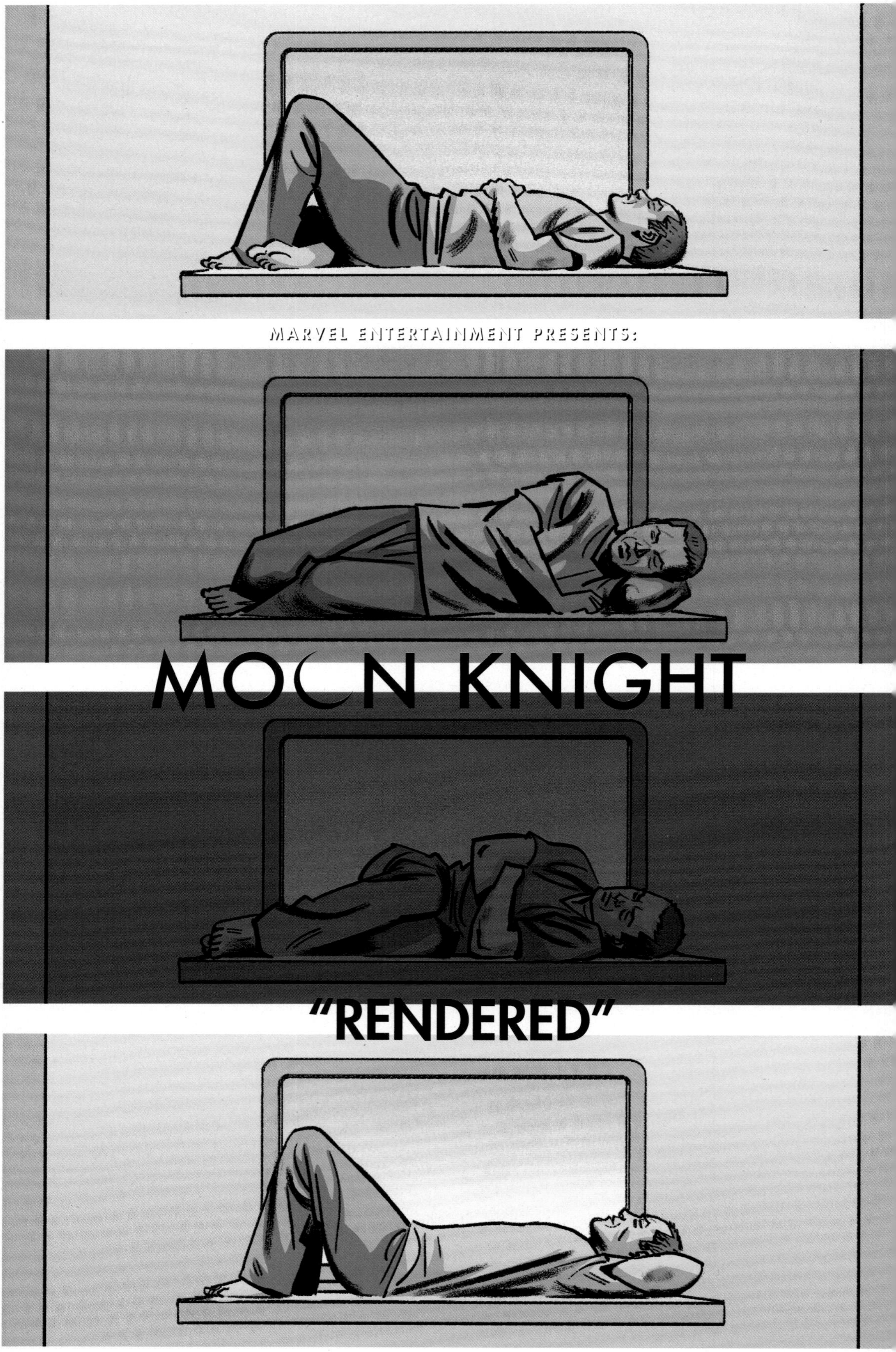
MARVEL ENTERTAINMENT PRESENTS:
MOON KNIGHT
"RENDERED"

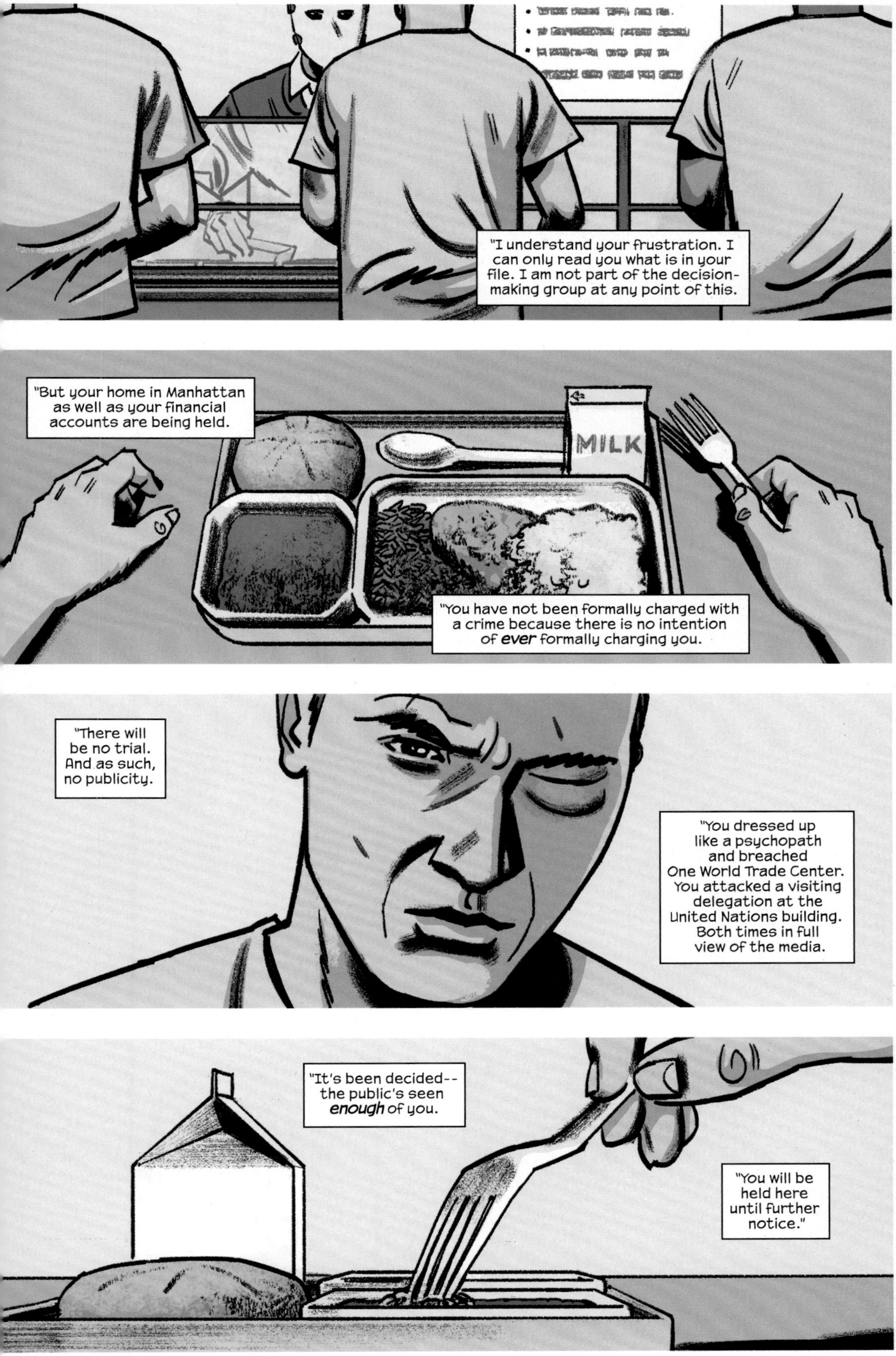
"I understand your frustration. I can only read you what is in your file. I am not part of the decision-making group at any point of this.
"But your home in Manhattan as well as your financial accounts are being held.
MILK
"You have not been formally charged with a crime because there is no intention of *ever* formally charging you.
"There will be no trial. And as such, no publicity.
"You dressed up like a psychopath and breached One World Trade Center. You attacked a visiting delegation at the United Nations building. Both times in full view of the media.
"It's been decided-- the public's seen *enough* of you.
"You will be held here until further notice."

How is that possible, legally? What is this place?

Am I in Guantanamo?

No, this isn't Guantanamo.

And I assure you, American law is not being broken here.

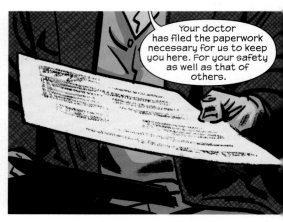

Your doctor has filed the paperwork necessary for us to keep you here. For your safety as well as that of others.

You're a dangerous man.

The good news is, I'm here to help you.

My doctor is insane.

Mr. Spector.

You *blew up* her *house.*

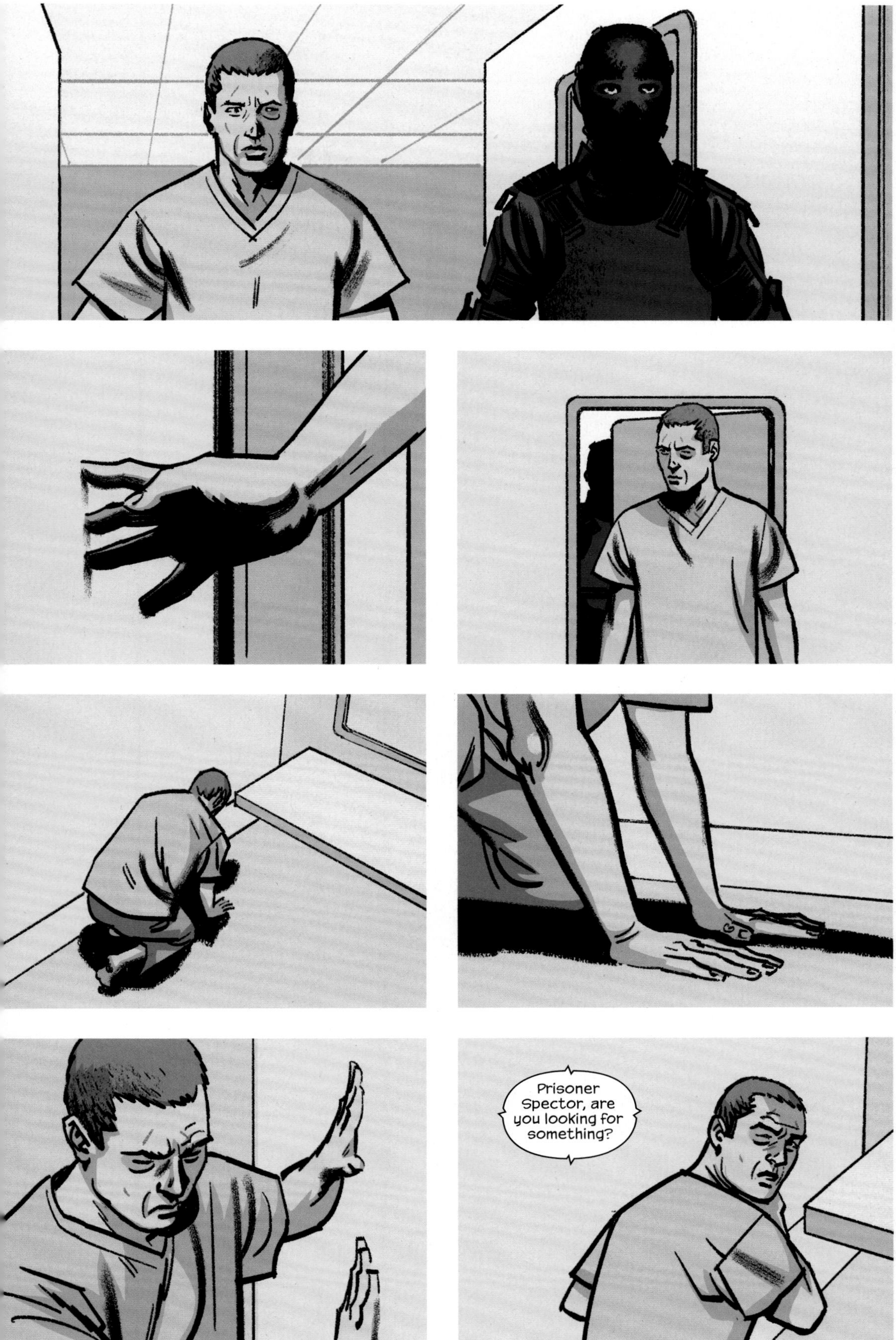
Prisoner Spector, are you looking for something?

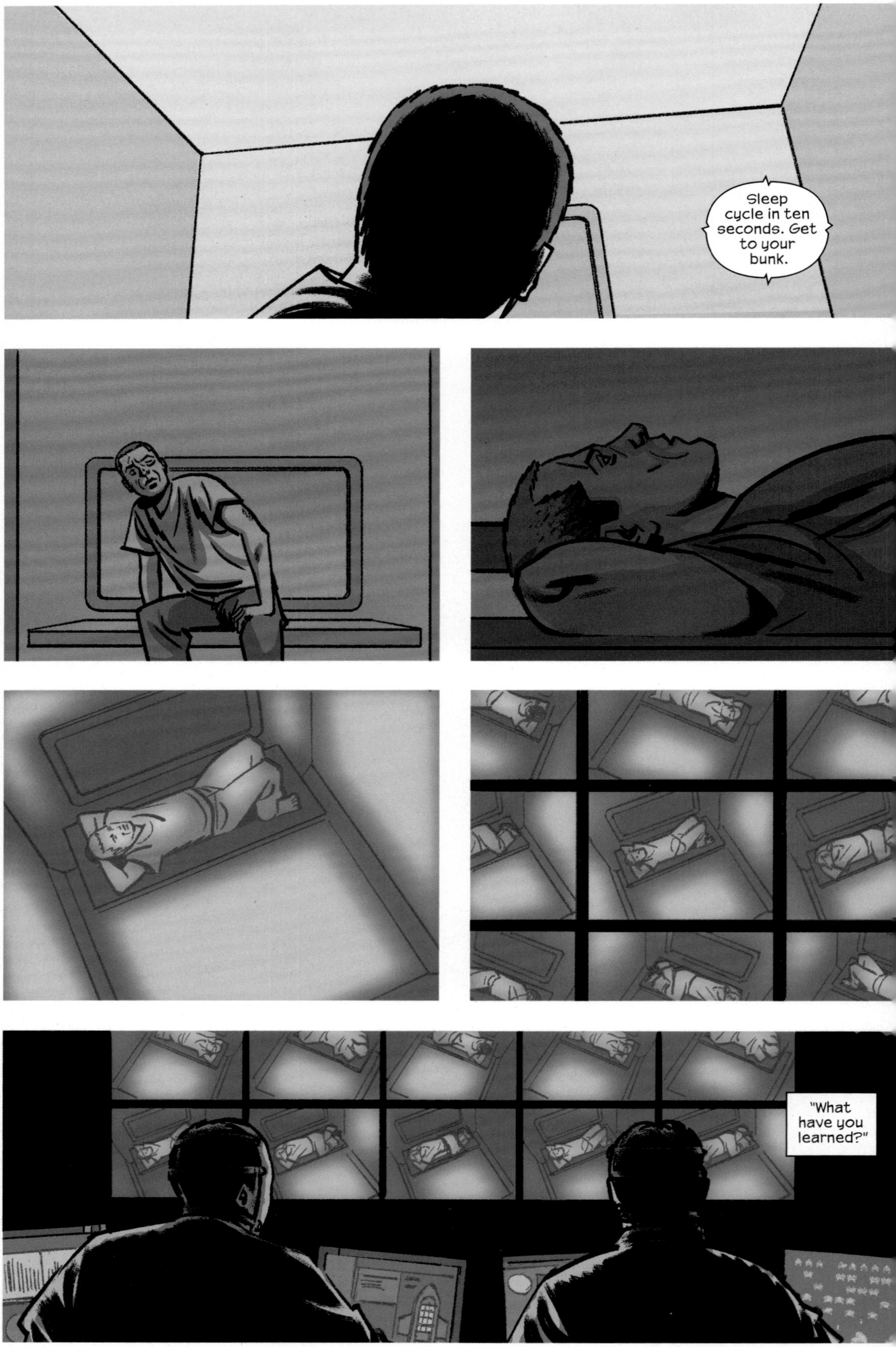
Sleep cycle in ten seconds. Get to your bunk.
"What have you learned?"

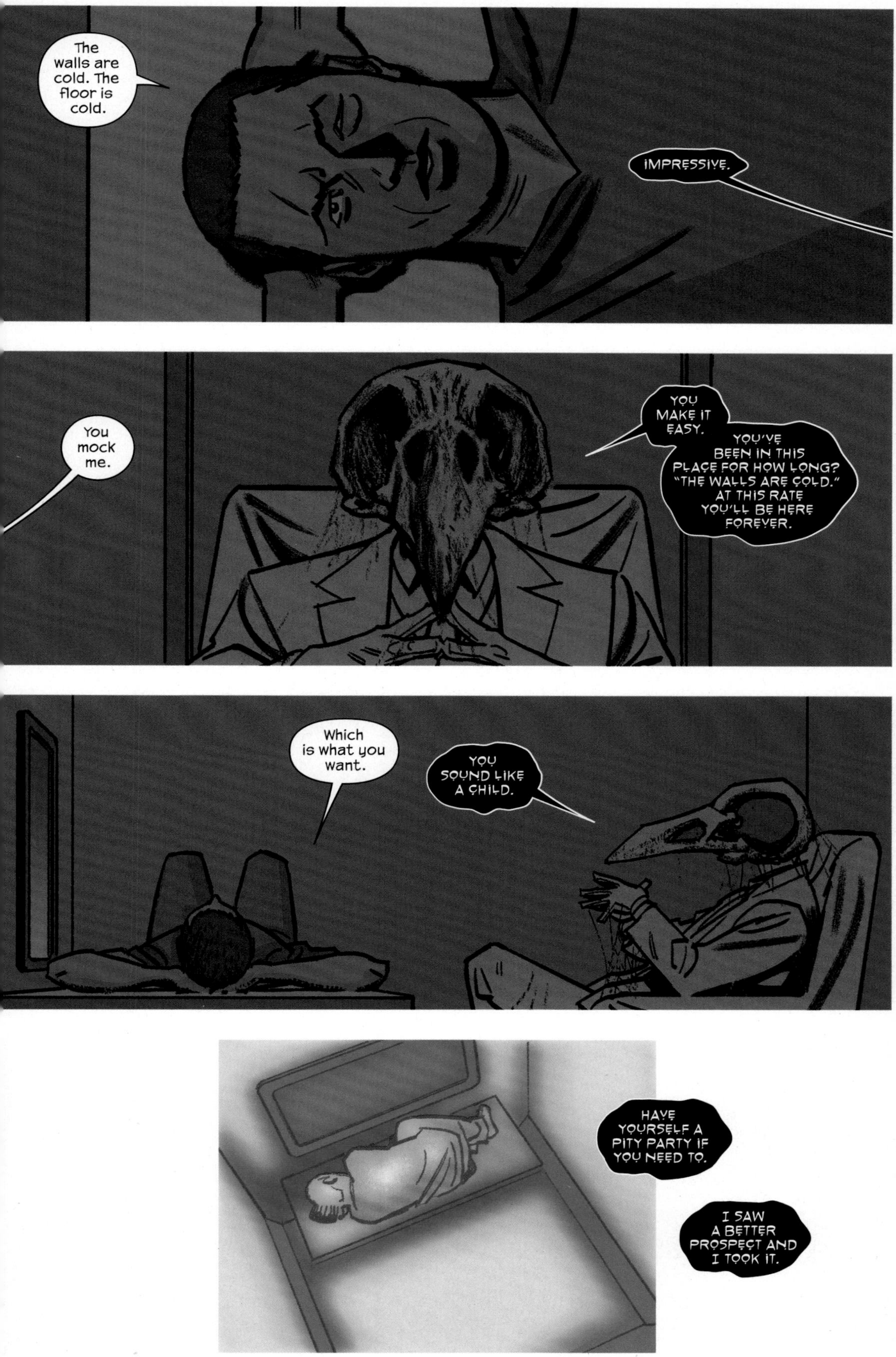
The walls are cold. The floor is cold.
IMPRESSIVE.
You mock me.
YOU MAKE IT EASY.
YOU'VE BEEN IN THIS PLACE FOR HOW LONG? "THE WALLS ARE COLD." AT THIS RATE YOU'LL BE HERE FOREVER.
Which is what you want.
YOU SOUND LIKE A CHILD.
HAVE YOURSELF A PITY PARTY IF YOU NEED TO.
I SAW A BETTER PROSPECT AND I TOOK IT.

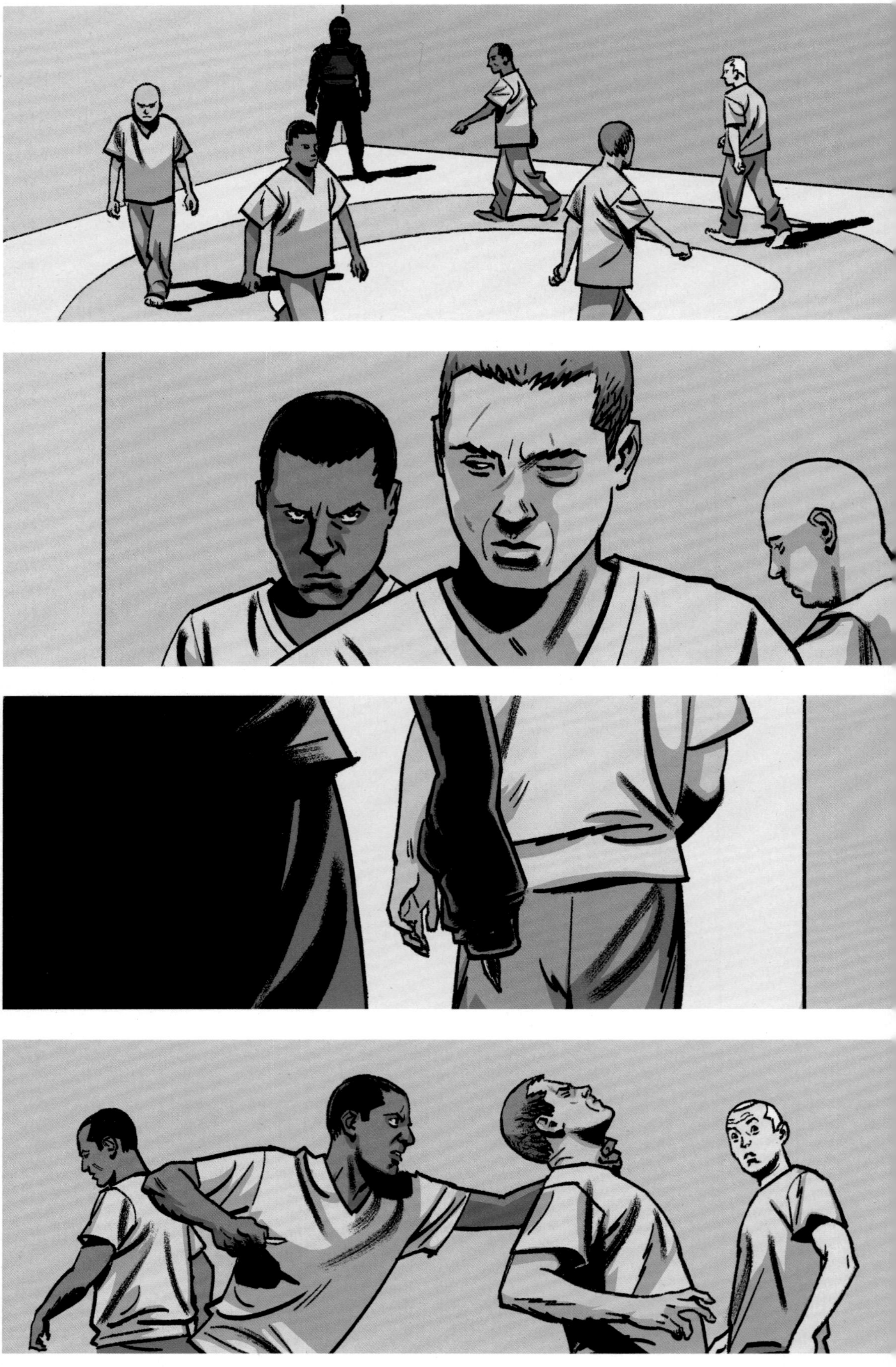

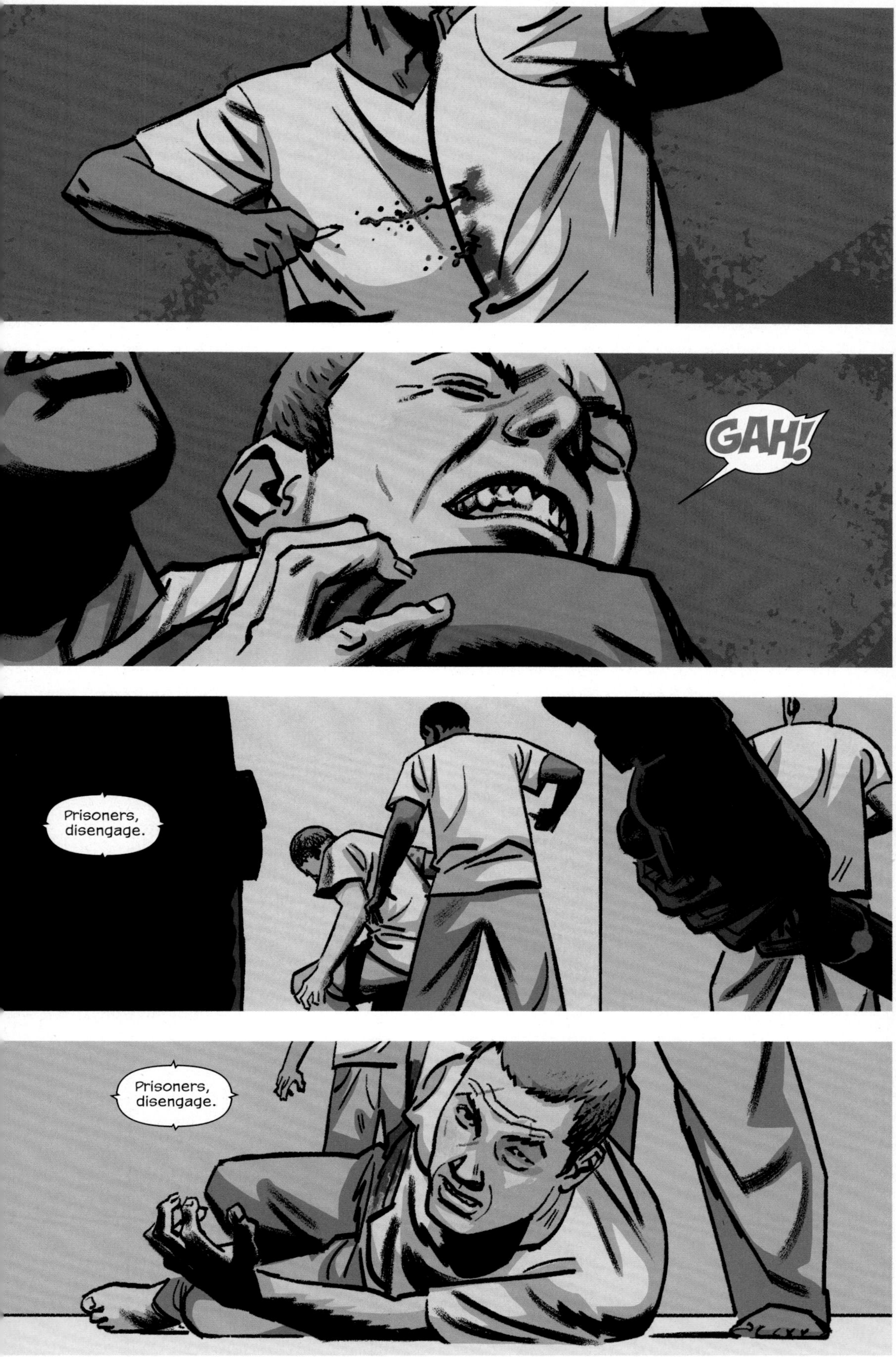
GAH!
Prisoners, disengage.
Prisoners, disengage.

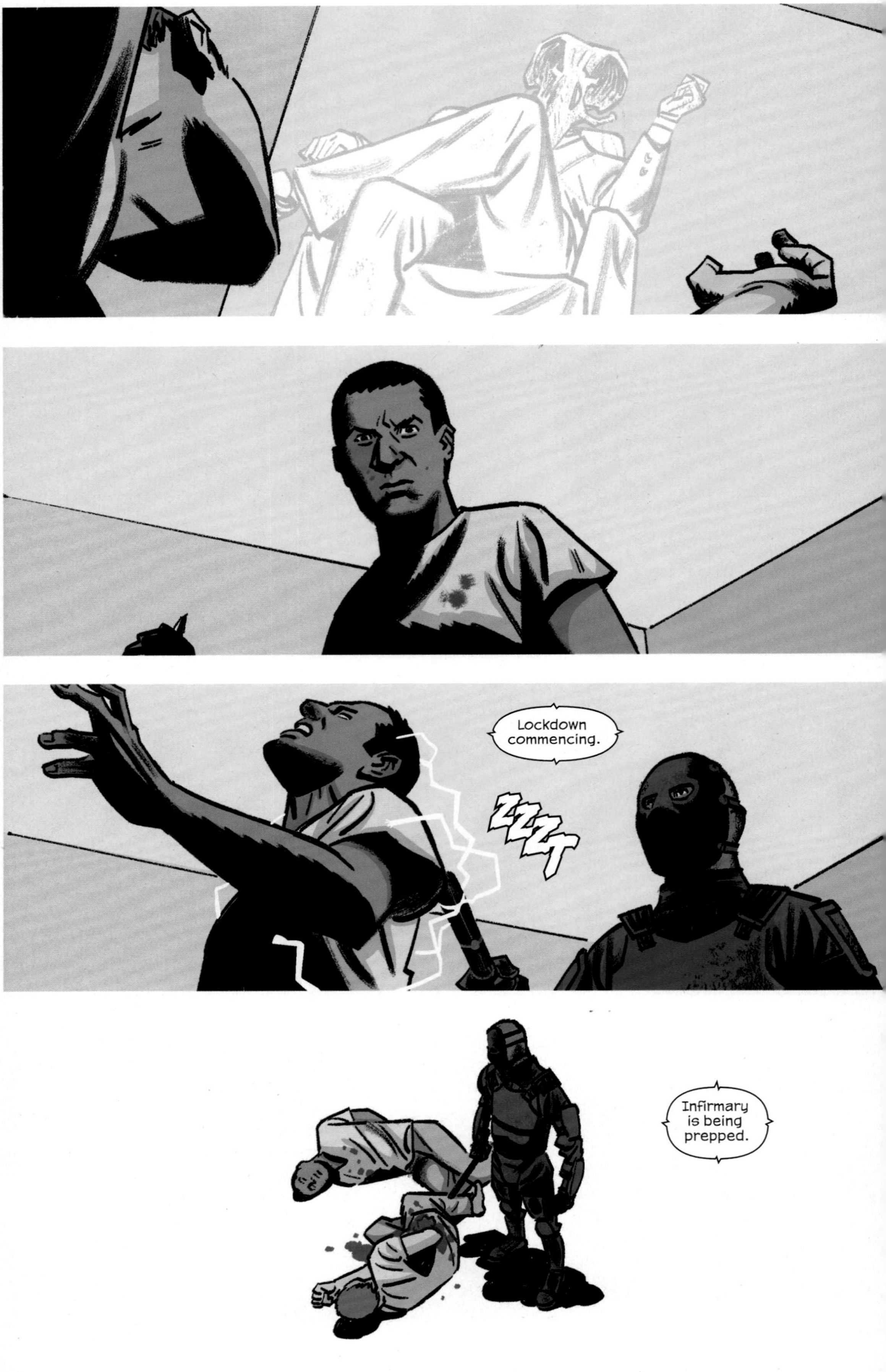
Lockdown commencing.
ZZZT
Infirmary is being prepped.

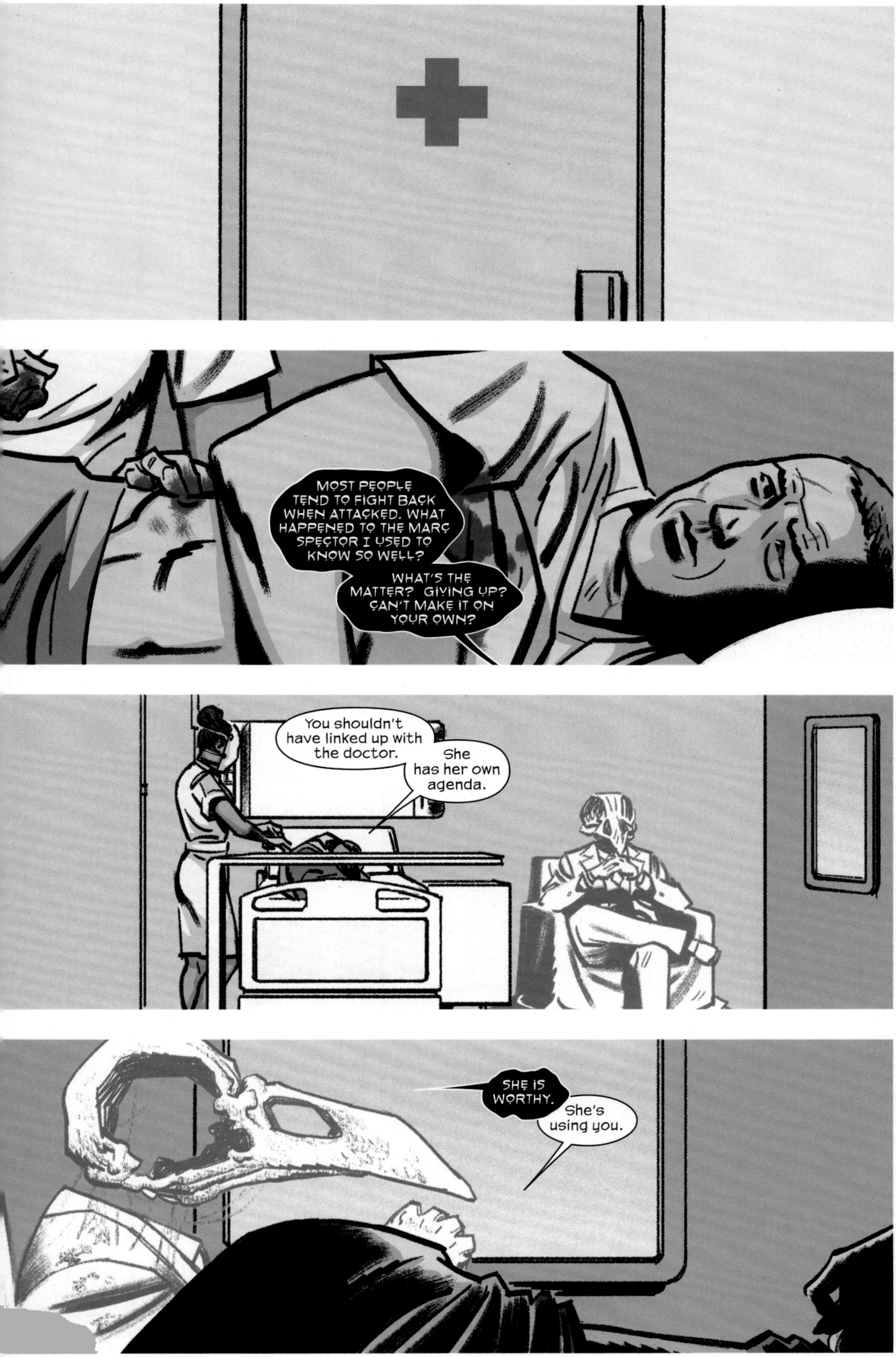
MOST PEOPLE TEND TO FIGHT BACK WHEN ATTACKED. WHAT HAPPENED TO THE MARC SPECTOR I USED TO KNOW SO WELL?
WHAT'S THE MATTER? GIVING UP? CAN'T MAKE IT ON YOUR OWN?
You shouldn't have linked up with the doctor.
She has her own agenda.
SHE IS WORTHY.
She's using you.

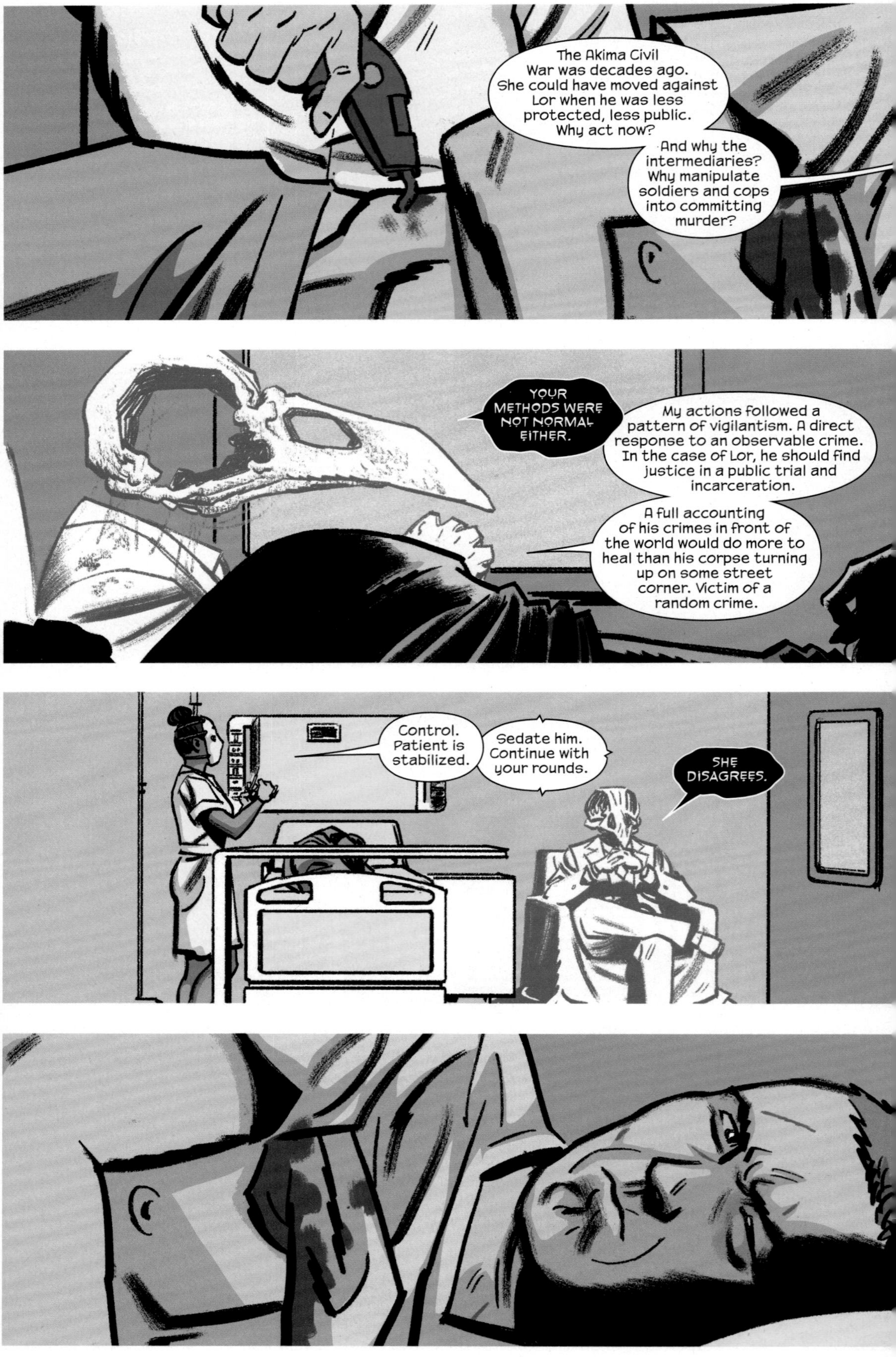
The Akima Civil War was decades ago. She could have moved against Lor when he was less protected, less public. Why act now?
And why the intermediaries? Why manipulate soldiers and cops into committing murder?
YOUR METHODS WERE NOT NORMAL EITHER.
My actions followed a pattern of vigilantism. A direct response to an observable crime. In the case of Lor, he should find justice in a public trial and incarceration.
A full accounting of his crimes in front of the world would do more to heal than his corpse turning up on some street corner. Victim of a random crime.
Control. Patient is stabilized.
Sedate him. Continue with your rounds.
SHE DISAGREES.

She's wrong. Look into it.
You may be a god...
...but you need to vet your candidates a little better.

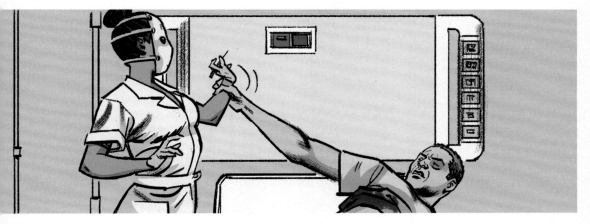

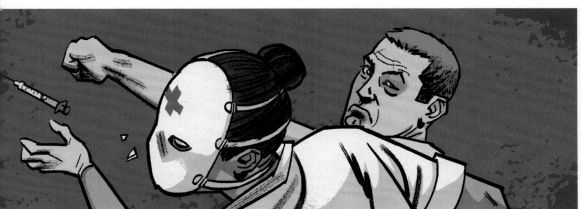

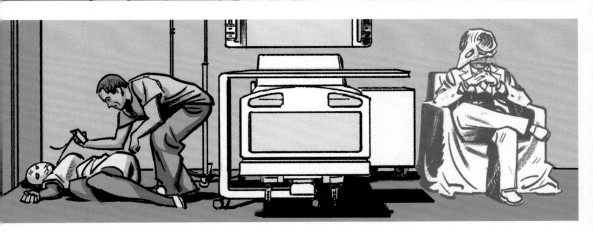

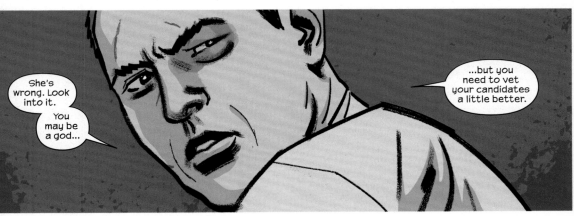

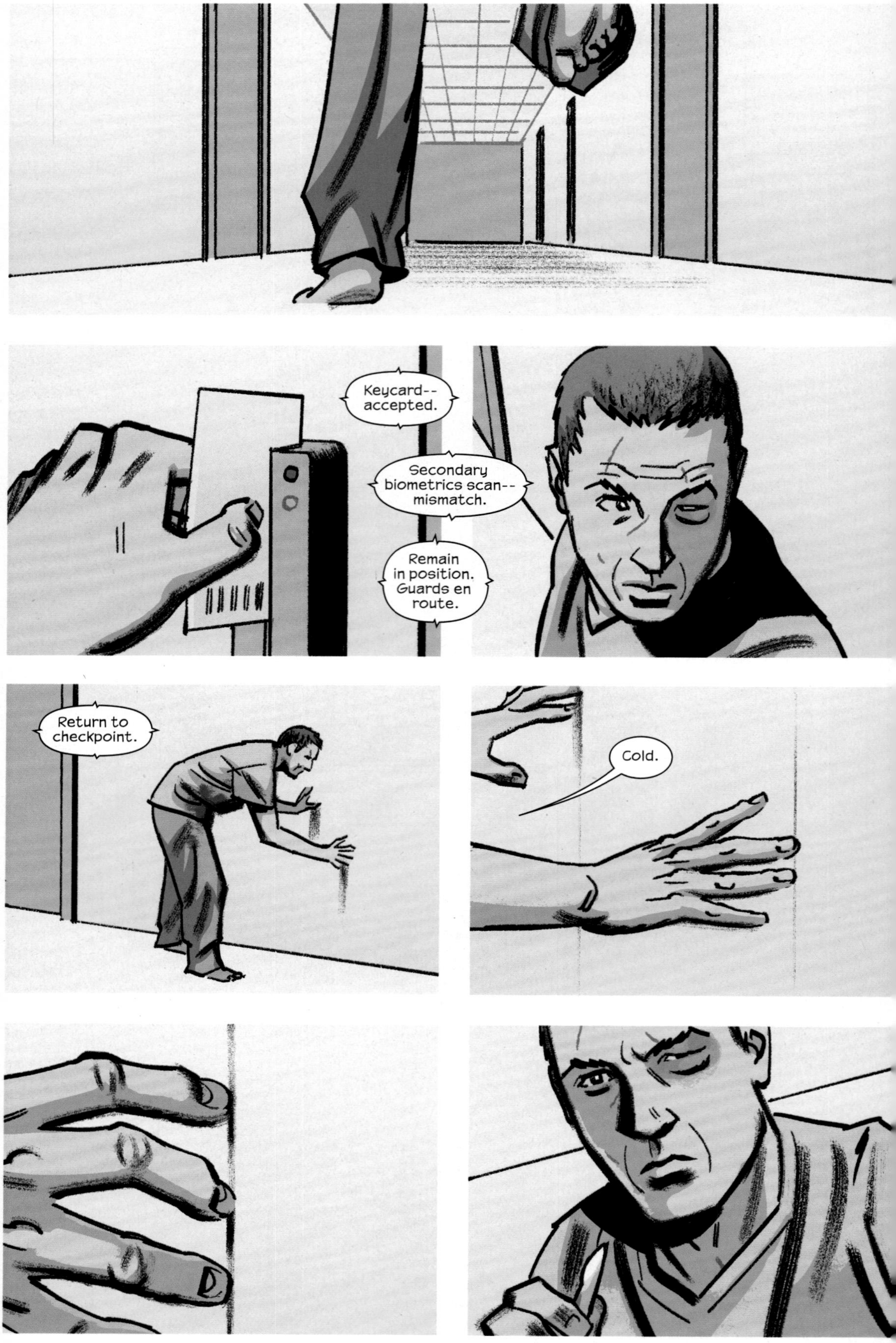
Keycard--
accepted.
Secondary biometrics scan--mismatch.
Remain in position. Guards en route.
Return to checkpoint.
Cold.

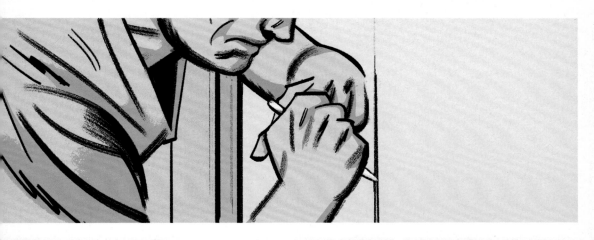

Alert. Unauthorized access.

SSSSSSSS

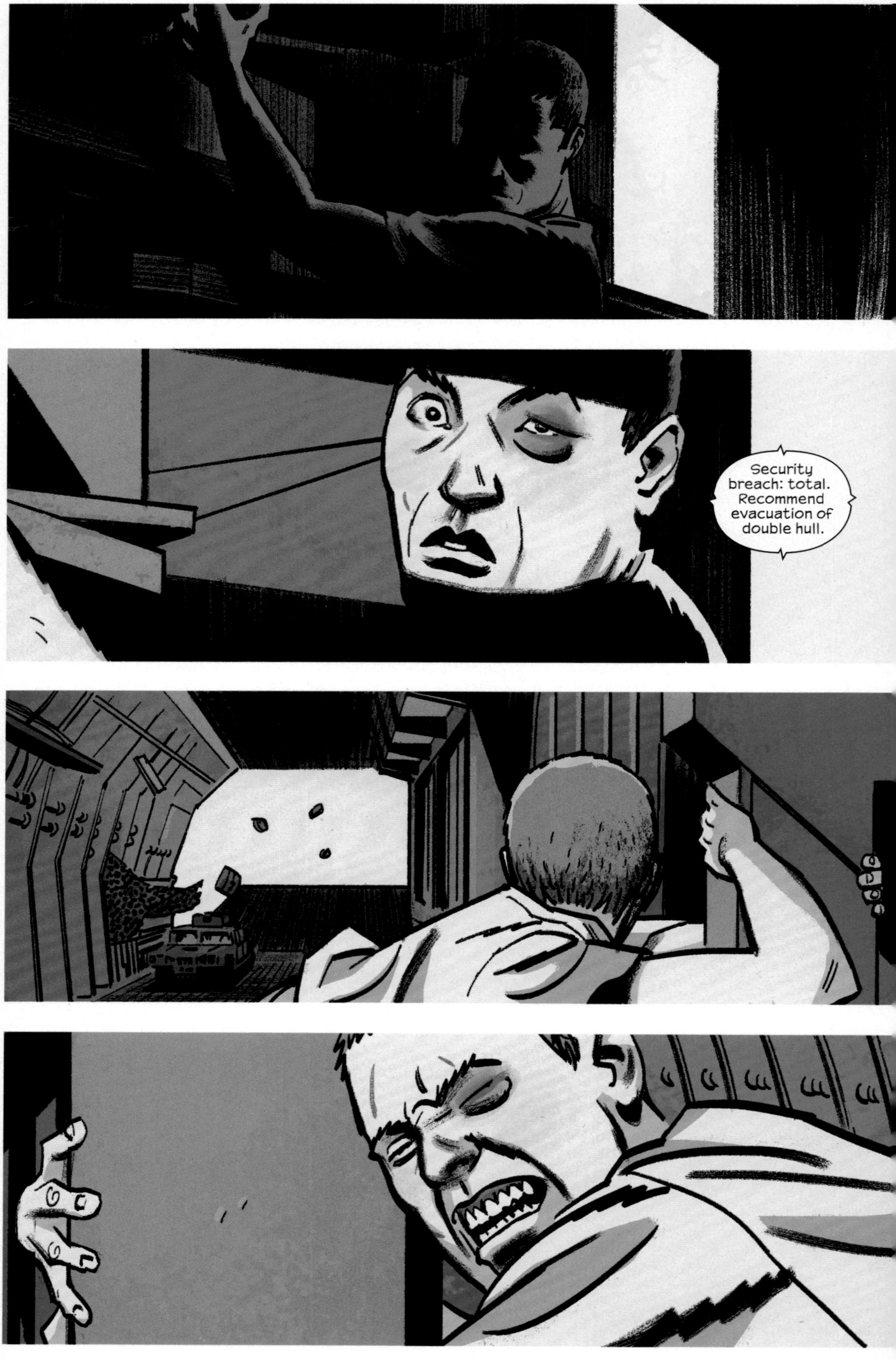
Security breach: total. Recommend evacuation of double hull.

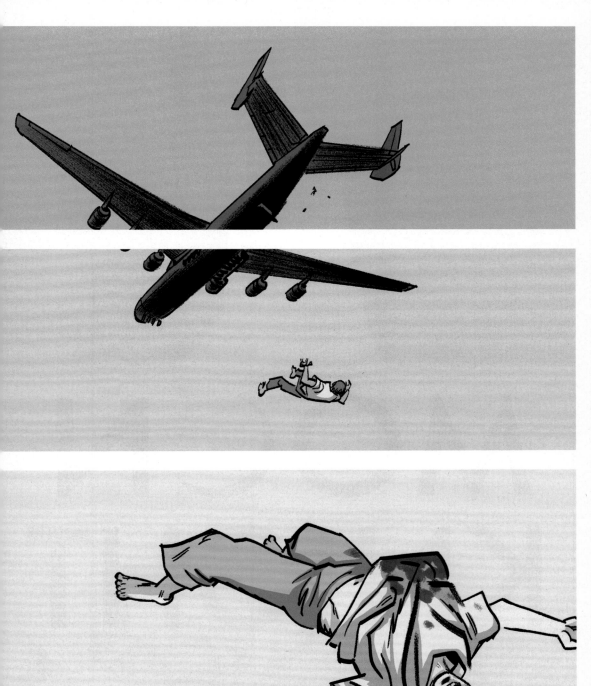

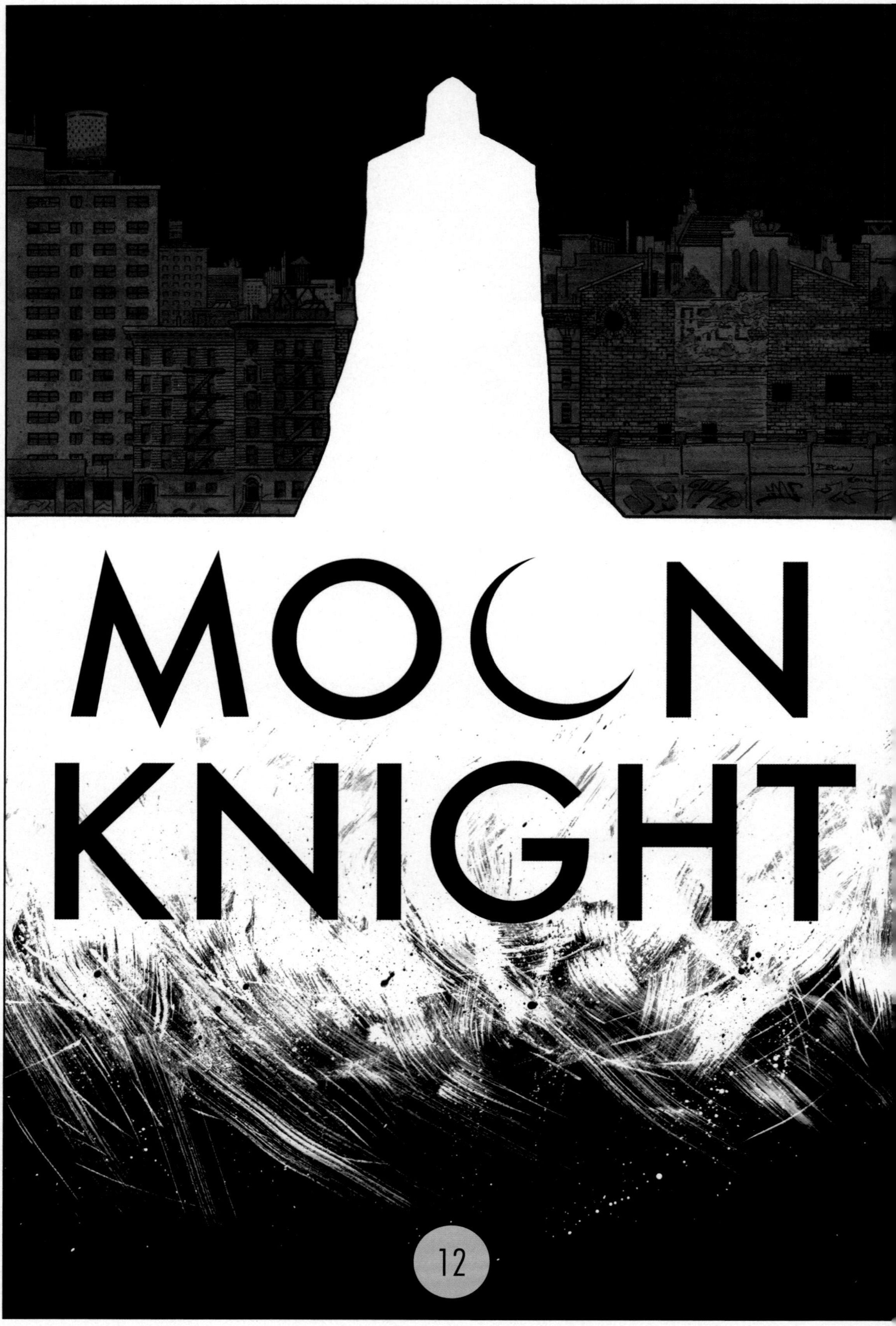
MOON KNIGHT
12

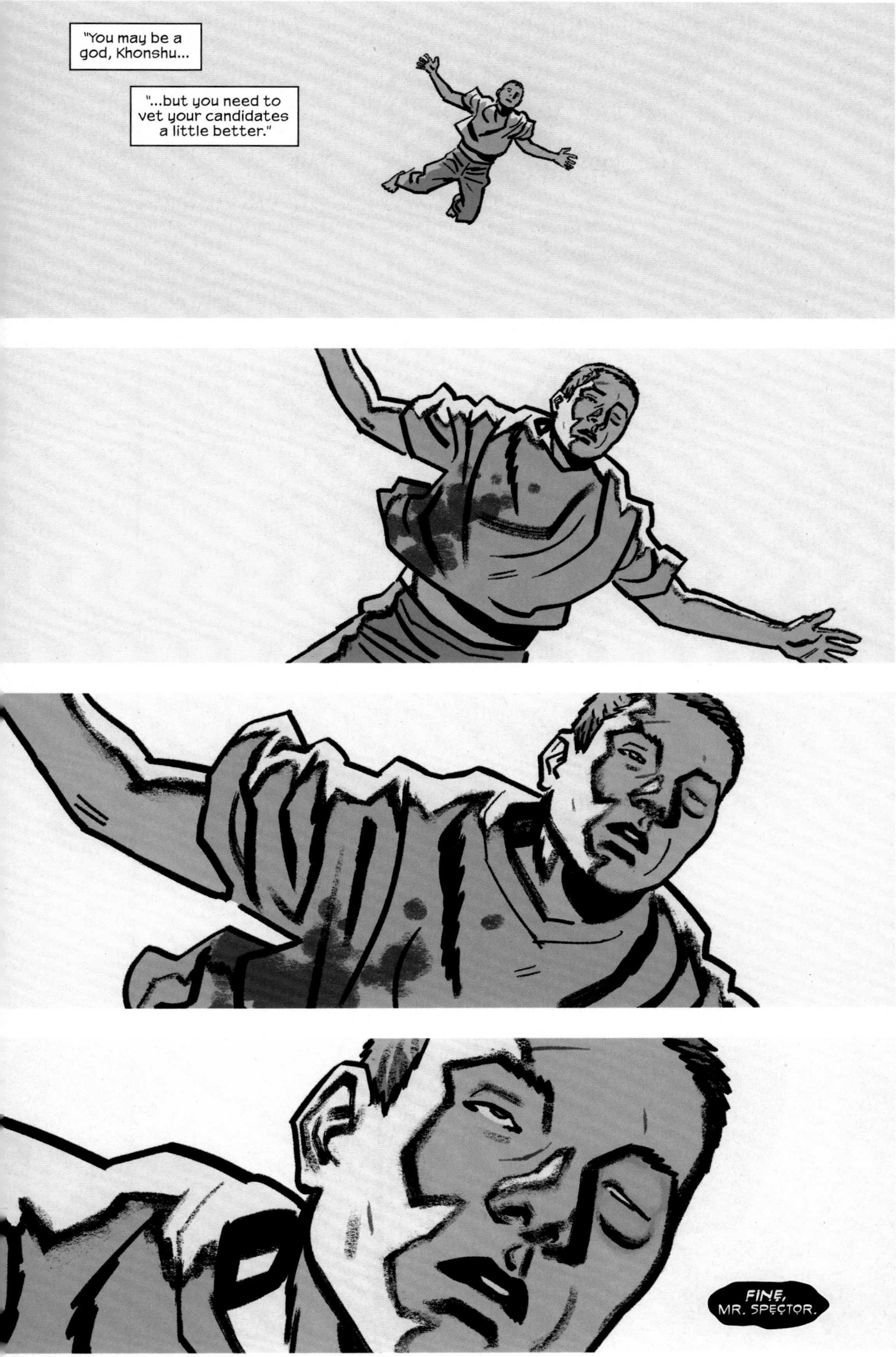
"You may be a god, Khonshu...
"...but you need to vet your candidates a little better."
FINE, MR. SPECTOR.

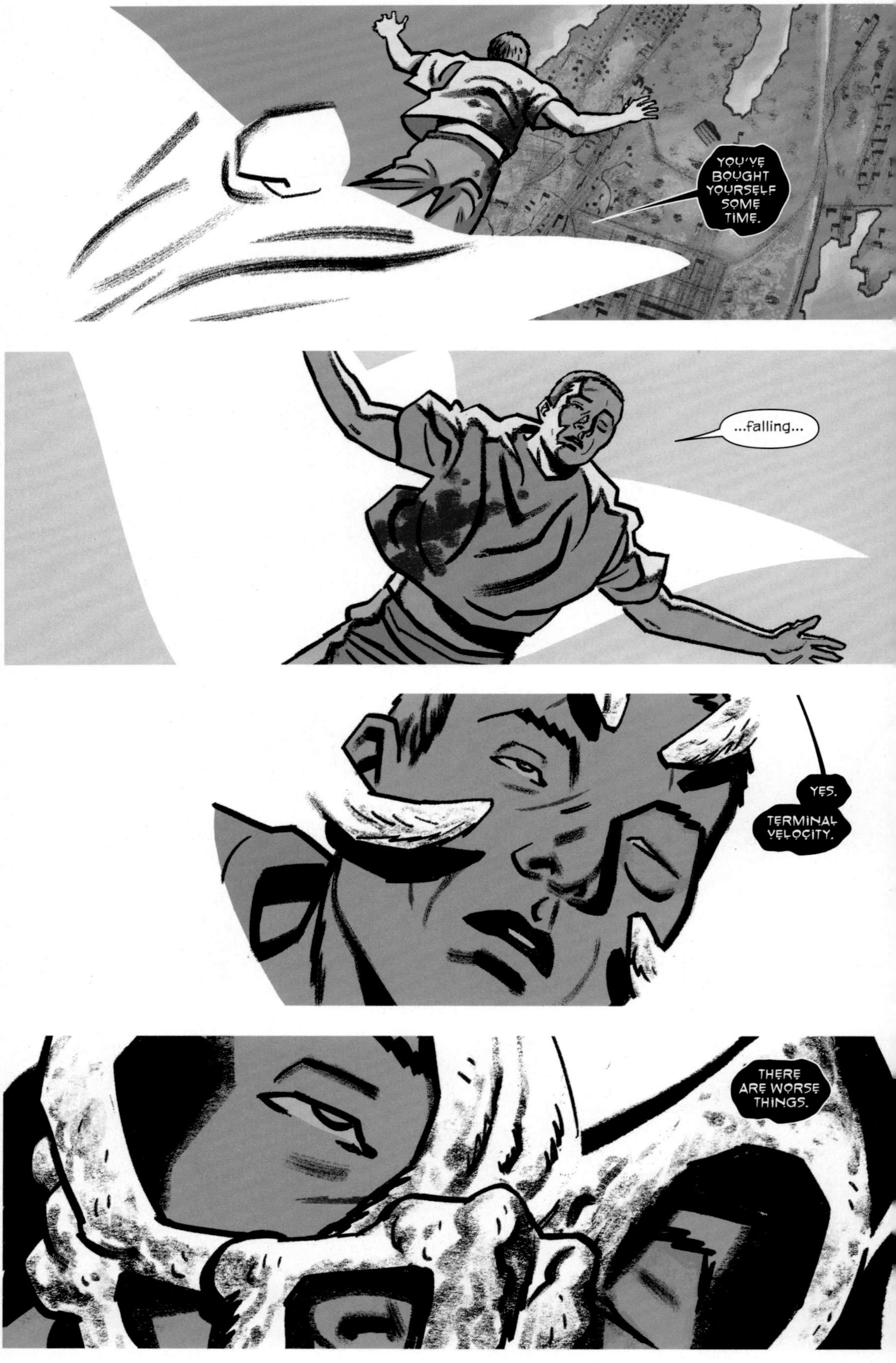
YOU'VE BOUGHT YOURSELF SOME TIME.
...falling...
YES.
TERMINAL VELOCITY.
THERE ARE WORSE THINGS.

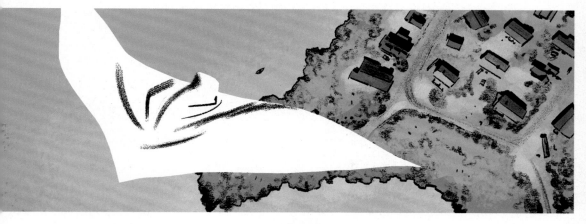

...how... survive...?

DO YOU WANT TO KNOW?

No.

THE CLOCK STARTS NOW.

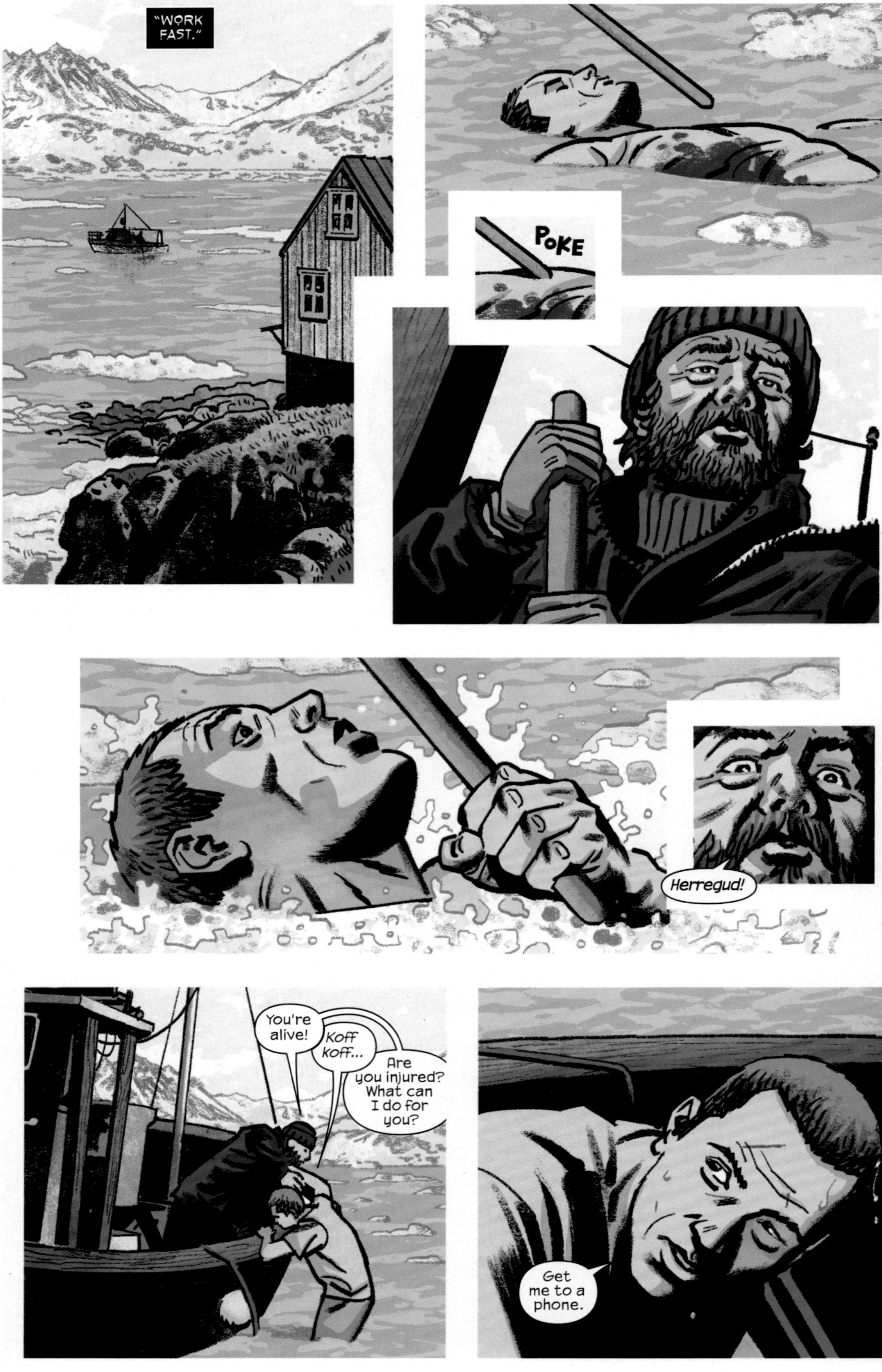
"WORK FAST."
POKE
Herregud!
You're alive!
Koff koff...
Are you injured? What can I do for you?
Get me to a phone.

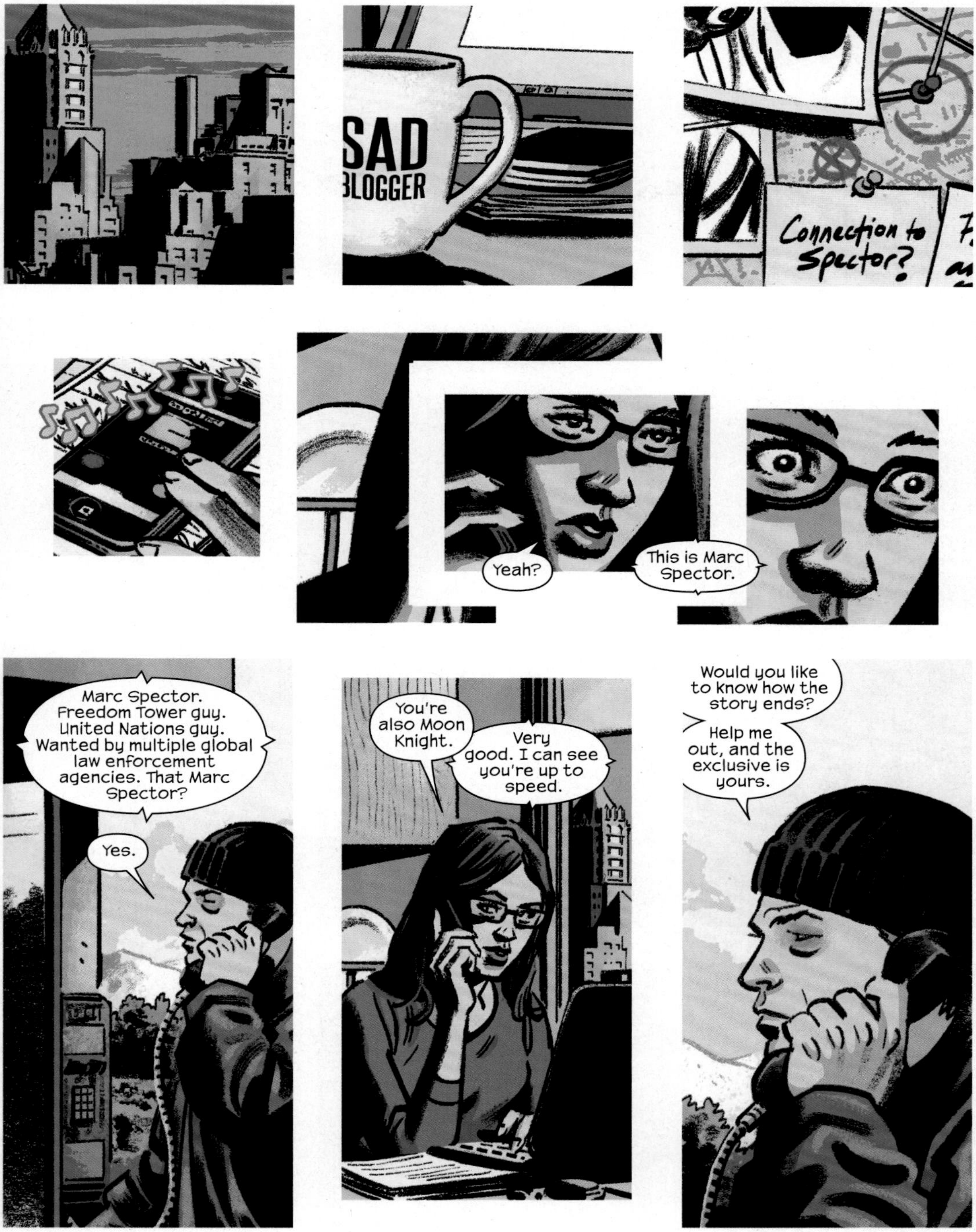
SAD
BLOGGER
Connection to Spector?
Yeah?
This is Marc Spector.
Marc Spector. Freedom Tower guy. United Nations guy. Wanted by multiple global law enforcement agencies. That Marc Spector?
Yes.
You're also Moon Knight.
Very good. I can see you're up to speed.
Would you like to know how the story ends?
Help me out, and the exclusive is yours.

MARVEL ENTERTAINMENT PRESENTS:

MOON KNIGHT

"DIASPORA"

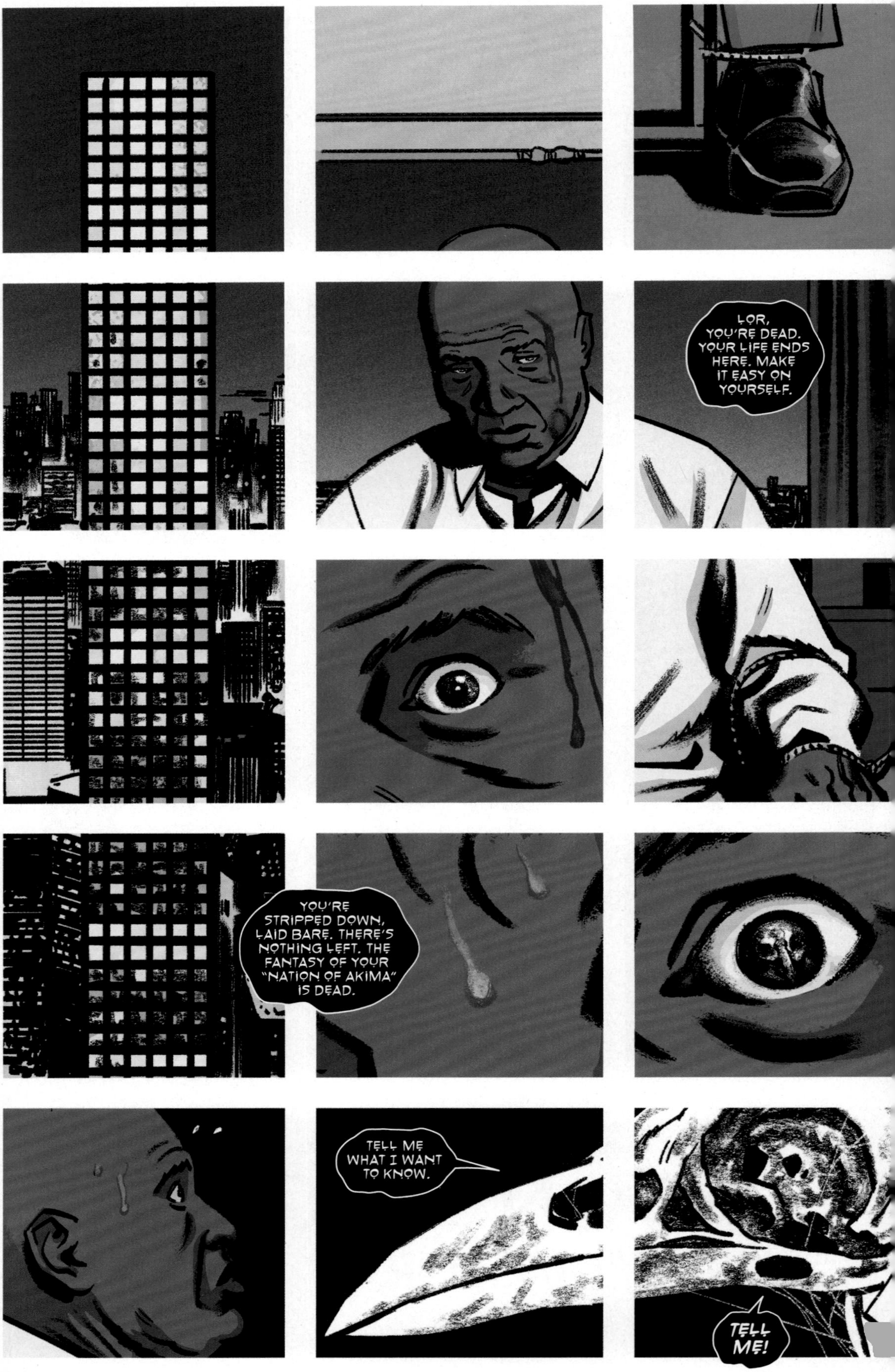
LOR, YOU'RE DEAD. YOUR LIFE ENDS HERE. MAKE IT EASY ON YOURSELF.
YOU'RE STRIPPED DOWN, LAID BARE. THERE'S NOTHING LEFT. THE FANTASY OF YOUR "NATION OF AKIMA" IS DEAD.
TELL ME WHAT I WANT TO KNOW.
TELL ME!

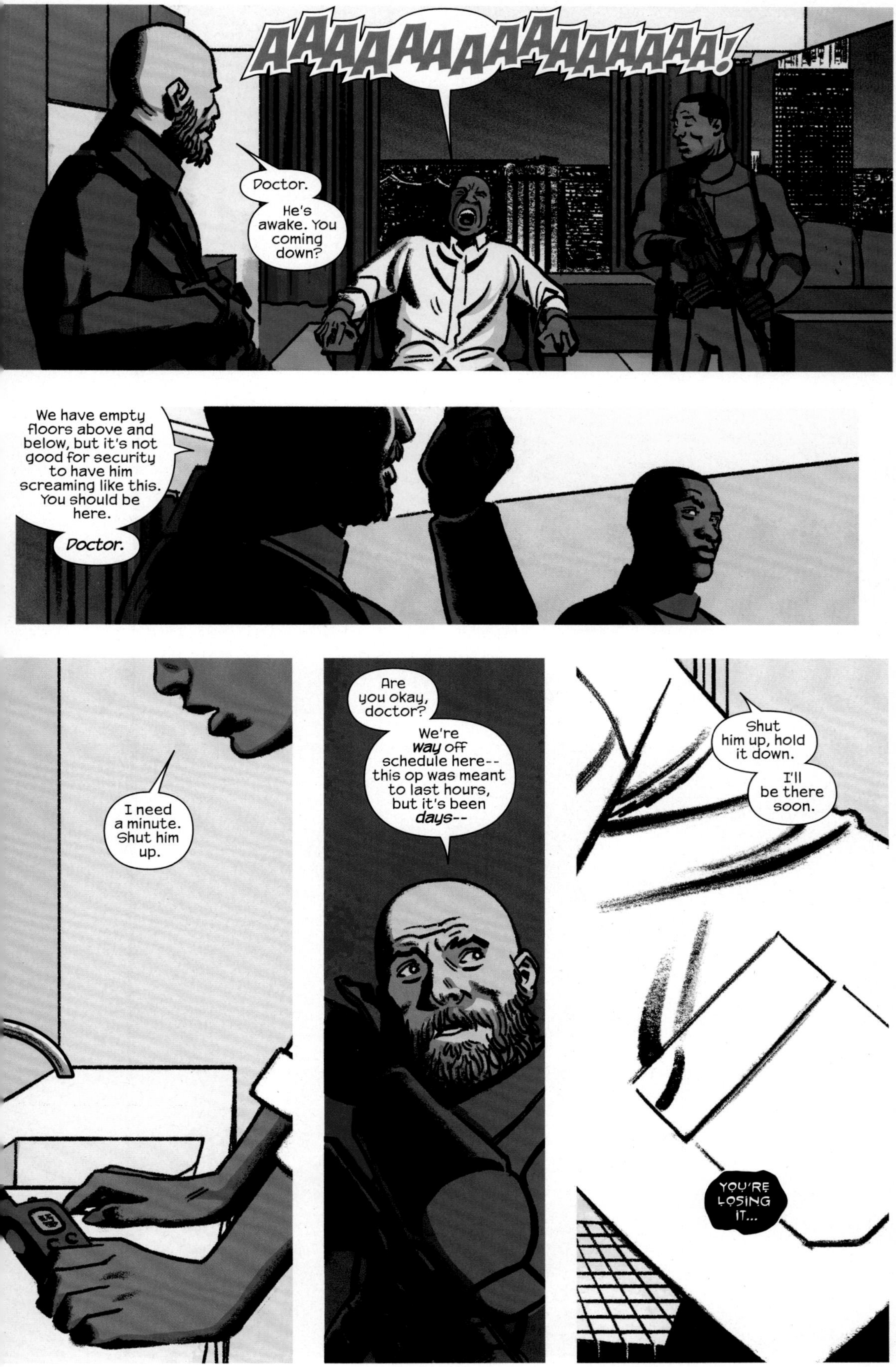
AAAAAAAAAAAAAA!
Doctor.
He's awake. You coming down?
We have empty floors above and below, but it's not good for security to have him screaming like this. You should be here.
Doctor.
I need a minute. Shut him up.
Are you okay, doctor?
We're way off schedule here--this op was meant to last hours, but it's been days--
Shut him up, hold it down.
I'll be there soon.
YOU'RE LOSING IT...

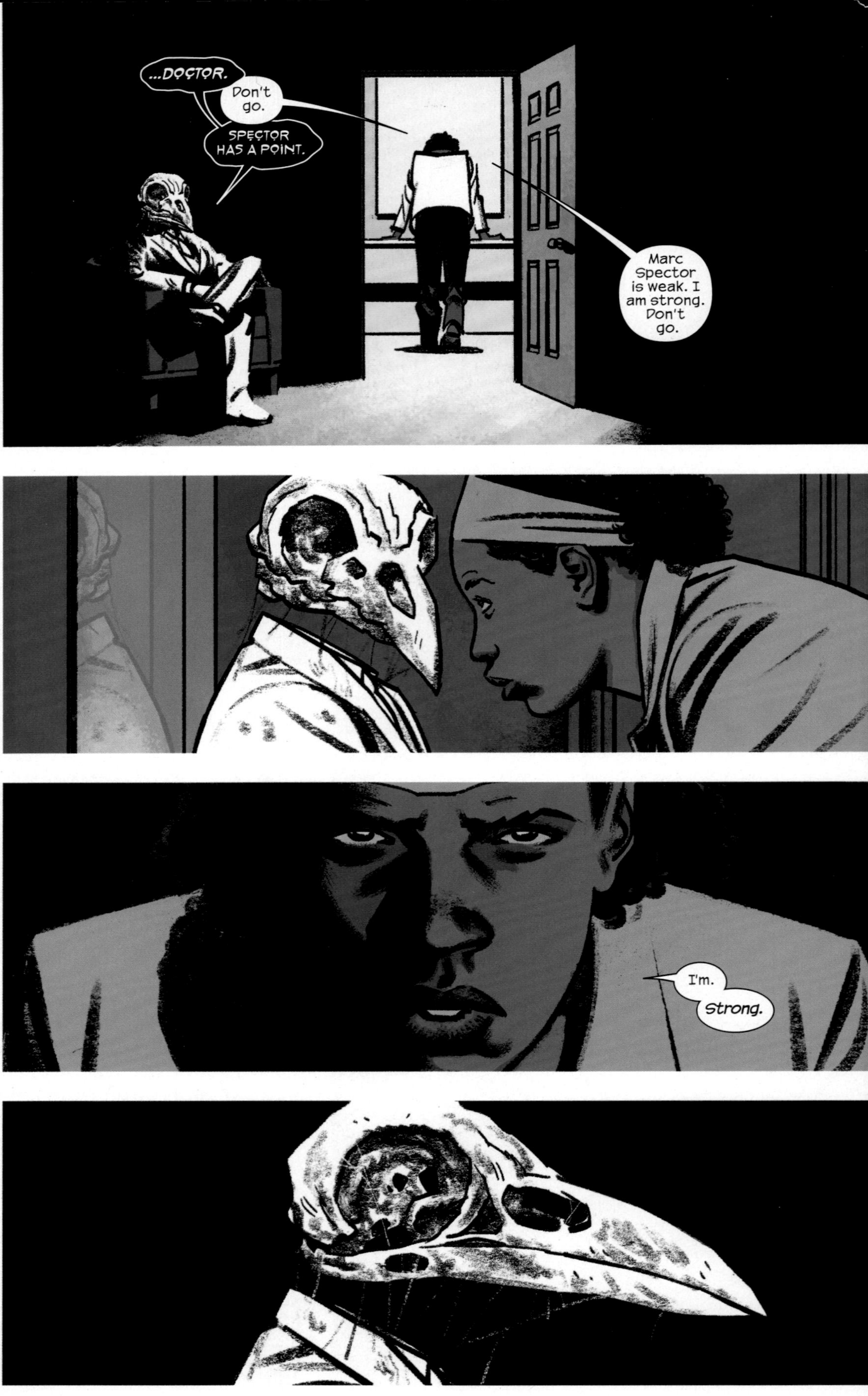
...DOCTOR.
Don't go.
SPECTOR HAS A POINT.
Marc Spector is weak. I am strong. Don't go.
I'm.
Strong.

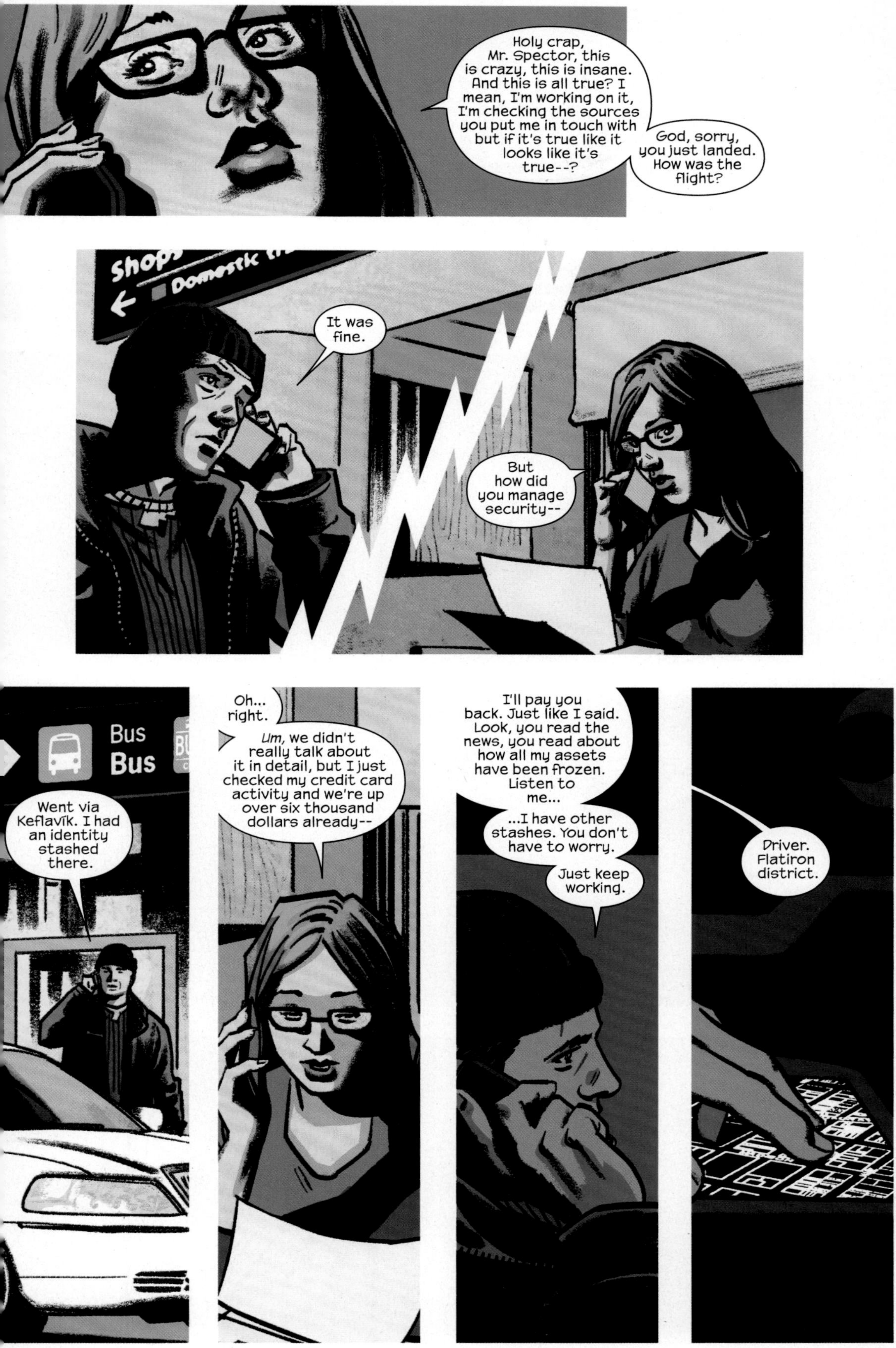
Holy crap, Mr. Spector, this is crazy, this is insane. And this is all true? I mean, I'm working on it, I'm checking the sources you put me in touch with but if it's true like it looks like it's true--?
God, sorry, you just landed. How was the flight?
Shops
Domestic
It was fine.
But how did you manage security--
Bus
Bus
Went via Keflavík. I had an identity stashed there.
Oh... right.
Um, we didn't really talk about it in detail, but I just checked my credit card activity and we're up over six thousand dollars already--
I'll pay you back. Just like I said. Look, you read the news, you read about how all my assets have been frozen. Listen to me...
...I have other stashes. You don't have to worry.
Just keep working.
Driver. Flatiron district.

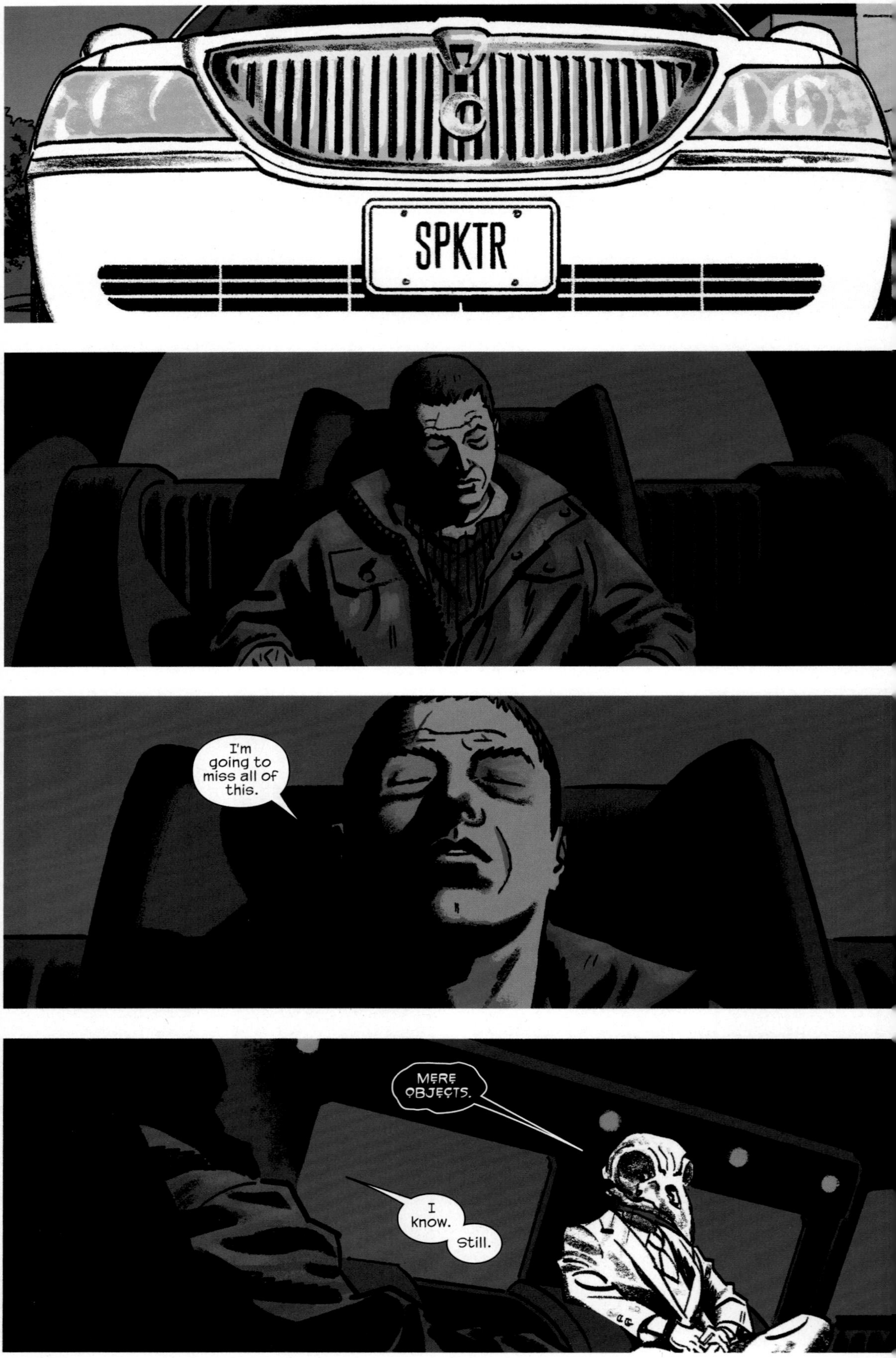
SPKTR
I'm going to miss all of this.
MERE OBJECTS.
I know.
Still.

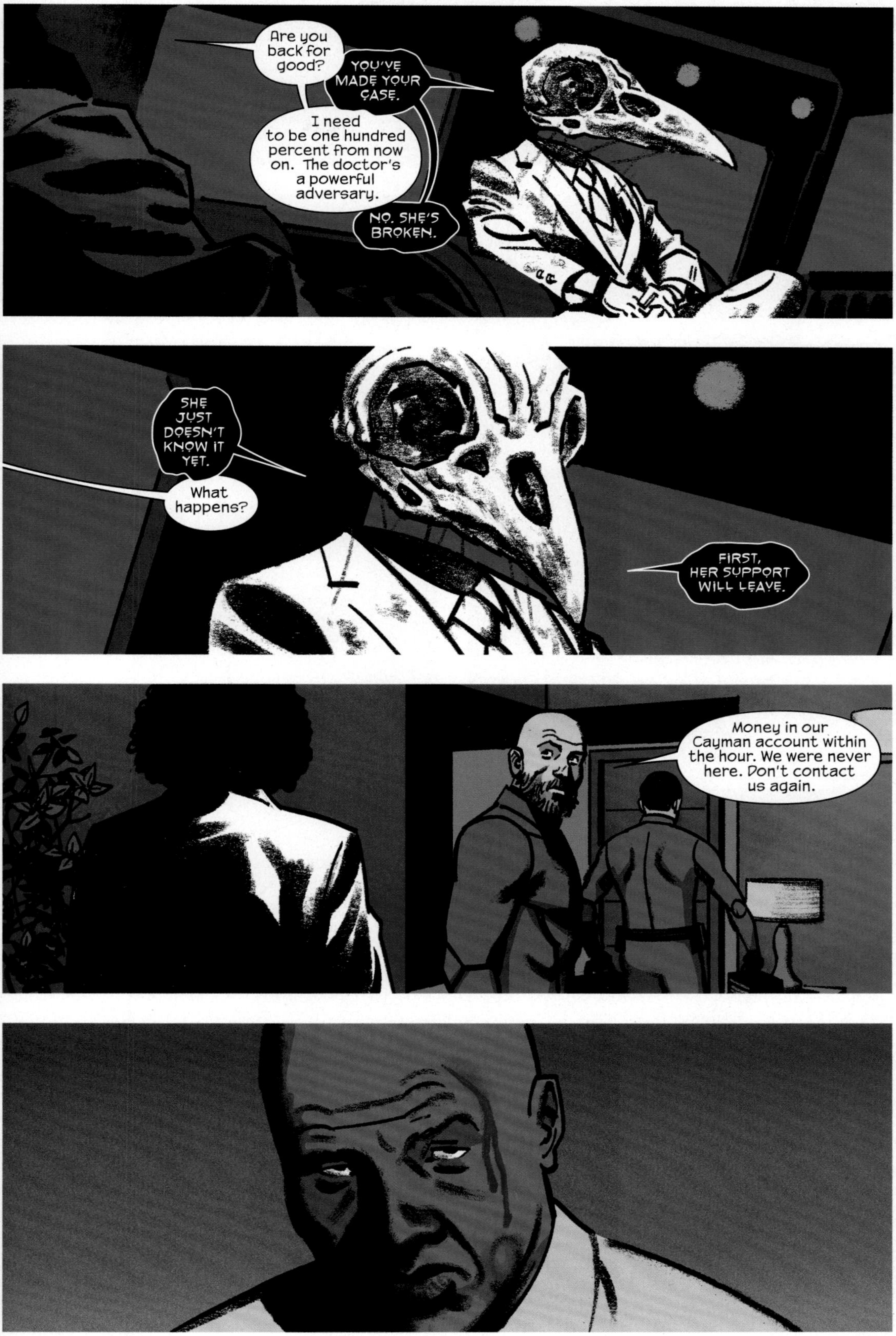
Are you back for good?
YOU'VE MADE YOUR CASE.
I need to be one hundred percent from now on. The doctor's a powerful adversary.
NO. SHE'S BROKEN.
SHE JUST DOESN'T KNOW IT YET.
What happens?
FIRST, HER SUPPORT WILL LEAVE.
Money in our Cayman account within the hour. We were never here. Don't contact us again.

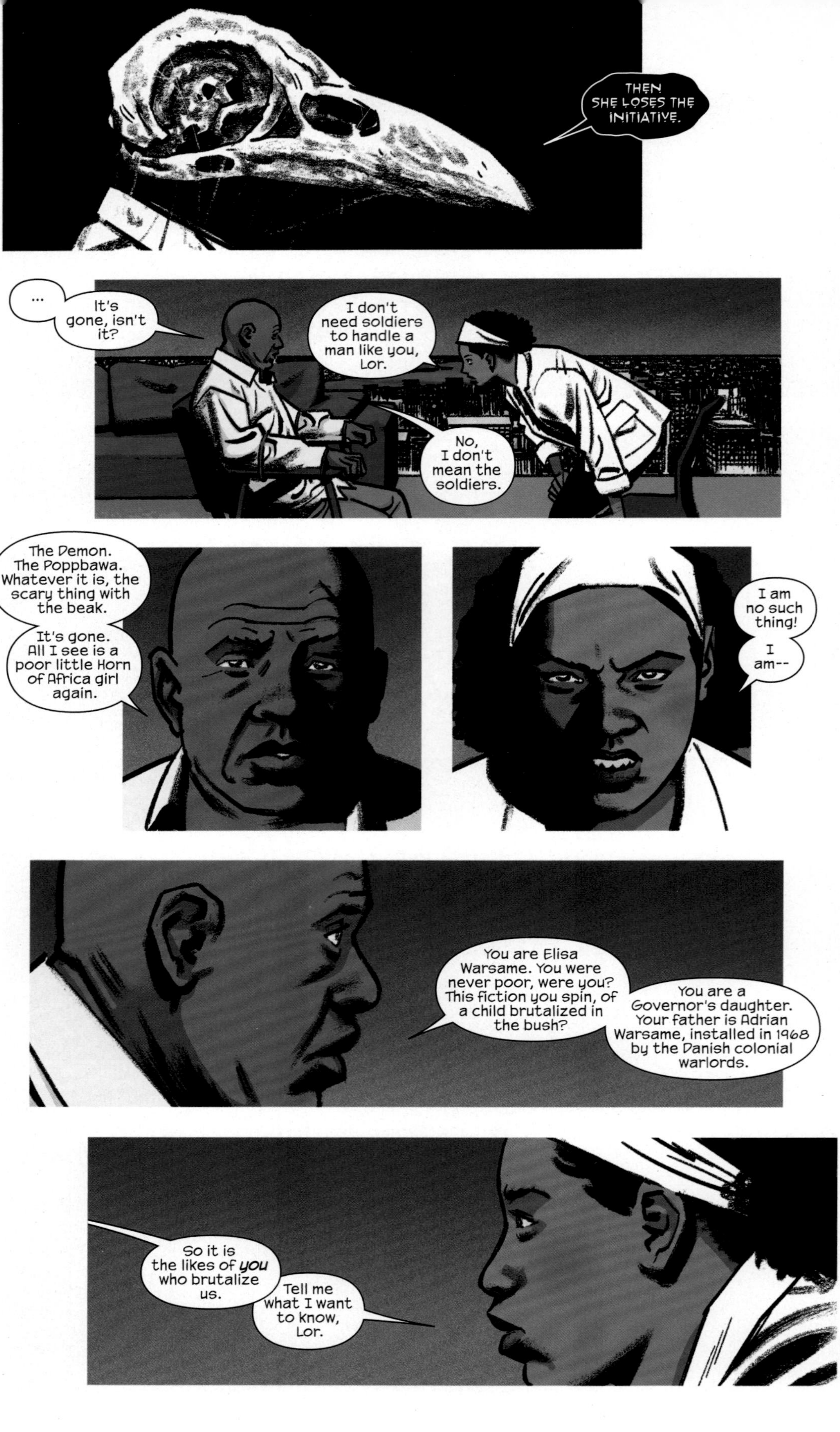
THEN SHE LOSES THE INITIATIVE.
...
It's gone, isn't it?
I don't need soldiers to handle a man like you, Lor.
No, I don't mean the soldiers.
The Demon. The Poppbawa. Whatever it is, the scary thing with the beak.
It's gone. All I see is a poor little Horn of Africa girl again.
I am no such thing!
I am--
You are Elisa Warsame. You were never poor, were you? This fiction you spin, of a child brutalized in the bush?
You are a Governor's daughter. Your father is Adrian Warsame, installed in 1968 by the Danish colonial warlords.
So it is the likes of *you* who brutalize us.
Tell me what I want to know, Lor.

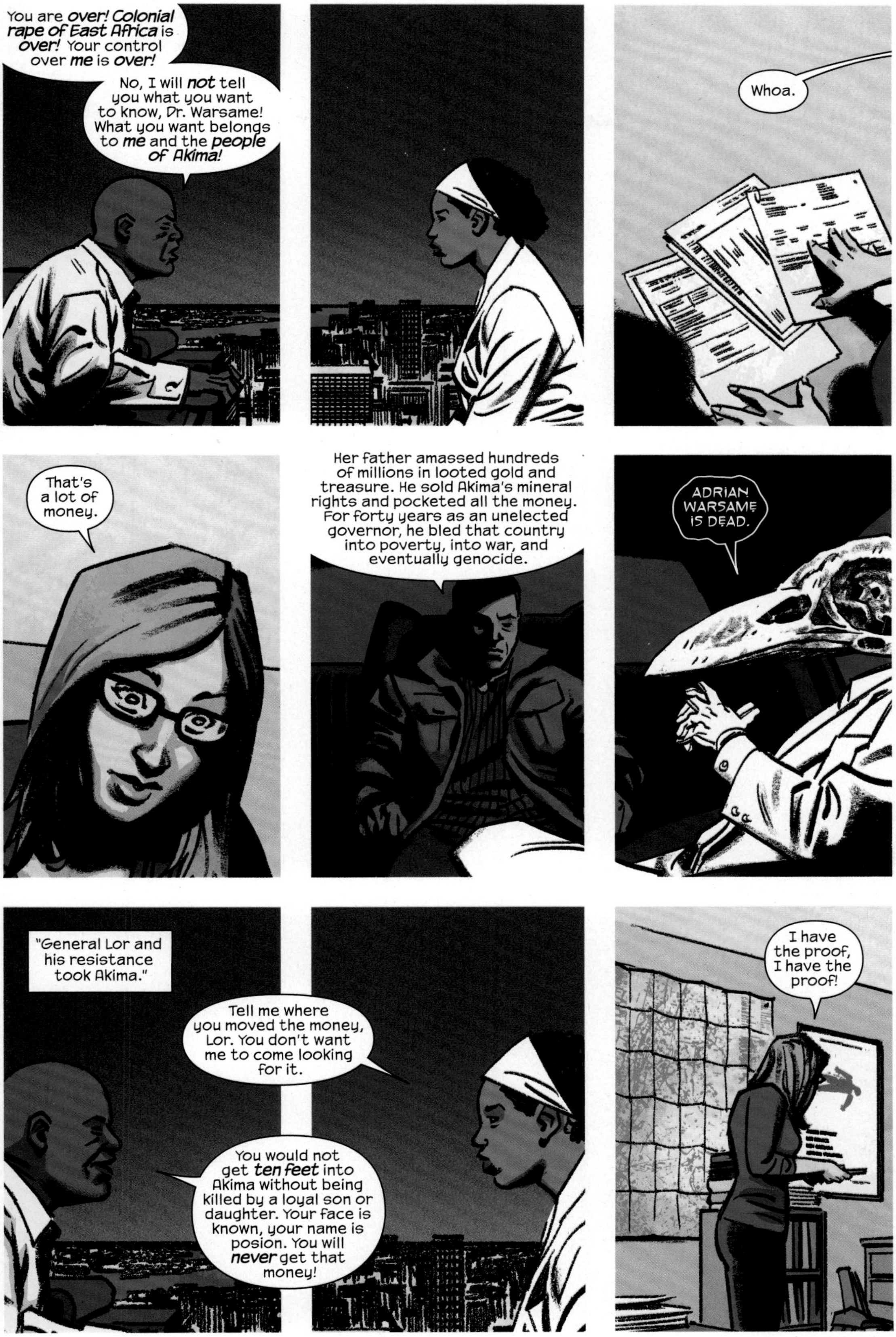
You are over! Colonial rape of East Africa is over! Your control over me is over!
No, I will not tell you what you want to know, Dr. Warsame! What you want belongs to me and the people of Akima!
Whoa.
That's a lot of money.
Her father amassed hundreds of millions in looted gold and treasure. He sold Akima's mineral rights and pocketed all the money. For forty years as an unelected governor, he bled that country into poverty, into war, and eventually genocide.
ADRIAN WARSAME IS DEAD.
"General Lor and his resistance took Akima."
Tell me where you moved the money, Lor. You don't want me to come looking for it.
You would not get ten feet into Akima without being killed by a loyal son or daughter. Your face is known, your name is posion. You will never get that money!
I have the proof, I have the proof!

What do you have?

I was trying to figure it out, the accounts you gave me of the attempted assassinations of Lor...why would she try and kill him if he's holding the money?

"Or implicate you?"

Chaos.

Chaos.

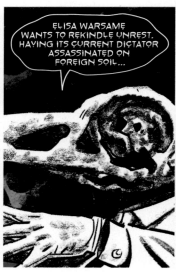

ELISA WARSAME WANTS TO REKINDLE UNREST. HAVING ITS CURRENT DICTATOR ASSASSINATED ON FOREIGN SOIL...

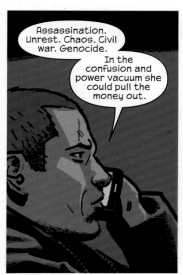

Assassination. Unrest. Chaos. Civil war. Genocide.

In the confusion and power vacuum she could pull the money out.

Then she'll kill him in the end!

THEN SHE'LL KILL HIM.

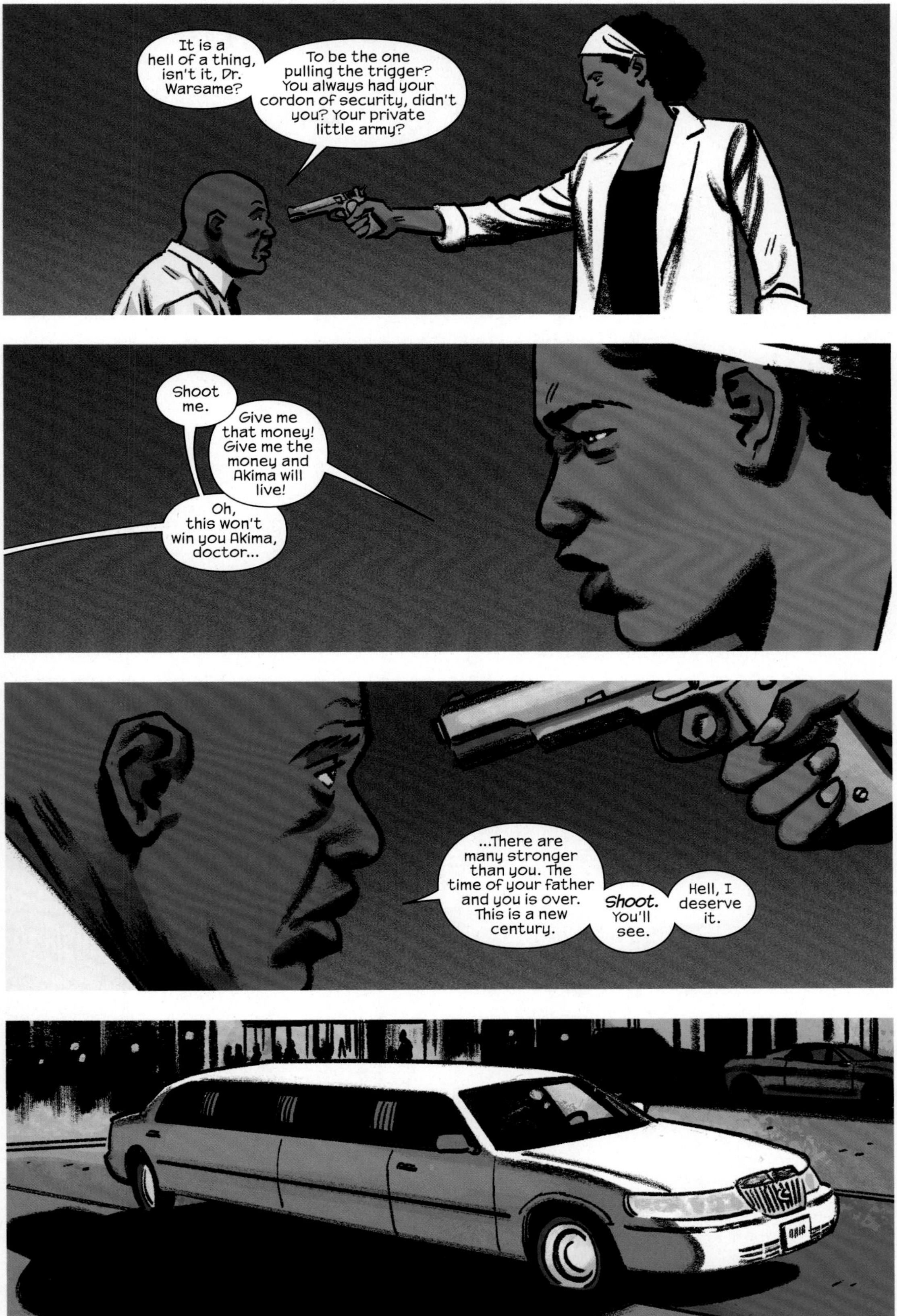
It is a hell of a thing, isn't it, Dr. Warsame?
To be the one pulling the trigger? You always had your cordon of security, didn't you? Your private little army?
Shoot me.
Give me that money! Give me the money and Akima will live!
Oh, this won't win you Akima, doctor...
...There are many stronger than you. The time of your father and you is over. This is a new century.
Shoot. You'll see.
Hell, I deserve it.

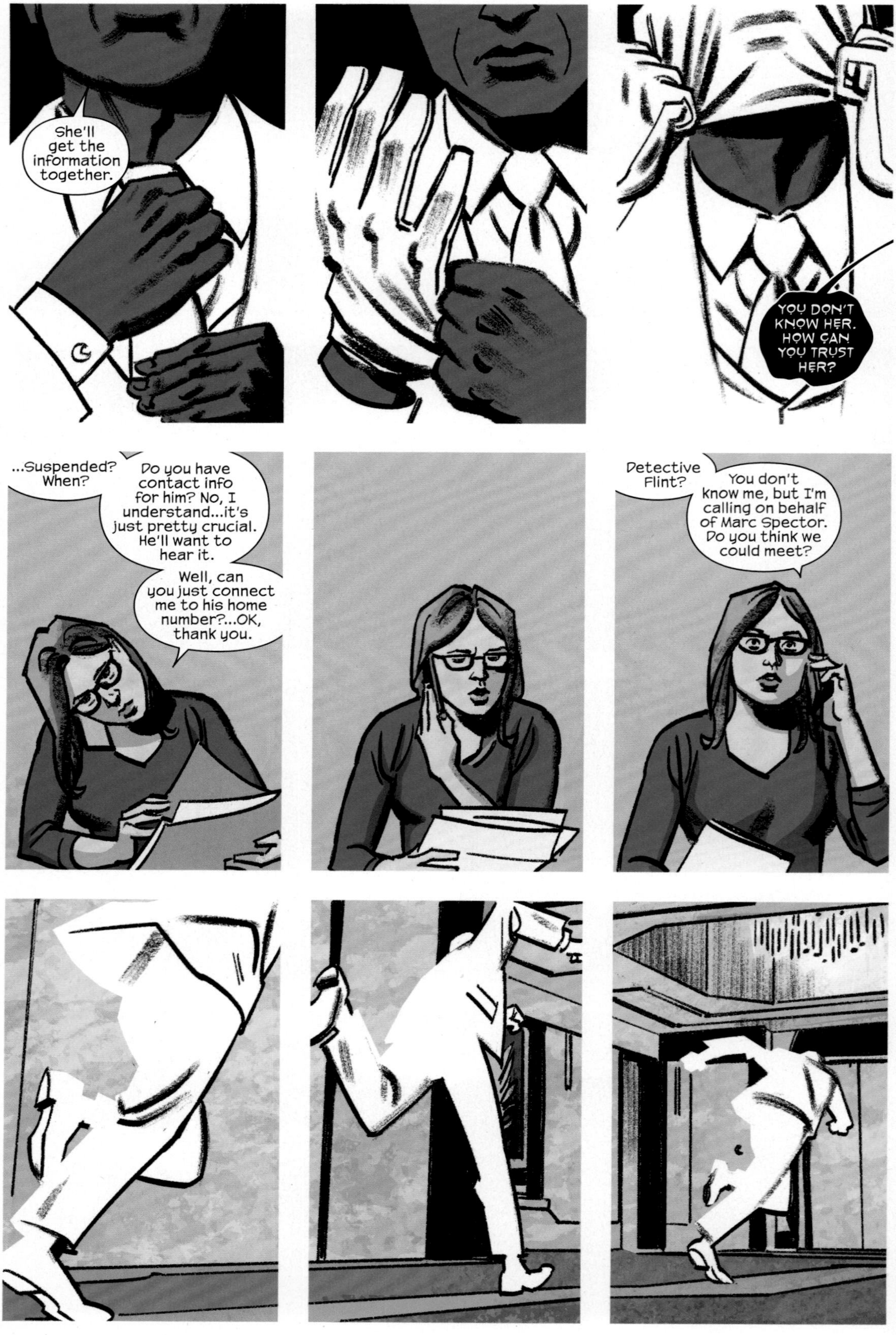
She'll get the information together.
YOU DON'T KNOW HER. HOW CAN YOU TRUST HER?
...Suspended? When?
Do you have contact info for him? No, I understand...it's just pretty crucial. He'll want to hear it.
Well, can you just connect me to his home number?...OK, thank you.
Detective Flint?
You don't know me, but I'm calling on behalf of Marc Spector. Do you think we could meet?

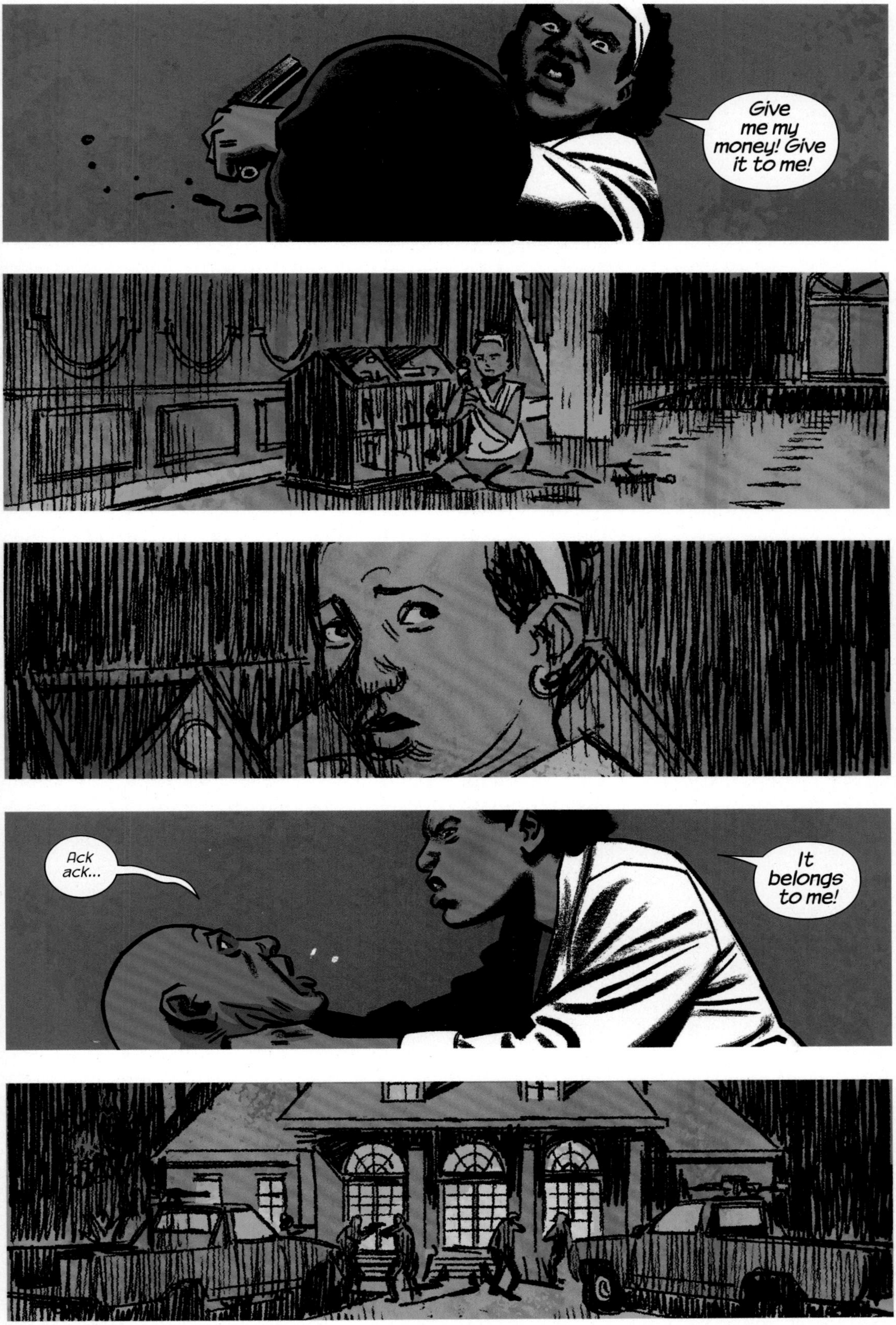
Give me my money! Give it to me!
Ack ack...
It belongs to me!

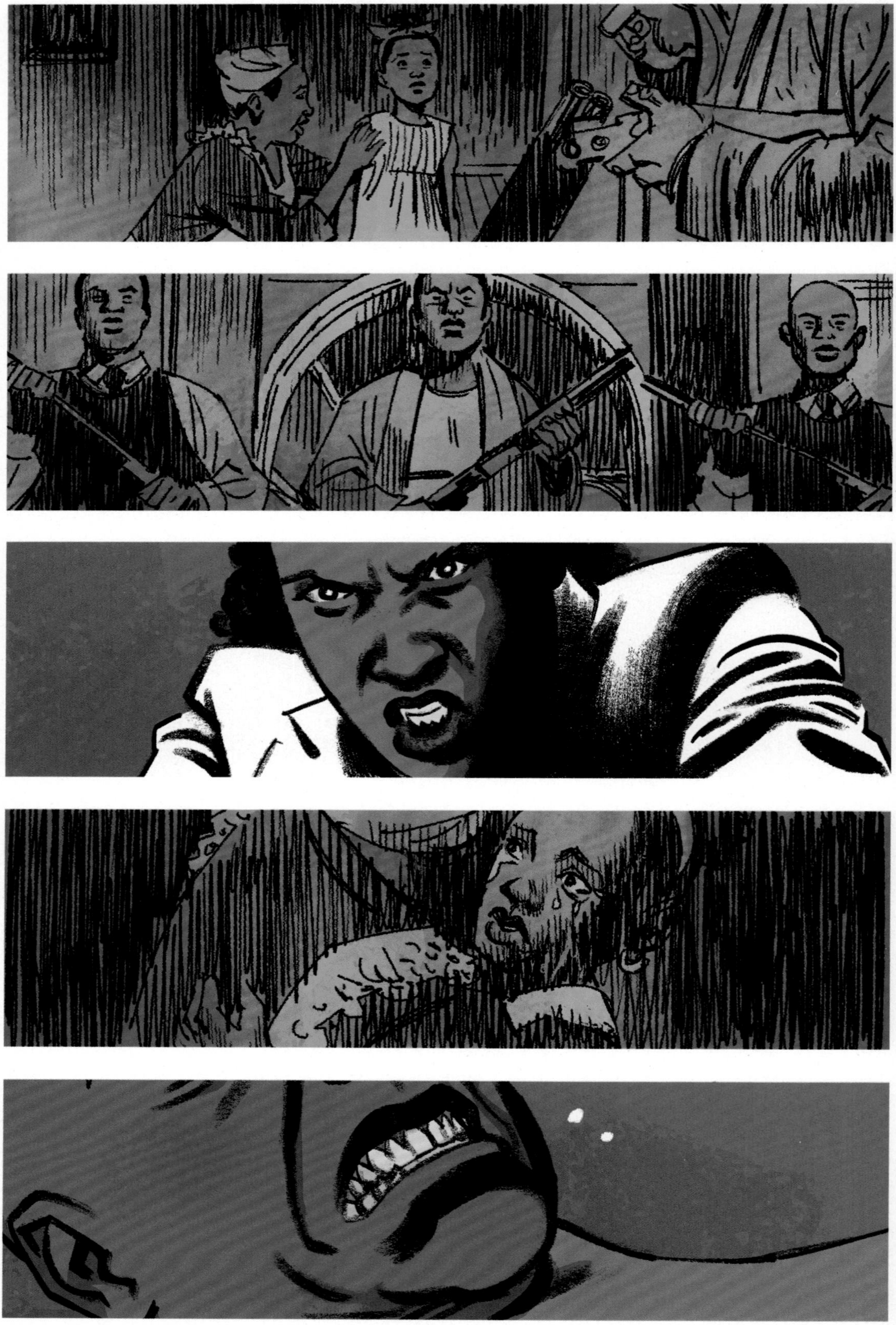

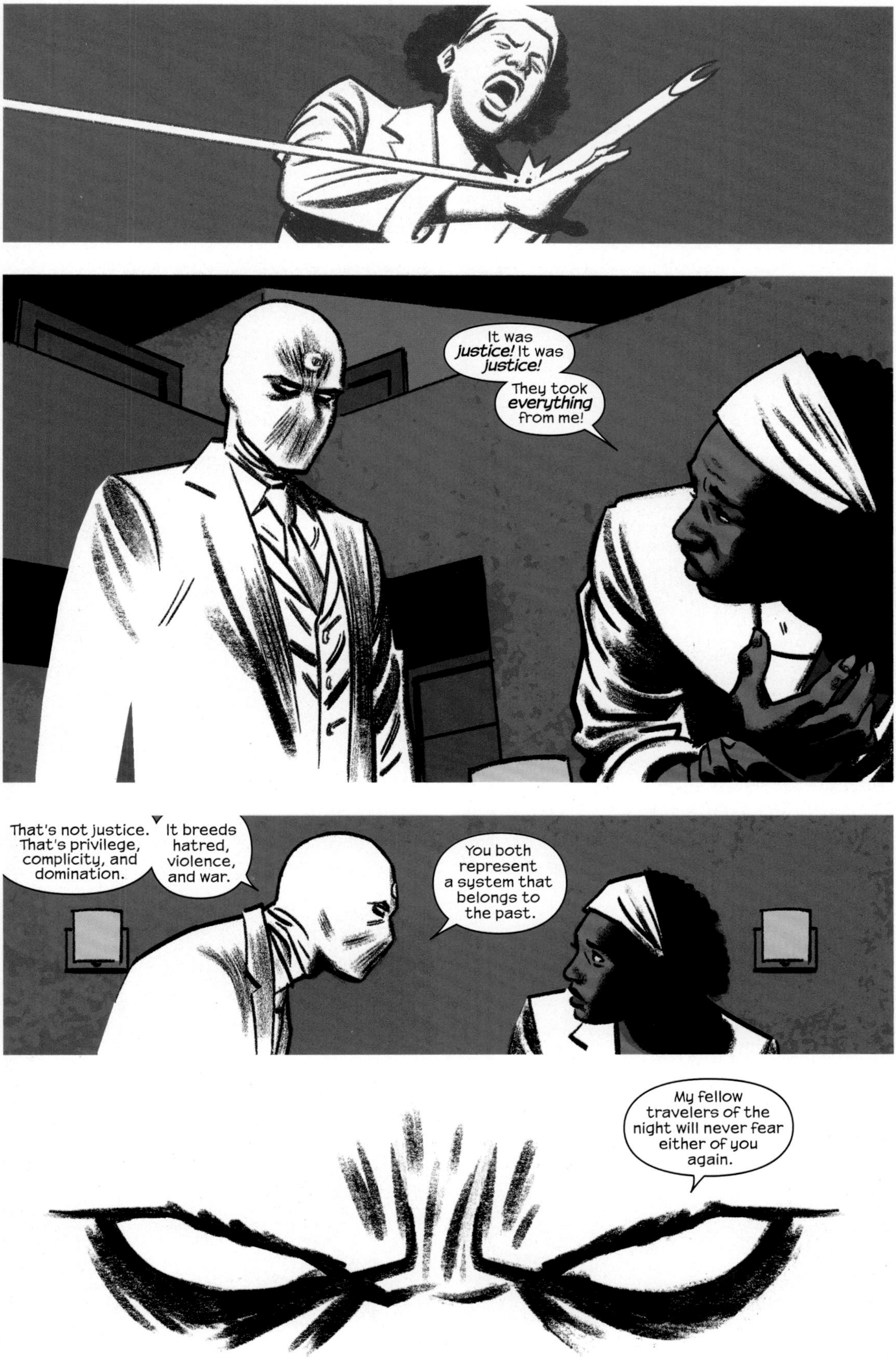
It was justice! It was justice!
They took everything from me!
That's not justice. That's privilege, complicity, and domination.
It breeds hatred, violence, and war.
You both represent a system that belongs to the past.
My fellow travelers of the night will never fear either of you again.

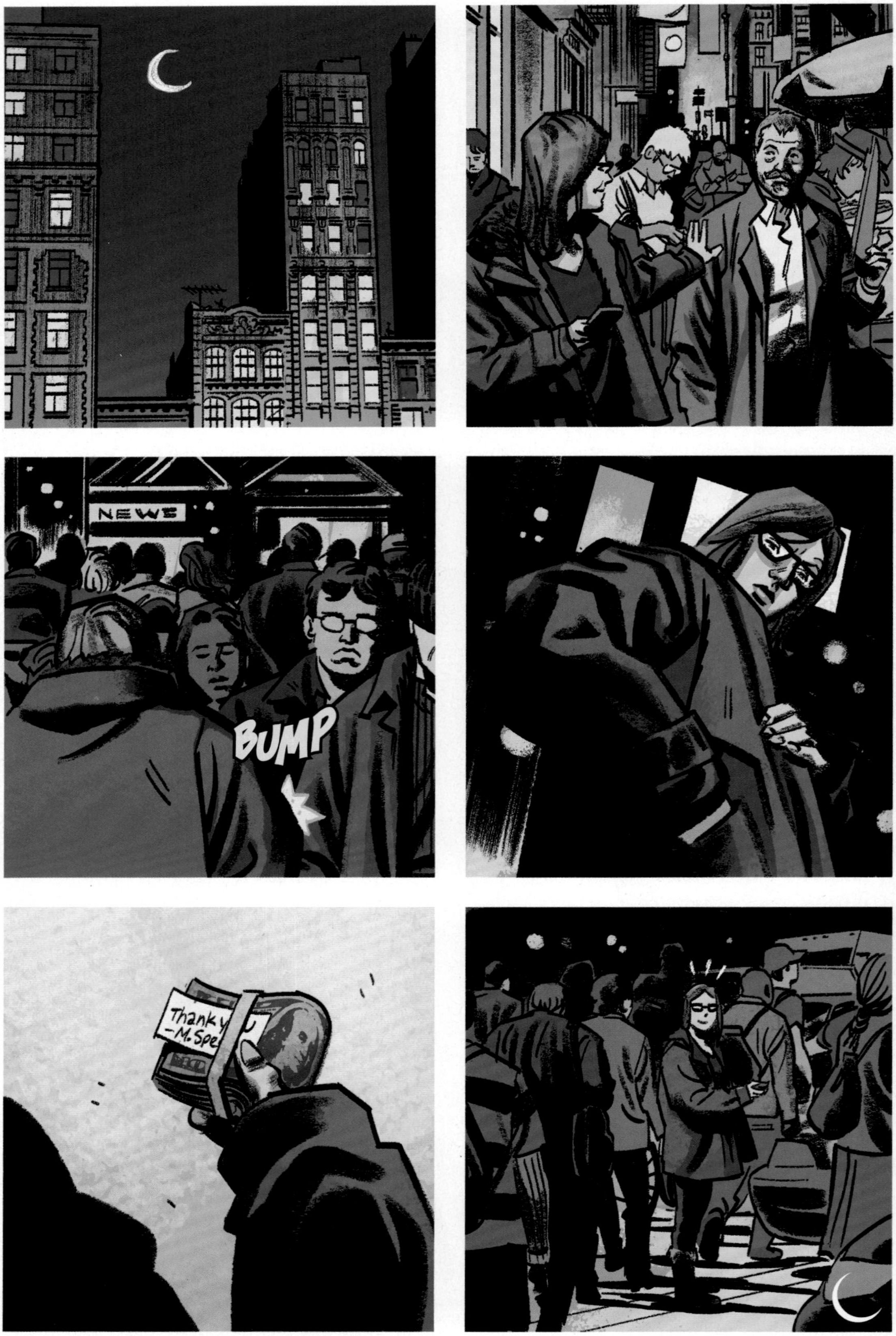
NEWS
BUMP
Thank y
—M. Spe

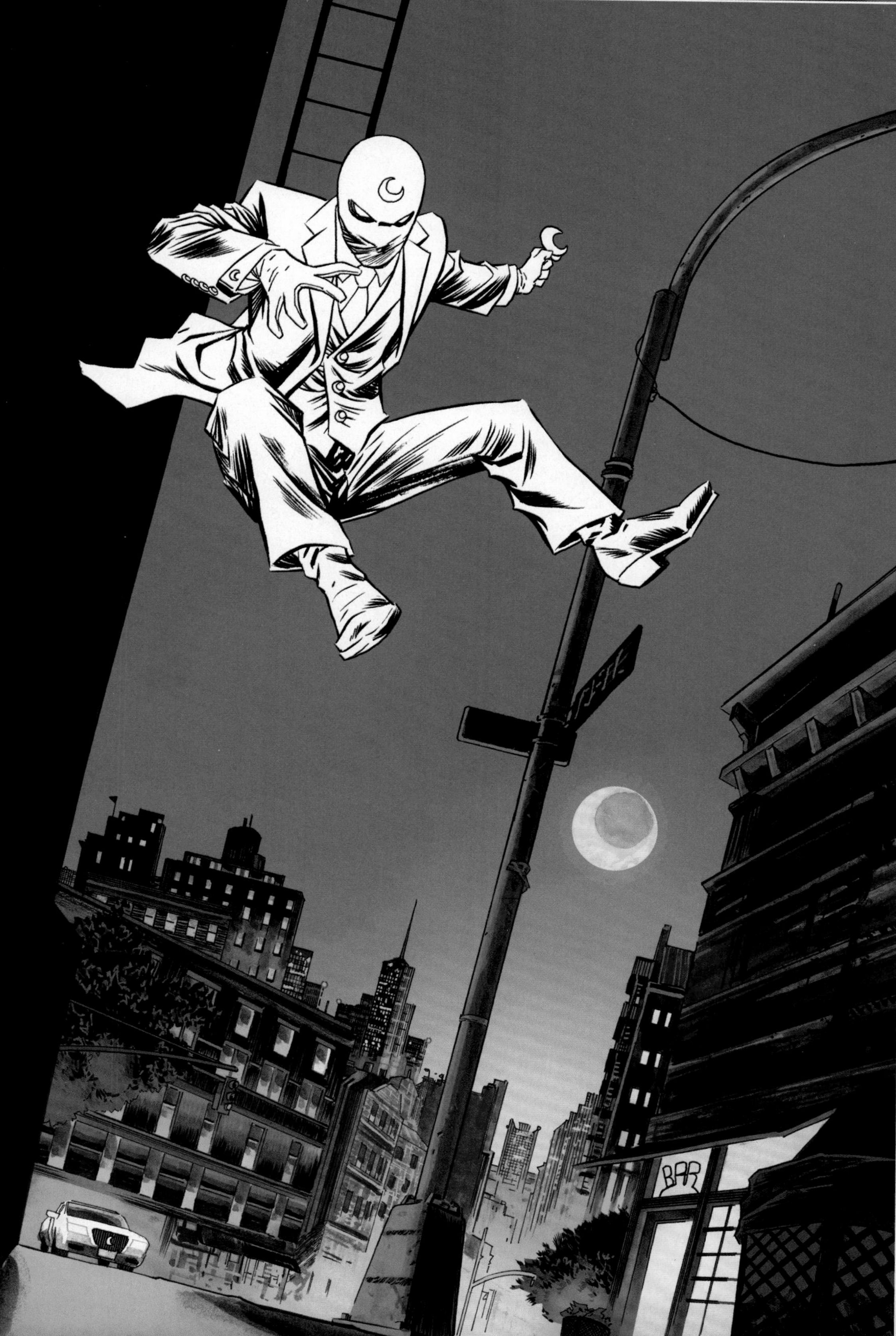
BAR

MOON KNIGHT #7 VARIANT BY DECLAN SHALVEY & JORDIE BELLAIRE

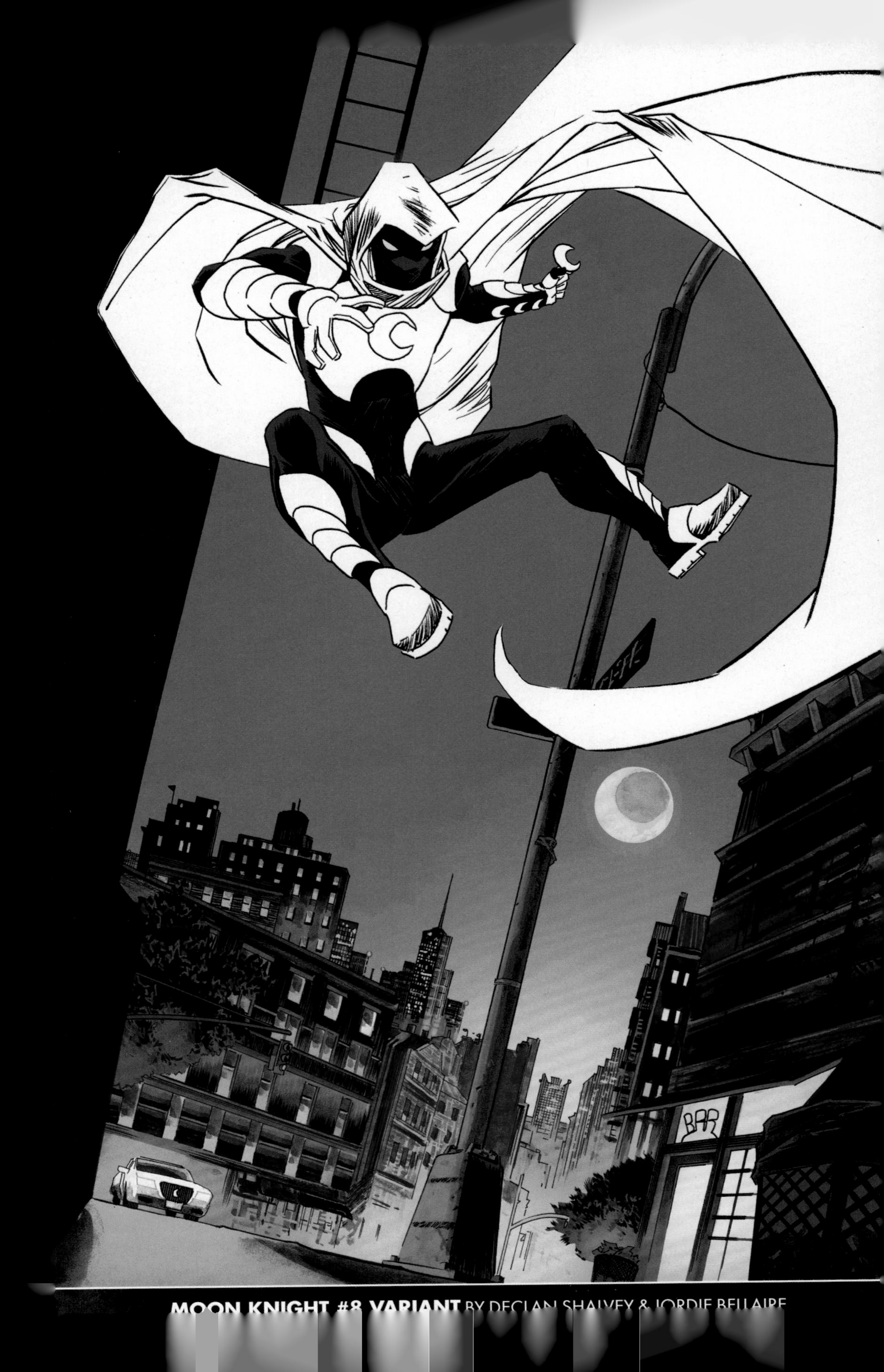
BAR

MOON KNIGHT #8 VARIANT BY DECLAN SHALVEY & JORDIE BELLAIRE

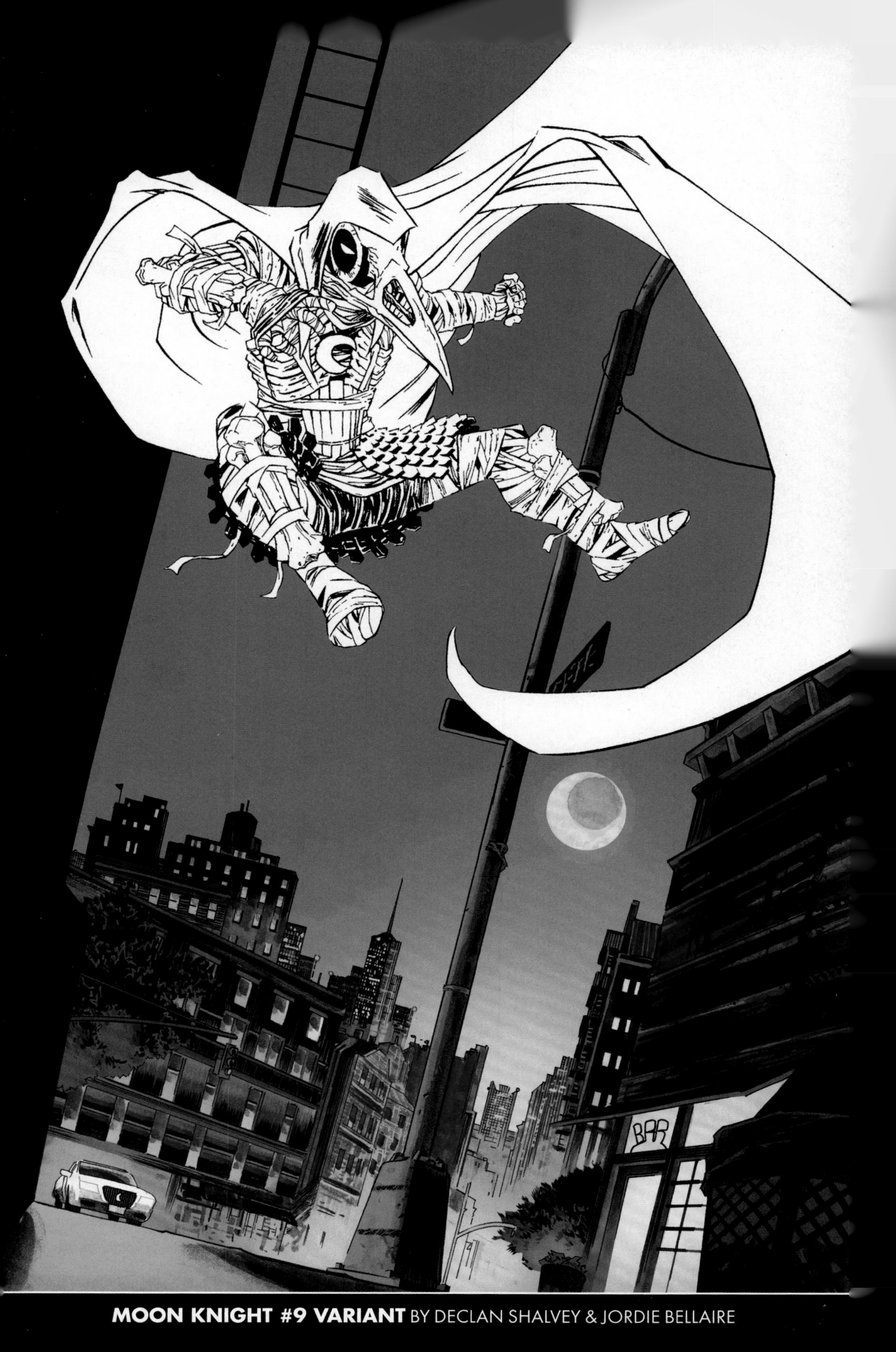
BAR

MOON KNIGHT #9 VARIANT BY DECLAN SHALVEY & JORDIE BELLAIRE

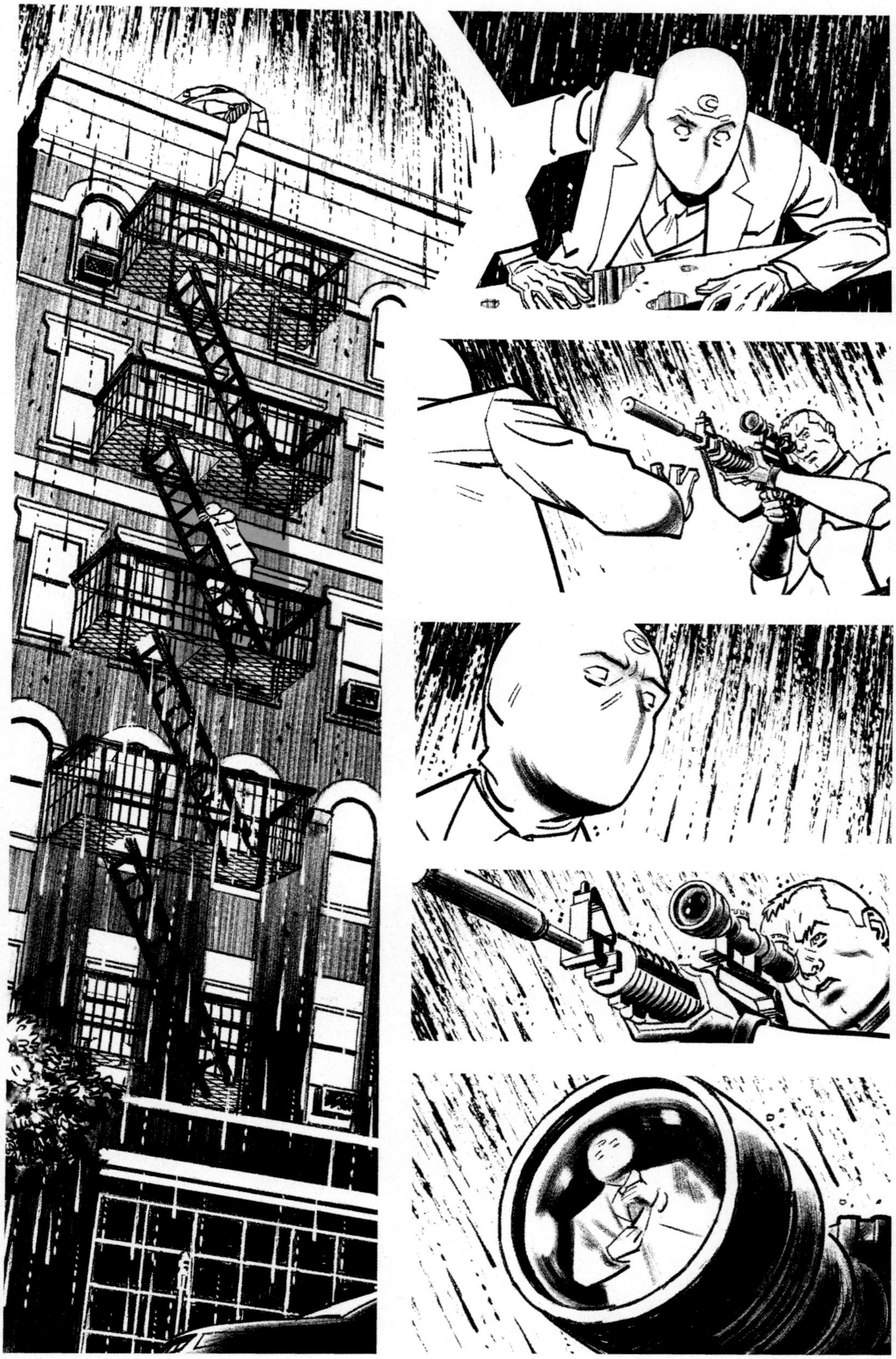

MOON KNIGHT #7, PAGE 15 BY GREG SMALLWOOD

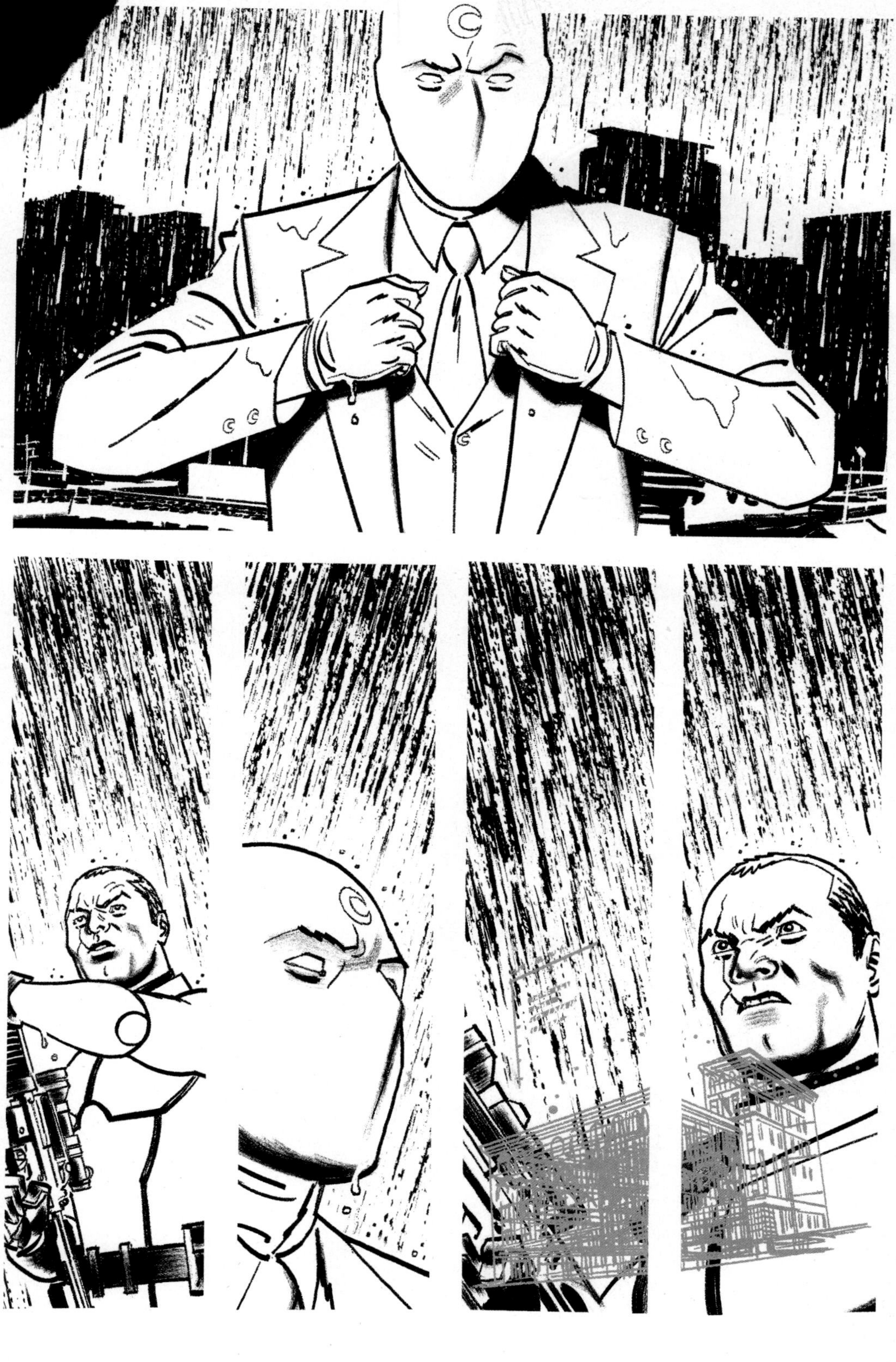

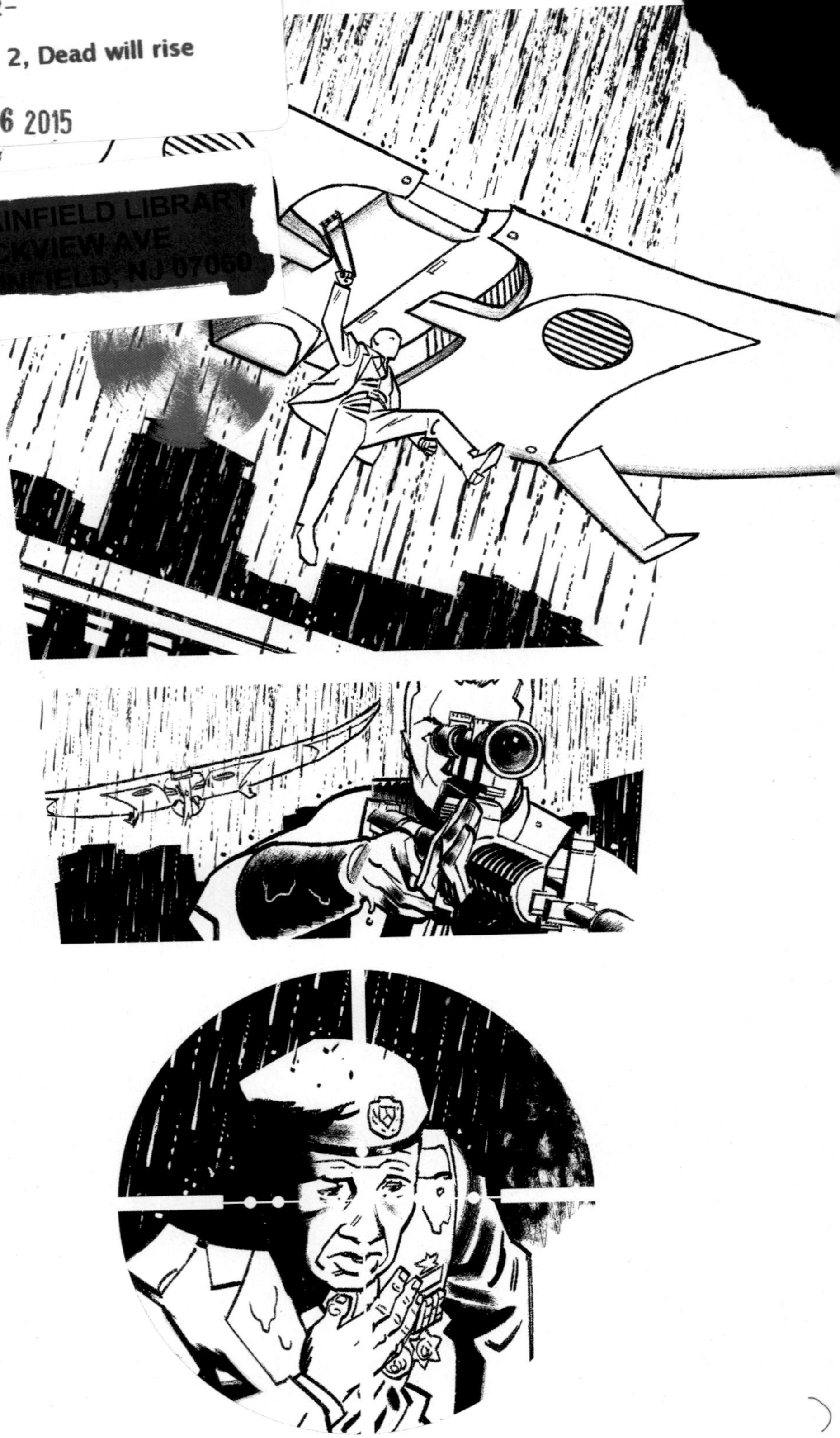

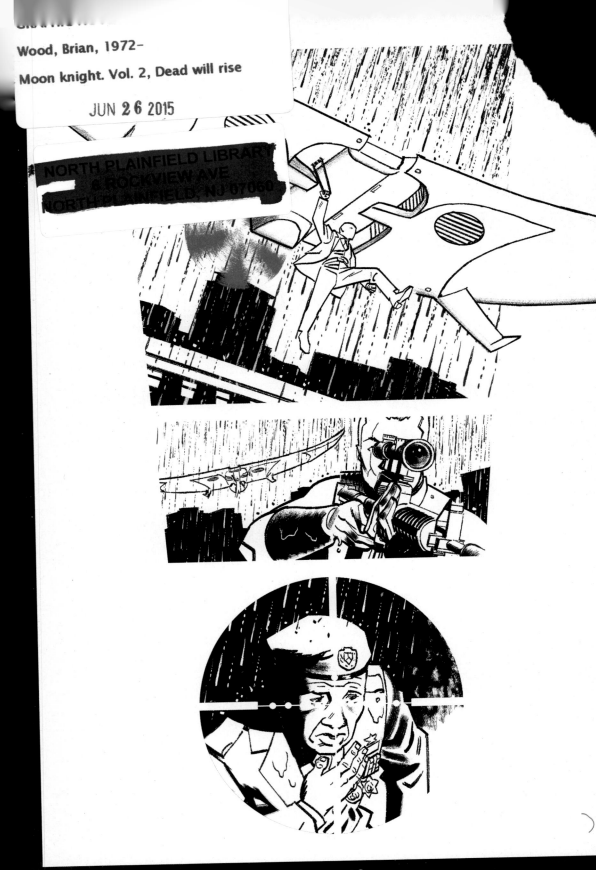